LIKE ONLY YESTERDAY

THE MEMOIRS OF DONALD E. NOBLE

D1253476

DONALD E. NOBLE
CHIEF EXECUTIVE OFFICER EMERITUS
RUBBERMAID INCORPORATED

The Wooster Book Company, Wooster, Ohio 44691

ISBN 1-888683-15-5

Library of Congress Cataloging-in-Publication Data

Noble, Donald E., 1915-
  Like only yesterday : the memoirs of Donald E. Noble / Donald E. Noble
    p.   cm.
  Includes index.
  ISBN 1-888683-15-5 (trade pbk.)
    1. Noble, Donald E. 2. Executives—United States—Biography.
3. Rubbermaid Incorporated—History. 4. Rubber industry and trade—
United States—History.   I. Title.
HD9161.U52N636   1996
338.7'6783'092—dc20
[B]   96-42180
                                                                    CIP

Printed by Watt Printing Company, Cleveland, Ohio

"Don Noble's memoirs are a fascinating look at the early life and subsequent business career of an extraordinary man. In addition to its historical interest, the book is filled with perceptive insights and lessons for aspiring young managers and professionals."
DR. R. STANTON HALES, PRESIDENT, THE COLLEGE OF WOOSTER

"This is the story of the growth of a very successful company and the personal growth of the man who guided it as Chief Executive Officer for 20 years told in interesting detail with personal warmth and great insight. A truly good read."
JOHN C. JOHNSTON, OF COUNSEL, CRITCHFIELD, CRITCHFIELD AND JOHNSTON

"All of the associates of Rubbermaid continue to benefit from the values that Don instilled into our corporation, not only through the Statement of Philosophy and Fundamental Principles, *but most importantly, through his leadership and personal example."*
WOLFGANG R. SCHMITT, CHAIRMAN OF THE BOARD AND CHIEF EXECUTIVE OFFICER, RUBBERMAID INCORPORATED

"I am grateful that Don Noble has published Like Only Yesterday, *a very readable book which chronicles an extraordinarily successful business career reminiscent of a Horatio Alger story."*
R. VICTOR DIX, PUBLISHER, THE DAILY RECORD

LIKE ONLY YESTERDAY

DONALD E. NOBLE was born in 1915 and began his business career in 1933 as an 18-year old bank messenger during the depths of the Depression. After completing a hard-won college education, he joined The Wooster Rubber Company (later Rubbermaid Incorporated) as an accountant and rose through the ranks to become President and Chief Executive Officer in 1959. He was elected Chairman of the Board in 1974 and continued to serve as the Chief Executive Officer of Rubbermaid Incorporated until he retired in 1980.

DEDICATION

Dedicated to my wife, Alice, whose support and wise counsel
were vital to whatever I may have accomplished and to our
children David, Richard, Jeanne, and Nancy who have been
a great joy and inspiration to me.

This book is also dedicated to our grandchildren.
I became motivated to write my memoirs only after our children
asked me to write down the stories that I had told them when
they were young. They wanted their own children – our
grandchildren – to be able to share in these stories
of my experiences.

Our Grandchildren

David Noble's children:	Donald II, Robinson, Elizabeth, and Matthew
Richard Noble's son:	Andrew
Jeanne Langford's children:	Katherine, Sarah, and Laura
Nancy Holland's children:	Lily and Stephen

CONTENTS

CONTENTS

PREFACE

In this book of memoirs, it has been possible to recognize by name only a few of the wonderful people who have had such a positive impact on my life and my career. I wish space would have permitted acknowledgment of all those exceptionally fine and generous individuals who have helped me and have contributed so much to Rubbermaid's success over the years. Since I could not mention everyone, I want to take this opportunity to express my heartfelt thanks to them and their families.

I also want to thank George F. Thompson, a former Rubbermaid employee who is now a free-lance writer in Cleveland, for providing me with his professional editing services and for repeatedly giving me the inspiration to continue working on this book.

While these are my personal memoirs, they contain substantial coverage of my business career, particularly at Rubbermaid Incorporated which was the focal point of my life for almost 40 years. During my years in management at Rubbermaid, I learned many lessons that go beyond the theories and technical training provided by business schools. These include the need for senior executives to treat all employees with dignity and respect, to communicate a written statement of philosophy and fundamental principles throughout the organization, and perhaps most important to conduct themselves in accordance with the same rules and ethical principles which they expect others to follow.

Because I have benefited so greatly from those lessons, I want to share them with young people considering a career in business. If our free enterprise system is to continue as the powerful engine that drives our national economic growth, we must have people working in our corporations who adhere to the highest ethical principles. I have tried to make the point by personal example that it is not necessary to sacrifice one's principles in order to succeed and, that, in fact, adherence to principles and a strong work ethic is the surest way to achieve success and promotion. One of the most rewarding responsibilities of every executive is helping to develop young managers by giving them the training and responsibilities they need to grow and mature into effective leaders. I hope some of the suggestions in this book will be useful in that process.

Wherever possible in this book, I have used both "he" and "she" in referring to executive employees. In some cases, however, the use of both words becomes cumbersome to the point of making the text less readable. For that reason, I emphasize that when I use the word "he" alone in that connection it is for improved readability and both genders are intended.

My mother, Mary Martha Meiche, was born on June 17, 1882, in Cleveland, Ohio. She was raised on a farm about two miles south of North Royalton, Ohio, on Akins Road, and attended a one-room school house in North Royalton going through only the eighth grade. Although my mother had only an eighth-grade education, I consider her to have been a very bright, well-informed lady who instilled in her children a wonderful philosophy and a strong desire to get a good education. Many of the proverbs which she repeated over and over again to us children are still indelibly etched in my memory and I quote them frequently. Many of her quotations were taken from either the Bible or Benjamin Franklin, while others were out of poems by Henry Wadsworth Longfellow.

My father, Philip Edgar Noble, was born on July 31, 1886, in Prospect, Ohio, and grew up on his parents' farm near Prospect, in Delaware County, Ohio. In 1902, my paternal grandparents, Reuben and Ida Noble, moved from Prospect, Ohio, to a farm just south of North Royalton, Ohio. Their farmhouse – a very substantial brick house which is still standing today – was located on the east side of State Road, about two miles south of the intersection of Akins Road and State Road. At the time of the move, my father would have been about 16 years old, his brother Lloyd about 13 years old, and his sister Clara about six years old. Lloyd died three years after the move at age 16.

My father graduated from North Royalton High School in the very first graduating class of the school, a class consisting of two people – a girl and my father – in the year 1907. He then went on to attend Ohio State University and graduated in 1909 from a two-year course at the Ohio State University School of Agriculture. For a period of time prior to her marriage to my father, my mother worked as an upstairs maid in the home of Dr. George Crile on Euclid Avenue in Cleveland. Dr. Crile was the famous doctor who established the Crile Clinic at 90th Street and Euclid Avenue in

Cleveland, which later became world-famous as The Cleveland Clinic. She told many stories about her experiences in helping to bring up the Crile children.

My mother and father undoubtedly met as young people at church since both of their families attended the North Royalton Methodist Church, a small church in the rural Ohio town where they both lived. In any event, we have a photograph of my mother and father before they were married that was taken when they were standing on some rocks near a creek, a tributary of the Cuyahoga River, about a mile east of the center of Brecksville. The spot is located where State Route 82 crosses that creek and is now a part of the Cleveland Metropolitan Park System. I was there recently and it looks just the same as it did in the picture which must have been taken sometime prior to their marriage in August 1910. I have to assume that they came over by horse and buggy from North Royalton, which was about six miles west of Brecksville.

Even though my mother's first language was German and only German had been spoken in her parents' home, she would not teach us German because she said she wanted her children to be Americans. When I started traveling to Germany on business, I often wished that she had taught us German because it would have come in handy. My mother was a beautiful, stately lady, five feet, eight inches tall with a round, pleasant, kindly face. She was somewhat overweight, but carried herself erectly and always looked very dignified. She wore her hair in loose, fluffy waves, but always neat, and with a bun at the neck. Her Sunday church clothes, although I am sure they were not expensive, gave her a very "dressed up" look. At home she wore house dresses, always clean, and a full front apron with straps over her shoulders and tied in back. My mother never raised her voice to any of us but whenever she addressed me as "Donald Edgar," I knew I should pay very close attention to what she was about to say.

I never heard a cross word between my mother and father and, in fact, I remember them having only one disagreement. One Sunday afternoon, mother wanted to go to one church for evening services while father wanted to attend services at another church. I do not recall how that minor dispute was resolved, but I do know that it involved a friendly and quiet discussion between my parents.

My father was a very handsome man five feet, ten inches tall. He had a slight wave in his brown hair which was always neatly combed and parted on the side. Mother said that when they lived on the dairy farm my father would never go out to do the 5:30 a.m. milking and chores until he had first carefully combed his hair.

Another thing about my father that sticks out in my memory is that he was always neatly dressed. Even when working on his bread delivery route, he wore clean, neat-looking work clothes. After he started selling insurance, he was always immaculately dressed on weekdays and Sundays. He wore stiffly starched detached shirt collars, which I would take to a Chinese laundry on 14th Street. Mother would launder and iron his shirts. The stiff collars were attached to the shirts by means of a separate metal collar button at the back and a slightly longer one at the front. These collar buttons were separate, that is, not attached to either the shirt or the collar. He wore three-piece suits with a watch chain across the vest. In the summer he often wore very light colored suits which, together with his straw hat, made him look elegant.

Perhaps because he had grown up on a farm, my father had a great liking for draft horses (the large, heavy horses used for pulling heavy loads, that are also sometimes called work horses). He knew the names of the various kinds of draft horses, such as the Belgian, which is a lovely light golden tan in color; the Percheron which originated in France; and each of the other kinds of draft horses including the giant Clydesdales. If father was driving along a country road and saw draft horses plowing or working in the fields or even when they had just been turned out in a pasture, he would always stop to admire them.

My mother and father lived with Grandma and Grandpa Noble on their family farm in North Royalton, Ohio, for two-and-a-half years after they were married. In 1913, they moved to East Lansing, Michigan, where my father became the manager of a large dairy farm. I can remember in later years my mother talking about how upset Grandpa Noble had been by their departure. He felt that father was leaving him alone to do all of the farm work, which up until then they had shared.

I was born on January 21, 1915, in East Lansing, Michigan. Since my family moved from Michigan to Ohio when I was only four years old, I have very few memories of East Lansing. I do remember when we were returning to Michigan from an automobile trip to Ohio, my mother exclaiming as we drove into the drive how much her canna lily plants had grown while we were gone. I remember that I also was impressed by the big plants.

In 1917, when I was two years old, my father and mother moved from the dairy farm, where they had lived in a house on the property, to a small bungalow in East Lansing and my father worked in a metal fabricating shop making military products for World War I. I have no idea why they made this move, but it may have been because my father wanted to get into war production.

My parents and their four children left East Lansing and moved back to Ohio in 1919 to live in Cleveland. At that time, Grandpa Noble was working at the Star Bakery Company on Clark Avenue near Scranton Road in Cleveland. My impression is that during the period from 1913 to 1919, when my parents were living in Michigan, my grandparents had sold their farm and moved to Cleveland. Although it is only a guess, Grandpa Noble may have arranged for my father to get a job at the Star Bakery, and may have done so even before my parents left Michigan.

In any event, Grandpa Noble did not continue working at the bakery for very long after my parents moved to Cleveland. Again, I am guessing that it was about 1921 when my grandparents either bought a house at the corner of Akins Road and State Road near North Royalton or bought the land and had the house built on it. After they had moved back to North Royalton, Grandpa Noble went into the real estate business. I can remember later seeing "For Sale" signs all around the area in which they lived with large letters "R. S. NOBLE, REAL ESTATE" on them.

When we moved to Cleveland in 1919, we lived in a house at 1422 Mentor Avenue which my parents had bought in a poor residential neighborhood, located less than a mile from the steel mills and only 2.2 miles from the Public Square in downtown Cleveland. It was a two-family, Victorian-style house in which Miss Hart – a retired school teacher, who in those days was called a "maiden lady" – lived upstairs while we lived downstairs. My mother and father and eventually a total of six children lived in what amounted to half a house (the first floor), with three-bedrooms, a small living room, a small dining room, and a small kitchen.

When we moved into the Cleveland house, the first floor had just been wired for electricity, but the upstairs flat where Miss Hart lived did not yet have electricity and she still used the gas lamps which were on the walls of each room in her apartment. She also used coal oil table lamps. Electric street lights had not yet been installed in our neighborhood and every evening at dusk a lamplighter walked up and down the street to light the gas street-lights, including the one that was located right on the corner in front of our house. The lamplighter carried a long pole with a torch on the end of it which he used to light the gas mantle inside the glass globe of the streetlights. Each morning either the same man or another man would come along to turn off the streetlights.

For several years, there was no telephone in the house. After a few years, Miss Hart had a telephone installed which we were allowed to use, but my recollection is that we used it for emergencies only. I doubt that we placed more than three or four calls per month and received only one or two calls per month. When we received a phone call, Miss Hart would pound on the top step of the back staircase with a broom stick to call us.

Living in a poor neighborhood, I learned very early about the value of money and that you had to work to earn it. When I was only five years old, I can remember my sister, Hazel, who was three-and-a-half years older than I was, being asked by a neighbor to help shell elderberries. This meant taking the elderberries off the stems – a very tedious task. For some reason I went along with her and, although I am sure I was of no help, the neighbor let me believe I was helping her and at the end gave me five pennies. I can remember being very proud of receiving those pennies and my mother put them into a padded box, I presume from some piece of jewelry, and saved them for me for many years. It was the first pay I can remember getting.

Another very vivid memory about the value of money was the time my Aunt Helen (my mother's sister) took me for a walk to the bank on West 25th Street, about seven blocks from our house. As we approached the bank she pointed to the sign which read in very large letters "Pearl Street Bank – 6% Interest." Aunt Helen carefully explained to me the meaning of six percent interest, saying that if a person put a dollar in the bank today, a year from today the bank would pay that person six cents for the use of the dollar. This made a tremendous impression on me and I can remember thinking that it sounded a lot better than working to get paid five cents as I had when I had helped Hazel. I think that had a lasting impact in making me want to save money because collecting interest seemed to be such a terrific idea.

Not long after these memorable experiences, I got a regular job. Miss Hart would bang on the staircase with her broom stick when she wanted me to run an errand for her, and soon my regular job every Saturday morning was to get Miss Hart's rubbish and put it into the garbage cans. For this I would get a nickel. As I grew older, there were some other opportunities to work for pay. For example, in the winter when there had been a big snowstorm, I would go out early in the morning before school and knock on the doors to see if anyone wanted their walks shoveled. I soon found that it was best to head toward the big houses on West 14th Street where elderly people lived and the pay was better.

All of my siblings also developed a strong work ethic quite early. During berry season my father would sometimes bring back from his bread route several quarts of red or black raspberries which he had purchased from some of his farmer customers. My sister, Hazel, and I would take the raspberries out in our coaster wagon and go from door to door around our neighborhood selling them. Since Hazel was older, she took responsibility for managing the business and did all the selling and handled the cash transactions.

One reason we worked hard was that all the people in our neighborhood were on a tight budget and were careful about spending the little money they had. For example, the bakery where my father worked as a route salesman had a room where the bakery sold what was called "day-old bread." Actually, by evening the day-old bread was the same bread that had been sold a few hours earlier as fresh bread for more money. When my mother needed bread, she sent us children to buy this day-old bread. The room in which it was sold was only 12 feet by 18 feet. People would stand crowded into this small space five or six deep as they pushed up to be waited on at the counter. Sometimes the people were packed all the way to the door so that it was hard to even get into the room. This presented a big challenge for us children because of our small size; we would be almost lost down among the legs of the grownups and would have trouble getting up to the counter to be waited on. Once we were successful in getting up there and making our purchase, it was then hard to work our way back through the crowd to reach the door to get out. But we, as well as many of our neighbors, did it over and over again to save half the price of a loaf of fresh bread.

Another reason for our strong work ethic was the fact that the public schools in those days taught about the great contributions made by the men who had built America's industries through hard work. I can remember very vividly at about the age of 12 getting a biography of Andrew Carnegie from the library. I read with great interest how he came to this country from Scotland as a poor boy with very little education but succeeded in building a great steel company and became an extremely wealthy man. I was very impressed with Carnegie's many accomplishments and he became something of a hero for me.

When I was growing up, Americans were unabashedly patriotic. Memorial Day stands out in my memory as a time when every house in our neighborhood flew the American flag. Early in the morning, Civil War veterans could be seen coming out of their houses in their Union Army soldier and officer uniforms and walking up the street to catch the streetcar to go downtown for the Memorial Day parade. Since this was more than 55 years after the Civil War ended, these men had to be a minimum of 70 years old but they marched proudly erect to honor the heroes of the Civil War to whom a huge memorial stood in Cleveland's Public Square.

About Thanksgiving time each year, our parents would give each of us children two or three dollars with which to buy Christmas presents for our siblings. All of our shopping was done, with some help from mother, through the Sears Roebuck and Montgomery Ward catalogs. I can remember shopping very carefully for toys for my siblings, usually setting a maximum of 39 or 49 cents for each purchase. One of my favorite purchases as a Christmas gift for one of my siblings was a toy gyroscope for 39 cents.

Christmas was always an exciting time. At Sunday school on the Sunday before Christmas, we were always given one orange and a small bag of hard candy. This represented an extremely big and eagerly awaited treat for me. Our family could not afford oranges and this Christmas orange was the only orange I got all year and, like any other child, I really liked hard candy.

My father, of course, always bought used cars. The first one I remember was an open touring car, a Maxwell, which was built before the day of self-starters so it had to be cranked every time we started out. It had side curtains with small isinglass panels that allowed you to see out. These side curtains had to be snapped into place each time it started to rain. When it was not raining, they would be taken down and stored under the back seat of the car.

The Maxwell had one manually operated windshield wiper. This consisted of a handle which projected down on the inside of the passenger compartment in exactly the same spot as the windshield wiper was on the outside. The handle had to be moved back and forth manually to wipe the water off the windshield. I can remember operating this handle back and forth for my father when he was driving so he could see out the windshield and still keep both of his hands on the steering wheel.

Automobiles have always held a great fascination for me. Miss Hart had a lady friend who visited her periodically and drove an electric car. This intrigued me because the car arrived making no sound whatsoever and she would drive it away in equal silence. The electric car looked like a square box with large glass windows on all four sides. There was no steering wheel on the car but instead it had a stick, called a "rudder," that was about 18 inches long and attached to a post that went down into the car's steering mechanism. Whenever the lady wanted to turn to the right, she moved the stick to the left, and when she wanted to turn left, she moved the stick to the right – just like sailing a boat.

A neighbor, who lived less than a block away from our house, was visited by a man who drove a Stanley Steamer, a big automobile with lots of brass tubing. Before the owner could start the car, he had to come out and turn on the fuel which burned beneath a boiler to create steam. When he pulled a lever, the steam made a great hissing sound and the car would lumber forward.

My mother bought her fruits and vegetables from a man who drove a truck loaded with fresh produce around our Mentor Avenue neighborhood twice a week. Depending on the season, she would order a bushel of apples, a bushel of peaches, or a half bushel of grapes to can in Mason jars for the winter. At these times, our kitchen would be turned into a work area for peeling apples or peaches, or squeezing grapes for the canning process. There would be an area set aside for the peeling, a big pot on the stove boiling whatever the produce was, and then an even larger kettle with boiling water for the Mason jars and the actual canning process.

The smell from whatever was being canned would permeate the entire house and, of course, all of this made for good eating during the winter months. During the canning season, there would be baskets of fruit sitting on the back porch. I can remember looking forward to coming home from school and eating an apple or a peach or a bunch of Concord blue grapes. After my snack of fruit, I would go next door to play with Morris (Morrie) Wright, who was one year older than I. Our house was on the corner and had a very small yard, but the Wrights had what seemed to us then to be a very large back yard. It actually was not that big. My guess was that it was 50 feet wide and perhaps 70 feet from the back of their house to the end of the lot.

The Wright family had three boys. Morrie, who as I said was a year older than I; Francis, who was two years older than Morrie; and Edwin, who was two years older than Francis. Mr. Wright had a chicken wire fence built up around the yard about 16 feet high so that we could play baseball or other ball games without the ball going outside of the yard – usually. Obviously, the ball occasionally did go into the next yard and then we would have to run around the wire fence to retrieve it.

Many of the clothes I wore were hand-me-downs from the Wright boys and I never minded getting hand-me-downs from them. The quality of their clothing – even after they had worn it – was so much better than anything purchased new which my folks could have afforded, that I really enjoyed and prized the items of apparel I received from them.

On Thanksgiving weekend each year, we would dig a trench around the Wright's yard, about ten inches wide and six inches deep, and would throw the dirt toward the inside of the yard to serve as a dike for water so that the yard could be flooded for ice-skating. Mr. Wright worked for the City of Cleveland Public Utilities, and, after the first freezing weather arrived, he would have the utility department come out, attach a hose to the fire hydrant at the street, and flood the back yard with water which would freeze to make an ice-skating pond. From then on we would flood the

Institute for Divorce Financial Analysts™
24901 Northwestern Hwy., Suite 710
Southfield, MI 48075

"CDFAs can provide invaluable information that allows the court to arrive at a fair, equitable, and just resolution – not just at the moment of trial, but down the road as well."
– Honorable Kathleen M. McCarthy, JD, Family Court Division Judge

A new source of year-round income can be yours for years to come

- Create a new source of revenue and business referrals
- Increase your expertise in the financial aspects of divorce – from spousal and child support to tax and insurance issues
- Get referrals from lawyers and mediators
- Learn to illustrate different financial settlements
- Be part of our "Client Referral Program"
- Receive CE Credits; check out our website for details
- CDFA™ is the most recognized and time-tested designation

Register for our course today!

☏ (800) 875-1760
☏ (989) 631-3605
www.InstituteDFA.com

Don't Gamble with the Divorce Market...
...when there's a sure way to win!

Certified Divorce Financial Analysts™ are in demand

- More than two million North Americans will divorce this year

- 100% of divorces involve financial settlements

- Many lawyers, mediators, and separated individuals are now seeking the services of a CDFA™

- CDFA™ is the only comprehensive divorce-planning designation listed by the CFP Board in its listing of professional certification programs. *

A CDFA™ is trained and qualified to:

- Serve as a financial expert on divorce cases

- Present powerful data to back up an argument

- Offer financially sound settlement options

* CFP Board does not endorse or otherwise approve any specific certification programs and CFP Board's listing of any certification program does not constitute an endorsement or approval of that program.

Institute for Divorce Financial Analysts™

We take your future into account.

pond with a garden hose to keep the surface as smooth as possible.

The Wrights had handed down to the Noble children the kind of ice skates that clamped onto the sole of a shoe in the same way that roller skates fastened to the sole of a shoe. We had many happy times ice-skating on this pond, playing some form of hockey, crack the whip, or just skating. Mrs. Wright was a saintly woman who permitted us – with our skates still on – to come into her kitchen, where she had a well-scrubbed, wooden floor. We would walk in and sit down and she would invariably bring out a plate of cookies for us to eat. If our feet were cold, she would light the oven and we would actually stick our feet, skates and all, into the oven to get our feet warm. I grew up thinking that all women would permit children to enter their kitchen, walk around the kitchen floor on ice skates, and put their feet in the oven, while serving them cookies.

I also have vivid memories of the ice man delivering ice to our house in Cleveland. The ice man came in a very high, horse-drawn wagon which was closed on three sides and at the top except for the back which was open. He came every other day, three times a week. My mother would place a card in the window which indicated whether she wanted 25, 50, 75, or 100 pounds of ice delivered. When the ice man arrived at our house and saw the sign, he would hoist himself up onto a step at the back of his wagon and, using an ice pick, he would cut off the proper chunk of ice, depending on how much ice my mother wanted. He would then carry this block of ice on his shoulder right into our house and put it into the top space of the ice box (it was not called a refrigerator in those days). There was a space underneath the ice box left for a shallow pan that was put there to catch the dripping water from the melting ice. This pan had to be emptied daily or it would overflow and spill out onto the floor, which happened frequently.

When the ice man went into the house, we would jump on a step at the back of the wagon and take small pieces of ice to suck on and eat. The ice man was usually a young man with bulging muscles which he needed to handle the large blocks of ice. He never seemed to mind us helping ourselves to the small chunks of ice. I imagine the ice man took it for granted that kids would take a little ice, which had no commercial value but was wonderfully refresing on a hot day.

When I was about eight years old, the house of Walter Mason, one of my playmates, burned down. Walter lived in a very large house at the corner of Mentor and West 14th Street just one block from where we lived. Late one evening, after we had gone to bed, the house caught on fire and burned so furiously that it gutted the entire house. Mother and father permitted us to put on our clothes and go across the street from the burning house to see the flames leaping up out of its roof. Walter's father produced and sold ink for use with dip pens. We never knew whether some of the chemicals he used to make ink or something else had caused the fire. The Masons had to move to live somewhere else which abruptly ended my association with this very fine playmate.

At the back of our house, across our small yard of only about 30 feet, was another house where a boy named Bobby Ham lived. I believe he was two years younger than I was. I remember well having done something to Bobby Ham which made him very unhappy. I do not remember what it was, but I can remember my father coming home, hearing about whatever it was that I had done, and insisting that I go over to apologize. I think I was seven years old, and it was a long trip across that yard, and a difficult thing for me to ring the doorbell and then to apologize. But it was a lesson that I remember very distinctly and have thought of many times since, that when a person makes a mistake, the quicker one admits it and apologizes or corrects it, the better.

Another similar incident occurred when I was approximately eight years old, and Morrie Wright and I got into some kind of spat. Each of us was called into our respective homes. I was scolded and told to go and apologize immediately to Morrie. I reluctantly shuffled out of the house and headed toward the Wright house, looking down at the ground. When I was almost to the fence dividing our two yards, I looked up and realized that Morrie was shuffling toward me. Each of us then realized that the other had been sent out to apologize and we broke out into gales of laughter. That was the end of our spat and I cannot imagine a better one.

Chapter Three • Early School Days

For my seven years in elementary school (kindergarten through sixth grade), I attended Scranton School which was five blocks from my home. The school was a stately, two-story brick building. The roof had four steep peaks, one going to each of the four sides of the building. There were three entrances, one at the front which opened onto a walkway down to the street, and one at the side and one at the back, both of which led to the playground. The building and playground covered the end of a city block facing Scranton Road. The school's playground had no equipment or basketball hoops, only a gravel surface.

There were four classrooms on each of the two floors, with one classroom located at each corner of the building on each floor. On the first floor there was a wide open space between the classrooms in the center, which was used for assemblies, where the students would all sit on the floor. The second floor had an open area with a railing around it, looking down on the first floor. This opening from the first floor all the way to the second floor ceiling gave the school a feeling of spaciousness. Each classroom had two doors from the big hall, one of which opened directly into the room while the other one opened into a cloakroom.

The cloakroom was a narrow room running the full length of the classroom with an opening into the classroom. In the morning, we entered through the cloakroom, hanging our hats and coats or jackets on a hook and – in winter – depositing our overshoes on the floor. When we left, we went out through the cloakroom, picking up our wraps on the way. I do not remember that there was ever a problem with anyone taking anything that did not belong to him or her, which is quite different from the situation today. I understand that many grade schools now have to have lockers for the students to lock up their belongings because otherwise they would be stolen.

I remember very few discipline problems at Scranton because the students had a very high degree of respect for their teachers. The few discipline problems that occurred were handled by the teacher asking the student to stay after class. As far as I know, this involved the teacher only talking to the student. Occasionally, a problem would be severe enough to tell the student to go to the principal's office. I do not know what happened there because I was never sent, but I do know that it was considered a very severe punishment to be sent to the principal's office.

I do not remember any bullies bothering me on the way walking to or from school but there must have been some bullies at the school. It may have been because I always walked to and from school with two older sisters until they went on to junior high school, by which time I was one of the older students myself.

My school day memories are primarily happy ones. I remember, of course, my mother taking me to kindergarten and leaving me there. I also can remember learning the multiplication tables while I was turning the handle on the clothes wringer as my mother fed the clothes from the wash water into the rinse water and then from the rinse water into the clothes basket to be hung outdoors. My mother would quiz me on multiplication problems, asking one after the other for me to answer. This was a great way to learn the multiplication tables and I am sure I learned addition and subtraction the same way.

During the seven-year period I attended Scranton School, the principal was Miss Edgerton. The school assemblies were held in the large central area between the classrooms with all the students sitting on the floor. Miss Edgerton, who did considerable traveling during the summer school vacation, would show slides of the places she had visited on a screen for us to look at as she gave us a travelogue. I remember how excited we were by this glimpse into what we youngsters thought were pretty exotic places.

In third grade, I remember that our teacher, Miss Schnabel,

immediately after she called the class to order each morning would have us sing this song:

"Good morning to you. Good morning to you.
We're all in our places. With sun-shiny faces.
Good morning to you. Good morning to you."

That song still buzzes through my head in the morning and I often sing it to the receptionists as I come into the Rubbermaid office building. Another pleasant elementary school memory is the taste of milk. Milk has never tasted so good to me as it did during our morning recess at the Scranton School when we would get a glass half-pint bottle of milk with a straw.

My favorite teacher in elementary school was Miss Lockwood, my sixth grade teacher. She gave me a very good foundation in English, Geography, and Mathematics. I remember her using a mechanical device to illustrate the earth's orbit. It had a ball which represented the sun and an arm out to the side with a smaller ball that represented the earth. As she rotated the arm around the sun, the earth rotated on its axis and tilted first toward the sun to indicate summer and then away from the sun to show winter. The seasons in the northern hemisphere were, of course, reversed in the southern hemisphere. I think her lessons with this excellent teaching device gave me a very good understanding of how our own solar system, and basically the whole universe, works.

My sixth grade classroom at Scranton School had a door at the rear corner of the room, through the cloak room, to the principal's office. It was understood that when Miss Edgerton, the principal, wanted an errand run, she would call on the boy who sat in the last seat in the row nearest the cloak room. I was assigned to that seat and, therefore, did the errands for the principal. This gave me breaks during the day which I rather enjoyed.

One day, Miss Edgerton called me into her office and said that there was a small grocery and candy store just one block from the school where the owner was selling cigarettes to elementary school pupils. She asked me to go to the store and buy a package of cigarettes for which she gave me the money. This made me quite nervous because there was no smoking in our family. I had heard many parental talks about the harm resulting from smoking and, of course, I had never purchased cigarettes. But I went and bought a pack and brought it back to Miss Edgerton. A few days later I was asked to appear in court in downtown Cleveland to testify that I had bought this pack of cigarettes. My mother went with me and I remember being questioned about the purchase. I think the store owner was fined and quit selling cigarettes to minors.

During my school years, up until about the time I entered high school, all of us children did our homework around the dining room table because nowhere else in the house was there a large enough surface on which to write. The table was lighted by only a single overhead dining room lighting fixture, which today would be considered inadequate for good vision. My memory, however, is that the arrangement worked quite well.

CHAPTER FOUR • LIFE AT HOME

My parents were very religious and we attended services at the Methodist Episcopal Church with great regularity. My father sang in the choir every Sunday morning and at times conducted the choir. In addition, he always served as a Sunday school teacher or Sunday school superintendent. I can remember mother and father walking together with us children the four long blocks to the church for both Sunday school and church.

Prior to leaving the house on Sunday morning, mother would have prepared a casserole or roast, which would be cooking in the oven while we were at church and would be ready for Sunday dinner when we came home at noon. These meals were always very special and were prepared with much loving care. They might consist of a standing rib-roast, a crown roast of pork chops, or what my mother called a "six-layer" dinner that combined six different foods, including potatoes and ground beef. We often had scalloped potatoes or sweet potatoes with marshmallows on top to go with whatever main dish she had prepared. Looking back, I am very impressed with my mother's ability to see to it that we had such good food on a very small budget. Sometimes our food was very plain, but it was always very good. An example is fried mush, which was one of our favorite dishes. In order to have fried mush, we would first have a meal of mush and milk. It was the mush left over from this meal that my mother fried and served with maple syrup, which made it a special treat. Our breakfast usually consisted of oatmeal or cream of wheat.

Also, each Sunday morning before we went go to church, we would make a big batch of ice cream in our four-gallon ice cream freezer. The ice cream was made from the cream mother had taken from the top of each of the many quarts of milk we used at our house. This was before the days of homogenized milk and so the cream rose to the top of the milk bottles. We would take a block of ice delivered by the ice man for our ice box and would put it into a burlap bag. Using a piece of cord wood, we would then pound the ice until it was smashed into small pieces. We would use these ice fragments along with rock salt to make the ice cream, taking turns cranking the crank on a continuous basis until the ice cream was frozen. Then it was always a treat to lick the paddles from the ice cream freezer. The ice cream was left in the ice cream freezer, carefully packed with more ice and rock salt, to be eaten as dessert at Sunday noon dinner and Sunday evening supper. This was a weekly ritual and one that we rarely missed.

Because we had a limited budget, it was a rule at our house that while you did not have to finish the food on your plate, if you did not, you got no dessert. As a result, we tended to clean our plates of whatever main course was served. This developed a life-long habit, and I still find it very difficult to leave any food on my plate.

My folks set up very rigid rules for our family and everyone living in the household was expected to follow them. There was no smoking, no drinking, no dancing, and no card playing – at least not bridge and poker. Other card games such as Flinch and Pit were okay. Nor were we permitted to go to the movies. Our play in the summer time consisted of riding scooters, pedaling our wagons, and roller-skating. We would have roller-skating races by starting two children in opposite directions going around the block on which we lived to see who would get back to the starting point first.

In the summer, there was also Daily Vacation Bible School in the mornings five days a week for about four weeks. I started attending the Bible School at a very early age and continued until I was 12 years old, when I became an assistant to the teachers of younger children. One of the crafts taught at the Bible School was pounding designs into copper sheets and cutting them out to make various things such as a bookmark, bookends, or a candlestick holder. I apparently became fairly good at working with the copper sheets because I was assigned to teach younger children how to do it. I also remember being sent by streetcar to the Revere Copper and Brass plant on the east side where I picked up the copper sheets.

I also remember when I was about 12 years old seeing Edwin Wright, who was about five years older than I, making a crystal radio set. He had bought the components and assembled them onto a thin piece of wood. The set had a piece of galena crystal no more than 3/8th of an inch in diameter and a tiny, very thin piece of wire. The end of the wire was dropped down onto the piece of crystal and when it hit a particular spot on the crystal, it brought in a radio station which could be listened to through earphones. Only two stations broadcasted within the set's range. One station was in Cleveland and the other in Pittsburgh – undoubtedly KDKA. Radio was still in its infancy, and it was the first time I had seen a radio set because there were still relatively few of them in existence.

Edwin graduated from Yale in 1932, when the country was in the depths of the Great Depression. I remember him going out to look for work every day for perhaps six months. He would trudge up and down the streets of Cleveland, applying for a job at any business that would even allow him to come in and ask for work. He finally was hired by a gasoline service station doing a job that we called back then "pumping gas," and he also lubricated automobiles. We called it "pumping gas" because each gasoline pump actually had a big four-foot long handle that had to be pumped vigorously back and forth to bring the gasoline up to a glass tank at the top of the pump. From there, gravity fed it through a hose into a car's gasoline tank. The filling station where Edwin got his job was owned by the Sinclair Oil Company. Starting from that very lowly position, Edwin worked his way up through the organization to an office job and then rose up through the management ranks to become a Vice President of Sinclair Oil.

Francis, who was a couple of years younger than Edwin, graduated from Yale in 1934 and also experienced difficulty in finding work. He eventually got a job with the East Ohio Gas Company and ended up as President of that corporation.

Morris went to University School in Shaker Heights for his high school education and then went on to Western Reserve University. He got a job with TRW in Cleveland and ended up in an executive position, heading up their automotive products division.

The fact that all of the Wright boys and I went on to successful business careers is in no small measure a reflection of the hard times in which we grew up. I believe the Depression era gave us the incentive to work hard and a real determination to succeed. That was certainly true in my case and, although they came from a much more prosperous family background, I am reasonably sure it motivated the Wrights as well, particularly Edwin.

CHAPTER FIVE • VISITING AND WORKING ON FARMS

Among my fondest memories are the visits I made for a couple of weeks each summer to the farm owned by my Uncle Will Meiche (my mother's brother) and Aunt Anna in North Royalton, about 15 miles south of Cleveland. I made these visits alone until my brother Milton – who was three-and-a-half years younger than I – was old enough to join me.

It was on Uncle Will's farm that I got my first taste of farm work which many people look back at as being hard, exhausting labor. For me, it was different and, therefore, a lot of fun. I enjoyed watching Uncle Will milk the cows every morning and night, and watching him feed the pigs and chickens. I particularly liked helping to make hay. I would ride the horse-drawn hay wagon and try to spread the hay around the wagon as my uncle, using a pitch fork, threw the hay up onto the wagon. Then I rode on top of the hay as my uncle drove the horses back to the barn and I also would help arrange the hay in the mow as he threw it with a pitch fork from the wagon up into the mow.

I also enjoyed helping Uncle Will put the bundles of wheat into shocks, which were thrown from the horse-drawn McCormick binder. I even enjoyed turning the milk separator by hand each evening after the milking was done. The separator separated the cream from the skim milk – the thin, watery skim milk would be fed to the pigs. I did *not* enjoy cleaning out the chicken coop, but I did it. Riding in Uncle Will's open Model T Ford each Sunday morning to attend church at the Methodist church in town was also fun.

Uncle Will was a tall, thin, lanky man with an Abraham Lincoln stature and appearance. He was a pleasant man and one of the kindest men I have ever known. During the week, he wore well-worn bib overalls with straps up over the shoulders and a work shirt. On Saturdays, when he drove into Cleveland to sell butter and eggs and other produce, he would wear a relatively new pair of overalls. On Sundays, he wore a suit with a shirt and tie, none of which seemed to fit properly. The shirt collar would be too big and the trouser legs would not be quite long enough, but people had such great respect for him that I always had the impression that none of these clothing problems really made any difference.

One spring my uncle and aunt invited me to spend my spring vacation week at the farm during maple sugar time and I have always looked back on this as a high point in my boyhood. My mother bought me a new pair of overalls and a pair of boots which came up to my knees. I helped gather the sap from the trees by going to each tree and emptying the accumulated sap into a bucket.

Then I emptied the bucket into the big drum on the mud sled which was drawn by horses. Eventually, I would ride the mud sled back to the sugar camp where the sap was being boiled. The taste of maple syrup directly from the trays where it was boiled is a memory never to be forgotten. And, of course, being able to slosh through the mud wearing boots was great fun.

In addition to the two weeks I spent with Uncle Will and Aunt Anna during the summer, my entire family also made occasional visits to their farm on Sunday afternoon. On these Sunday visits, all of us kids had happy times jumping from the rafters in the barn onto the hay in the haymow and riding a tire swing attached to a tree limb with a long rope which would swing us from a small cliff out across a creek and back. We also enjoyed walking out into the pasture or into the woods. Occasionally, Uncle Will would take us for bareback rides on his work horses, which were big, strong animals but very gentle.

Our family also used to alternate Thanksgiving Day with my father's sister, Aunt Clara, and her husband, Uncle Jim Hamlin, at their home in North Royalton. They had two children: Betty Jane (about ten years younger than I) and Dwight (about three years younger than I). We had sumptuous Thanksgiving meals with turkey and all the trimmings. Our grandparents – my father's mother and father – always joined us for Thanksgiving dinner.

One Thanksgiving, after it had been snowing all morning, all of us went out to ride a bobsled down a long hill on Royalton Road which is now State Route 82. There was no traffic at all and we rode the bobsled time and again down the hill and then dragged it back up for another turn. The bobsled consisted of two sleds connected together with a long wooden plank on top of them and a steering mechanism on the front sled. I doubt that anyone today would think such a thing would be safe to ride on, but we thought it was marvelous and had a great time.

Quite frequently, there were big snowstorms – close to being blizzards – on Thanksgiving Day which resulted in our driving back to Cleveland on snow-covered roads, often while the snow was continuing to come down heavily. Those driving conditions made for an exciting trip on the narrow two-lane roads of those days, but fortunately we never had an accident.

My first clear memories of Grandma and Grandpa Noble are at their house in North Royalton. About once a month on a Sunday afternoon, my mother and father would drive us out to visit Grandma and Grandpa Noble. We children – my sisters Hazel and Grace, my brother Milton, and I – were often left outdoors to play while the grownups talked inside.

On two occasions that I can remember, Hazel, Grace, Milton and I were left with our Grandparents for two or three days while my mother and father took trips to attend sales meetings of the New York Life Insurance Company, for which my father worked. A strong memory of these extended visits was the pleasant smell of coffee in the morning. Since we never had coffee at our house, the fragrant aroma of the coffee brewed in an old-fashioned perco- lator is still vivid in my memory.

I also remember early one morning when we children were using a walkway made of boards to go to the outhouse and we saw a snake crawling out from under the boards. We rushed back to the house to tell our grandparents about the snake. Grandpa immedi- ately went out to the barn, got a spade, and came back and removed the board where we had seen the snake. Under that walk- way was a whole nest of snakes, at least a dozen of them. Grandpa chopped those snakes into small pieces with his spade – watching him was something I will never forget.

I remember hearing the adults talking about Grandpa having had an automobile accident at the corner of Ridge Road and Pleasant Valley Road in which his automobile, which must have been a Model T, was totally destroyed. This accident occurred in about 1922. The next time we visited our grandparents, I remem- ber very distinctly seeing Grandpa's new car – a Model T Ford Sedan, which had only one door on the entire car. This door opened on the passenger side and was located between the back of the front passenger seat and the back seat. Both the driver and the person sitting in the front passenger seat had to enter at the center of the car and walk forward to their seats in the space between the driver's seat and the passenger's seat.

About 1927, Grandma and Grandpa Noble began building a new house facing onto State Road, about 200 feet south of their prior house at the corner of Akins and State Roads. First they built a garage and moved into it and lived there for an entire summer while their new house was being constructed. Apparently they had sold their old house before the new one was started. I can remember visiting them several times while they were still living in the garage.

One of my most vivid memories – and a very pleasant one – was Grandma going to her cupboard and taking down a cookie jar, which was full of her home-made cookies. They were drop cookies on which she had melted brown sugar and they tasted delicious.

During our Sunday afternoon visits, we often played croquet in the front yard. Father was pretty good at it and he seemed to take a special delight in driving our balls out of the yard. A drop in the front yard about midway between the house and the street added to the hazard of play. Another outstanding feature of our Sunday afternoon visits was gathering around the piano for a song fest with Grandma playing and all of the family singing together.

Grandma and Grandpa Noble usually had a dog which may have been a miniature bulldog – not too friendly an animal, as I remember. The people who lived across the street from our grandparents were, I believe, named Guest. We thought they must be rich because they actually had a swimming pool in their yard!

About once a year, when we visited Grandma and Grandpa Noble on a Sunday afternoon, we would find that Grandpa's brother, Will Noble, Allie his wife, and their daughters Elizabeth and Ruth were also there. I liked both Uncle Will and Aunt Allie very much. In fact, I was very much impressed with their entire family because they were sweet, considerate, happy, fun-loving people. I was also very much impressed with the very large Buick open touring car in which they drove to North Royalton from Delaware, Ohio, where Uncle Will owned a furniture store.

I remember when I accompanied my father on a trip he made to Columbus, Ohio, in connection with his business, and we stayed overnight at Uncle Will and Aunt Allie's house in Delaware. I must have been about 11 years old at the time, and I was very much impressed with their very large and beautifully furnished house. My eyes must have been like saucers when I saw the pony and pony cart that belonged to Elizabeth and Ruth!

CHAPTER SIX • MY INTRODUCTION TO WORK AND ALICE

In 1919, when I was four years old, my folks moved from East Lansing, Michigan, to Cleveland. For seven years, until 1926 when I was 11, my father drove a Star Bakery truck and sold bread from door to door out in the countryside. Sometimes on Saturdays and sometimes on regular work days during the summer vacation from school I would ride along with my father on his bread delivery route. He had two different routes which he alternated each day. One route went through Hinckley, Strongsville, Brunswick, and North Royalton. The other went further east through Brecksville, Richfield, Peninsula, Macedonia, Northfield Center, and Northfield.

My father was ill so seldom that there was no one else trained to know his routes. On one rare occasion when he was ill, he asked me to ride along with the man who was substituting for him to show him the route. He later told me that I had missed only three customers on the entire route. During the last couple of years of his driving the bread truck, I would get up and go with him at six o'clock in the morning to help him load the truck. Later my brother, Milton, would go with us and Milton would help my father while I would help some other driver load his truck for which I remember getting a quarter. Because I was small, I would be the one who would get into the truck and the driver would toss the loaves of bread to me so I could stack them in neat rows.

When my father first started driving a truck, he had an old Ford Model T truck without a self starter, which meant that he had to crank it by hand every time he started the engine. I can remember one time after father had finished his breakfast and was getting ready to start his route, the crank kicked back and broke his arm.

When I finished the sixth grade I moved to Lincoln High School, which had seventh grade through twelfth grade. The very first week my homeroom teacher asked me if I would be the room's representative for the school newspaper – *The Lincoln Log*. This meant that each Monday I would take orders for that week's issue of the paper and then early on Wednesday I would go up to the Lincoln Log Room – an attic room on the third floor – to get the number of papers I had ordered. I would bring the papers back to the homeroom, distribute them, and collect a nickel for each paper. Then, at some point during the day, I would take the money I had collected up to the Lincoln Log Room and turn it in. I had to be sure that I had collected enough money to pay for the number of papers I had taken in the morning. I did this during the entire time that I was in the seventh and eighth grades.

Apparently, I did it pretty well because, when I was in ninth grade, Miss McCoy, the faculty advisor in charge of *The Lincoln Log*, asked me if I would be circulation manager for the entire school. This meant that I had to take all the orders from all the homerooms on Monday and tabulate them to determine how many papers we needed. On Wednesday morning, I had to go into the school an hour and a half early to count out the papers for each of the homeroom representatives to pick up. I had to keep a record of how many each homeroom got and then at the end of the day I had to count all of the money that was turned in and be sure that each homeroom representative had turned in the proper amount of money for the number of papers he or she had taken out that morning. I served as *The Lincoln Log* circulation manager for three years until the end of my junior year.

This early experience of looking after other people's money and balancing the number of papers against the nickels turned in by the homerooms may have had some influence on my eventually choosing the occupation of an accountant. All I can remember feeling at the time, however, is a great sense of relief when the two figures matched. I believe the best indication that the work was something I enjoyed is the fact that I continued doing it throughout my junior year even though I also was working at the soda fountain of a nearby drug store every evening from 5:30 to 11:30.

In school I think mathematics came easier for me than other subjects. I particularly enjoyed algebra and plane and solid geometry. Plane and solid geometry seemed to me to be particularly easy subjects, I think partially because they seemed to be so logical. As a supplement to regular class work, our teachers at Lincoln High arranged some interesting field trips for us. My high school class made about three field trips per year; one to the Natural History Museum, one to the Cleveland Museum of Art, and one to hear the Cleveland Orchestra play at the Masonic Temple.

At the Art Museum, I remember having been most impressed with the life-sized models of knights wearing heavy steel armor for protection in battle. I also liked the life-sized model horses which wore protection made out of metal mesh while their riders wore even heavier looking armor.

During the time I attended high school, the Cleveland Orchestra had not yet moved to Severance Hall and still played at the Masonic Temple on Euclid Avenue at East 32nd Street. I was always impressed by this field trip and enjoyed listening to the Cleveland Orchestra. On one of these visits to the Masonic Temple, instead of hearing the Cleveland Orchestra, we heard John Philip Sousa and his band, which I think at that age impressed me much more than even the beautiful classical music of the Cleveland Orchestra.

At Lincoln High School, I played French horn in the high school band which primarily meant marching at football games, but we also had one trip to Akron to compete in a statewide high school band contest. I was never very good on the French horn, although I did take lessons every Saturday morning from a member of the Cleveland Orchestra at West Tech High School. It was quite a distance from where we lived and required changing streetcars to get there, so it took the entire morning when I went for lessons.

For us kids, doing work around the house was a big part of our lives. I remember that my brother Milton and I painted our entire house on Mentor Avenue in the summer of 1931, when I was 16 years old and Milton was 12. We borrowed two extension ladders and a plank that had brackets on it from a neighbor. When the brackets were attached to the ladders, the plank formed a kind of scaffold on which the two of us could stand while we painted. The plank was pretty sturdy and neither of us weighed all that much so it was relatively safe.

The house was a full two-story building which had very high roof peaks and, because it had been built in the 1890s, it had a great deal of decorative fretwork or "gingerbread" all along the roof line to the gables. This required a lot of careful, detailed painting at a very high level from the ground and we soon learned the wisdom of the adage about never looking down! My recollection is that it took us about three weeks to complete the painting. Being as young and inexperienced in handling a paint brush as we were, I think we did a very good job with no major accidents or paint spills, although we got a lot of paint on ourselves.

We had to make our own entertainment, of course, and that meant playing family games. Television was still more than two decades away. Although the radio had been invented a few years earlier, we could not afford to own one. So we played card games of Pit and Flinch and we had a Carom Board (a sort of miniature pool table with wooden rings instead of balls) and that was our entertainment at home. My favorite game was Pit, a very raucous, lively game where you bid or try to exchange your cards for someone else's cards. We had a lot of fun doing that.

When I was growing up, our front porch became an assembly place for the neighborhood children. There would frequently be a game of some kind going on, either with the Carom Board or Flinch or Pit cards, or, in the later years, playing Monopoly, a game which came out when I was about 14 years old.

We also had a lot of fun with the other young people at our church, which was a very big part of our lives and was to prove especially significant in my life. When I was 14 years old, our church had a special Sunday night service to welcome back the pastor's wife, who had been ill for three months. As part of the welcoming ceremony, young people were to hold up arches decorated with flowers through which she would enter the church and walk up to the platform. In order to have enough people, the young people's group from a nearby church had been invited to join us and help hold up the arches.

When we were lining up to get partners to hold the other end of our arch, I spotted a beautiful auburn-haired girl across the room who was from the other church. I angled over to arrange for her to hold the other end of my arch and that is how I met Alice Jackson, who was to become my wife ten years later. Because she attended another church, I did not see her except when she would occasionally visit our church and young people's group. Through those visits, she became acquainted with my sister, Grace, who was one year older than I.

I continued to think that Alice was the most beautiful girl I had ever seen and would spend whatever time I could talking to her before or after any church service or young people's meeting she happened to attend. One memorable afternoon, when I was working behind the soda fountain at the drug store, she stopped in on her way home from West Tech High School. She had walked a considerable distance from her high school to get the Clark Avenue streetcar so that she could transfer at the corner of West 25th Street and Clark and stop in to see me. I was very impressed by the trouble she had taken to see me. I prepared for her – and paid for – the biggest banana split sundae that she or I had ever seen.

When I was growing up, one of the important rituals of a boy becoming a young man was the purchase of his first pair of long pants. Until about the age of 14, all boys wore knickers with long socks coming up over the calf and under the elastic band of the knickers. It seemed to me that I had to wait longer than most of my friends for my folks to purchase my first pair of long trousers. But it was a memorable day when they did. They bought me a complete suit with a pair of long trousers and it was a proud day indeed for me. I wore the new suit only to church at first, continuing to wear knickers on all school days for a considerable time longer.

Along with the long pants came a greater level of responsibility. When I was about 14 years old, I remember a time when I was having trouble getting everything done that I needed to do. My father gave me a lesson in time management. He had me make a schedule of how my time would be spent from the time I got up in the morning until I went to bed at night. The schedule provided enough time for me to complete everything I needed to do. It not only helped me at that time, but ever since then the discipline it gave me has helped me in managing my time.

CHAPTER SEVEN • THE DEATHS OF MY FATHER AND MOTHER

One day in June 1930, when I was 15 years old, my father came home in the middle of the afternoon extremely ill with severe abdominal pains. He went to bed and my mother called the doctor who came and diagnosed the problem as acute appendicitis. My father was taken to the Deaconess Hospital in the Brooklyn section of Cleveland for an emergency appendectomy. Before the doctor arrived, my father called me into his bedroom and handed me the keys to his car and asked me if I thought I could drive the car around to put it into the rented garage two doors from where we lived. I said yes and took the keys.

I had never driven any car, other than sliding over to the middle of the seat when my father was driving and steering the car for a few minutes. I had never operated a gearshift, nor had I operated a clutch or the brake pedals on the floor. This was before the days of synchro-mesh gears so that shifting gears at that time was very tricky. I immediately went next door to tell Morrie Wright of my assignment and to get moral support from him. Even though he was a year older than I, he had never driven a car either. He came with me so that we could pool our collective lack of knowledge and to muster up my courage.

The car was a 1926 Chandler Sedan with a long-handled manual gearshift lever mounted on the floor. I got into the driver's seat and Morrie and I discussed for some time the best way to go about the job. The car was facing in the wrong direction on the street alongside our house. I decided that rather than trying to shift gears, first into reverse and then into a forward drive, I would go all the way around the block in first gear. That would permit me to go only in a forward direction. I further decided that I would never shift out of first gear so that I would not have to operate the shift lever more than once.

I depressed the clutch and got the gearshift into the position of the first gear and, with a mighty series of jerking motions, got the car going in a forward direction. I slowed down at each of the three corners I had to turn, but never did come to a total stop. I was very fortunate in that, as I approached each intersection, there were no cars coming so I could move around the corners without stopping and starting again. I successfully drove into the drive where our rented garage was and successfully pulled into the garage and properly put in the clutch and stopped the car in the proper place in the garage. I viewed this as a tremendous victory.

My father progressed slowly but satisfactorily in his recovery from surgery. After ten days of recuperation, he was scheduled to come home in a couple of days. At that point, my mother, grand-mother, and grandfather were all visiting in his room when he reported having stomach pains. An intern came in to examine him. After examining him, the intern asked my mother and grandparents to leave the room so he could pump out my father's stomach. They were told that the procedure would take 15 or 20 minutes. Forty-five minutes later a doctor came out to tell them that my father had died during the procedure.

I was at home when my mother returned and all that she said was, "Edgar is gone. It's all over." The undertaker told my mother that my father had drowned and that the intern must have placed the pump into his trachea instead of his esophagus where it belonged. The undertaker also told my mother that she could sue the hospital for what clearly had been negligence by one of its employees. I can remember my mother's reaction. She said simply, "Suing the hospital won't bring Edgar back."

My mother did an amazing job of carrying on following my father's death, providing a constructive family life for her six children as best she could. It must have been very difficult at times, but she instilled in us a strong work ethic and a desire to get a good education. It is a tribute to her efforts that all of us went on to successful careers in various professions.

Hazel became a chiropractor in Bethel, Kentucky. Grace became a nurse and during World War II she went to Hawaii as a Navy nurse. She stayed there, married, and reared a family. For many years, Grace supervised all the nurses at a large retirement village and nursing home. Milton spent most of his career as the manager of a branch bank in North Royalton. Paul graduated from Ohio University and got his Master's degree and Ph.D. degree at Ohio State University. He returned to Ohio University to teach accounting and became Dean of the School of Commerce. From there, Paul became President of the Printers' Association in the New York City area. Roger became a manufacturers' representative for large milling machines and steel processing equipment.

Following my father's death, our family did without a car for a year. We used the streetcar to go wherever we wanted to go, including to and from church which was about four miles away from our house (we had changed churches by then). Friends of the family were very kind and often took us to church and brought us back. I particularly remember Mr. and Mrs. Besserer who were so kind and jolly. Many children, including us, called them "Mom" and "Pop."

After a year of this, my mother decided it would help keep the family together to have an automobile so, in July 1931, she bought a used 1928 Dodge four-door sedan. The color was called cherry red. I thought that car was beautiful and I spent many hours using Simonize Cleaner and then Simonize Wax to keep it nice and shiny.

In 1931, the tire manufacturers had not yet developed tires that were durable enough to last very long. The average life of an automotive tire was anywhere from 8,000 to 10,000 miles and it was a great exception for a tire to last for 12,000 miles of use. At 8,000 to 10,000 miles, the tread on a tire was worn so thin that it was down to where the cord showed through. Because tire rubber was so soft and wore thin so quickly, tires frequently picked up tacks or nails or pieces of glass. All tires at that time had a rubber inner tube that inflated inside the tire body to hold air and cushion the ride. Any sharp object picked up on the soft rubber surface of the tire would quickly work its way in to the inner tube and puncture it so the air leaked out and the tire went flat.

This kind of puncture happened so frequently on our 1928 Dodge that I became quite expert at changing a flat tire and could usually do it in about 15 minutes. As soon as we would get home with a flat tire, we would repair the inner tube by first pumping it up outside the tire and then putting it in water so the air bubbles could help us locate the leaking puncture. We would then scrape the puncture spot with a piece of metal that was roughened on one side like a cheese grater. This prepared the surface for the glue which we put on the puncture and then attached a rubber patch over it. The little metal grater, the glue, and a number of patches came in a small kit that every motorist carried in those days.

It was a very difficult and dirty job to get the tire off the rim in order to get the inner tube out to be repaired, but few people could afford to have a garage do it. Most trucks in those days had solid rubber tires which were immune to punctures because there was no inner tube in them, but without the cushioning of the air-filled inner tube they made for a very hard, bumpy ride. That was, I expect, the origin of the statement, "It rides like a truck," to describe a car with a particularly uncomfortable ride.

In 1938, when I was 23 years old, my mother developed cancer of the esophagus and was ill for about six months, continually getting worse. For the last three months of her life, she was confined to her bed until her death. I can remember Alice and my going to her bedside and telling her that we had become engaged and that we were planning to be married the following summer.

At that point, we had not announced our engagement to anyone else. Due to the cancer, my mother's voice was gone, but she gave us what we interpreted as her enthusiastic consent, with a smile, a nod of her head, and holding each of our hands in hers. She died quietly about three weeks later.

The fall after my mother died, the brakes on our Dodge gave way and I did not have the money to have them repaired. I moved the Dodge to my Uncle Will's farm where it was stored for the winter in one of his sheds. Having no car meant that wherever any member of our family wanted to go, we either walked or took a streetcar and often a combination of both. For example, Alice lived about one mile from the nearest streetcar line, which meant that when I went to see her I walked a mile from the streetcar to her house and then a mile back to the streetcar. The return trip was a one-mile walk if I got to the streetcar stop by 11:10 p.m. to catch the last streetcar on the Pearl Road line. If not, I had to walk another mile to the State Road line which had a later schedule.

Shortly before Alice and I got married in 1939, we bought a black three-year-old 1936 Ford two-door sedan for $135. It served us well for two years until we moved to Wooster and for $722 bought a new 1941 Plymouth Coupe, which we kept several years because no civilian cars were made during World War II.

CHAPTER EIGHT • EDUCATION AND MY PERSONAL CODE

My mother wanted me to be a minister and, therefore, in the fall of 1931, she sent me to Allentown Bible School in Allentown, Pennsylvania, for my last year of high school. My two sisters, Hazel and Grace, went with me or, perhaps more accurately, I went with them. Hazel had been attending the Bible School for two years and Grace for one year prior to my going there. When we left, each of us took one medium-sized piece of luggage. I remember that this was not a problem, because I did not have anything more to take than would fit neatly into a single bag. I tell my grandchildren this when I see them packing a whole van full of luggage, electronic equipment, and a host of other belongings to haul away to college. But my sisters and I had no radios, television sets, record players, or refrigerators to take with us.

We made the trip to the Allentown Bible School by a route that was rather circuitous but very economical. First, we took a boat from Cleveland across the lake to Buffalo, New York. Then we took a bus from Buffalo to Allentown. The trip took many hours but there was a lot of good scenery so it was never boring.

At the Bible School, all students had to work an hour and a half per day so that the cost of tuition, room, and board could be held to a very low figure. My first job, along with two other boys, was peeling potatoes for the entire student body, which meant that I had to get up very early in the morning and peel what looked like a mountain of potatoes. I thought there had to be jobs that were less demanding, at least in terms of a better schedule if nothing else. So during the first semester I looked around the school to see what job I could do during the second semester. I applied for and got the job of dusting the library, a much less onerous form of employment, particularly since I did not do it very thoroughly. When I was dusting the library, the school's housekeeper, Miss Lukabeal, would come in periodically to see what kind of a job I was doing. She would rub her finger over the rung of a chair and, if she found dust on it, she would show me her finger with the dust smudge on it. My comment was always, "I must have missed that."

When I was 15 and 16 years old, I did some singing in the church choir and a little singing in a male quartet. When I went to Allentown Bible School I was invited to sing in the school's male quartet. We sang church music and were invited to sing in churches nearby and occasionally some distance from the school, using the school's automobile for transportation. In the quartet, I sang second tenor. When I went to Fort Wayne Bible Institute (see page 35), I was again invited to sing as second tenor in the school's male quartet, which also was invited to sing in local and distant churches. In both schools this was a wonderful association and a wonderful outlet for me. The other members of the quartets were very friendly, affable boys, and we had a great deal of fun together.

In June 1932, I was scheduled to graduate from high school in Allentown at age 17. So my mother could attend the graduation commencement, I took a bus from Allentown to Cleveland. As soon as I got to Cleveland, which was late in the afternoon, my mother and I got into our 1928 Dodge to make the 500-mile drive back to Allentown. My mother did not drive, so I had to do all the driving. I was pretty tired but we had to drive straight through without any stops except for gasoline. My mother had brought along quite a few oranges and she kept feeding me orange slices through the night, which helped keep me awake. We pulled up at the Bible School after dawn the next morning.

The next school year, during the winter of 1932-33, I attended the Fort Wayne Bible Institute in Fort Wayne, Indiana, studying both the Old Testament and the New Testament. I even studied Greek with the objective of being able to read the New Testament in the original language. During my time at Fort Wayne Bible Institute, I determined that I did not want to be a minister unless I could get a very good education. By that I meant a four-year college degree and some graduate work beyond it. I felt that way because I had heard too many ministers who did not have an adequate education and, therefore, in my opinion, did an inadequate job of preaching and ministering to their congregations. Since I could see no way that I could afford to get an education which I would consider adequate, I thought I might be able to do good in the world by proving that a person could earn a living while living up to Christian principles.

Mind you, I thought it would be a victory to be able to earn a living while practicing Christian principles. I never thought that a person who followed such principles could be successful in business, because I believed, like so many young people do, that in order to advance in business it would be necessary to compromise one's principles. This feeling, along with some other factors, made me believe that I was entering into business with a handicap compared to the young men with whom I was working.

Another reason I thought I was handicapped was the fact that, being from a poor family, I did not have any contacts with business people to whom I could look for advice, counsel, and help. Because I had never learned to dance or play cards, and because I did not believe in drinking or smoking, I also moved in quite a different circle of people. I felt, therefore, that I did not have the contacts which other young men had.

For all of these reasons, I began to develop a personal code that I have followed all my life. Part of that code was my conviction that in order to keep a job and make a living, it would be necessary for me to work longer hours than the young men with whom I was working. I remember thinking that if I worked 20 percent more hours for the same pay, it would put me on an even playing field with the other men despite their educational and financial advantages. As it turned out, I now believe that operating on the basis of Christian principles actually was an advantage for me in business and my personal code of working extra hours actually gave me another advantage over the people with whom I was competing in the business world.

CHAPTER NINE • BLACK FRIDAY AND THE GREAT DEPRESSION

On October 29, 1929, when I was 14 years old, the stock market crashed. I can remember my father sitting at the kitchen table and talking about newspaper articles concerning the crash. That October day became known as "Black Friday" and it was to usher in the Great Depression that would change the lives of everyone who lived through it. At the time, however, the stock market crash did not have an immediate effect on my family. My folks were very poor and they did not own a single share of stock in any company.

As I have described, my father died after surgery in June 1930 when I was 15 years old. Within three weeks after he died, I got a job working evenings at a soda fountain in a drug store seven blocks from our house, which was a 12-minute walk. I worked there from 5:30 p.m. to 11:30 p.m. six nights a week, Monday through Saturday, plus one Sunday per month from 9:00 a.m. to 11:30 p.m. I got an hour off for lunch and an hour off for dinner. I continued working there through my entire junior year in high school and throughout the next summer. The period that I worked at the soda fountain was during the early stages of the Depression and I made only $1.00 per night, or 16-2/3 cents per hour for the six hours I worked. I made $2.00 for the 12-1/2 hours I worked on Sunday once a month.

In the summer of 1930, following my father's death and after I got my job at the drug store, I started to cut my brother's hair to save the 50 cents a barber charged for a haircut in those days. I decided that I could do a better job and that it would pay off eventually for me to learn how to cut hair better, so I went downtown to a barber college and signed up for two weeks of training in how to cut hair. The regular course for barbers was nine months long, but I just wanted to learn the basic fundamentals so I signed up for only two weeks, which was all I could afford. To take the course, I had to buy all of the equipment for cutting hair, including a pair of hand-operated clippers, a pair of barber scissors, a barber comb, a straight razor, a shaving mug to hold the soap, and a shaving brush. (It was not until years later that I acquired a pair of electric clippers.) Men came into the barber college for hair cuts that were free if they used the beginning barbers. Thereafter, the price graduated up to 10 cents, 20 cents, and 25 cents, depending on the length of time a student barber had been in training. I, of course, could only work on those men who were willing to take a free hair cut from a rank beginner.

Following my two weeks of training, I cut my brother's hair and also the hair of a couple of boys for whom my Aunt Bertha (my mother's sister) provided a foster home. When I went away to the Allentown Bible School and later to the Fort Wayne Bible Institute, I cut hair for some of the students by setting up a stool in my room. I charged 25 cents for a haircut while the barbers were charging 50 cents. At Fort Wayne, even one of the instructors came in a couple of times for a haircut. Many years later, I cut my two sons' hair, giving them flat-top butch hair cuts until they went away to college.

While it was pretty tough working and going to high school, I do not want to make my teen years sound like something out of a Dickens novel. Families were a lot closer back then and, although we were poor, we enjoyed life as much as most people we knew.

President Roosevelt closed all the banks on March 6, 1933, but I do not think that this event had much of a direct impact on my family. I rather doubt that my mother even had a checking account because my parents always lived from hand to mouth, paying cash for what they bought. My mother may have lost a small amount if she had a savings account, but I do not know for sure. In retrospect, I think Roosevelt acted impulsively in declaring the so-called "Bank Holiday," closing many banks that never should have been closed. A lot of banks were in deep trouble by that time, but not all of them. He indiscriminately closed them all and then reopened only a few of them after the Bank Holiday. Banks that were perfectly sound and should have been re-opened were not. Many more people suffered than needed to suffer at that time as a result of hasty and not very well-conceived legislative action by the New Dealers in Roosevelt's administration.

When I returned home from the Fort Wayne Bible Institute in June 1933, I went out to look for a job. It was, of course, right in the middle of the lowest point in the Great Depression of the Thirties and there were literally thousands of people walking in and out of every business asking for jobs. That meant I was competing with thousands of unemployed people, many of them with substantial work experience, while I was an 18-year-old high school graduate whose experience consisted of one year and three months as – what we called in those days – a soda jerk.

So I considered myself very lucky when I was hired on June 12, 1933, by the National City Bank of Cleveland as a messenger boy for $25 a month. Prior to the Bank Holiday, which took place on March 6 of that year, messenger boys were paid a starting wage of $60 a month all the way up to $90 a month. I competed for that job with hundreds of young unemployed men who had lots of experience as bank messengers or clerks, but they were unwilling to go to work for only $25 a month because they thought it was beneath their dignity. That is why I got the job; I was willing to work for much less money than anyone else.

I was delighted to get that job because I reasoned that applying for a job at every business that was open meant that I would be walking around all over downtown Cleveland – walking up and down every street and using up shoe leather. I would be doing essentially the same thing that I would have done as a bank messenger, but I would be getting zero pay for it. To me, working at any job for $25 was a lot better than zero, so I reasoned that I would be ahead of the game by going to work at the bank.

It is difficult for young people today, in the middle of the 1990s, to understand the value of a dollar back in 1933. My salary of $25 a month gave me a little less than $6 a week to cover all my living expenses. That meant I had to economize in every way I could.

For example, I was not able to afford the fare for a streetcar which was only seven cents a ride. If I had ridden the streetcars from home to my downtown job, it would have cost me $3.64 a month or 15 percent of my $25 salary. So in the morning, I walked the 2.2 miles from where I lived to the bank and walked back at night, even though there were streetcars going right by me.

In the fall of 1933, when it began to get chilly, I went to an army surplus store that sold used clothing and I bought a heavy overcoat, fur-lined gloves, a wool cap, and a pair of galoshes. Bundled up against the cold in these warm clothes, I walked back and forth to work all winter long. Walking four and a half miles a day was not unusual back then and the exercise was probably better for me than riding the streetcars would have been.

I had to economize the same way on food because lunches in even the cheapest restaurants cost about 75 cents. If I had bought my lunch every day, it would have cost me $19.50 a month, or 78 percent of my monthly pay. So I carried my lunch from home, which I could do for only a few cents a day, and my diet was healthier because cheap restaurant food was starchy and greasy.

Clothing was another problem for my skimpy finances. Richman

Brothers was selling men's suits at that time for $22.50, which meant I could have bought one suit with almost all of my $25 and that was the cheapest suit available. The cheapest shoes at that time cost about $5 per pair. As a messenger, I was hard on shoes, but we made shoes last a long, long time by buying rubber half soles for 25 cents. The rubber half soles came with a tube of glue that I used to attach them to cover up the holes worn in my shoes.

I said earlier that the Depression changed the lives of the people who lived through it. I know it had several lasting effects on me. First, it gave me a very firm resolve never to be unemployed. I saw thousands of people walking around the streets without jobs while I was working only because I was willing to work for less than anyone else. So I determined that no matter what happened, I would take a job at any pay I could get rather than be jobless. Second, living through the Depression developed in me a much stronger work ethic than I might have had if I had graduated from high school during a normal period. I decided that in order to keep my job, I would work 20 percent more hours than was required, to be sure that I would not get laid off if there was a layoff. As it turned out, that way of thinking worked out very well for me because it helped open up a new career opportunity for me.

Three weeks after I was hired as a messenger boy at the bank, Earl Biggs, who was head of the Customer Securities Department, asked me whether I would be willing to do some posting in a ledger when I was not running messages and I said I would be happy to. I thought the new work was terrific – so much so that I was still posting when quitting time came around at 5:00 p.m., and I was so interested in what I was doing that I just kept on posting. About 20 minutes after five o'clock, Paul Minter, who later became head of the Mortgage Loan Department, came up, patted me on the back and said, "Don, if they find out that you're willing to work after hours, you'll be doing it for the rest of your life." He was right! To this day, I am still working after hours.

For a couple of months, I continued posting in a ledger when I was not delivering messages. Then Earl Biggs asked me to take a full-time clerk's job at a modest pay increase in the Customer Securities Department which he managed. The job consisted primarily of posting the day's debit and credit entries in a journal. Even better, in the fall I was able to begin attending night classes at Cleveland College with the bank paying my tuition. I continued to walk home after 9:00 p.m. when classes at the college ended.

While I worked primarily as a clerk, I still ran some errands but only for the Customer Securities Department. Those errands involved delivering stocks or bonds to brokerage houses or to the Federal Reserve Bank of Cleveland. The trips to the Federal Reserve Bank also were made to deliver U.S. Treasury bonds, notes, or certificates which had to be turned in because they were maturing or to pick up similar instruments that the bank had purchased for its own account or for a customer account. There were times on these trips when I carried very large amounts – in the hundreds of thousands of dollars up to half a million – of negotiable Treasury securities. I realized that this was a very big responsibility, and I took it very seriously. Eventually, the bank made a rule that no one could carry negotiable securities in excess of $10,000 without having an armed guard with them and that no one could carry more than $100,000 worth of such securities without being accompanied by two armed guards.

After I had been working at National City Bank for two years (I was 20 years old by that time), my boss, Earl Biggs, told me that Robert Blythe, who was a Vice President in the Securities Analysis Department, wanted to talk to me about an opening in his department. The job was operating the trading desk. Since it represented an opportunity for me to learn an entirely new field, I took the job after talking with Blythe.

The trading desk had 16 direct telephone lines to 16 brokerage firms in Cleveland, which meant all I had to do was flip a switch and I would be connected immediately to a trader at Bache & Company, Salomon Brothers, Merrill Lynch, Loeb & Company, or one of a dozen other brokerage houses. I placed orders for all the purchases and sales of securities for all the trusts in the Trust

Department and for all the purchases and sales of the bank's own securities. I did not make decisions regarding which securities were to be bought or sold, but I placed all of the orders with the brokers to execute the transactions.

The Securities Analysis Department was made up of 12 men, all of whom had their Masters in Business degrees from the Harvard Graduate School of Business and me, a high school graduate. It was humbling, but it was a wonderful experience to be associated with men of such high intellect and education. They treated me with great courtesy and it was a tremendous learning opportunity for which I have always been very grateful. The job taught me a great deal that was valuable because I had to become familiar with all of the bonds, notes, and certificates issued by the federal government. I also had to become familiar with the stocks that were being bought for the trusts and those which were being sold from the trusts. I had to become schooled in the art of getting the best price whether it was for the purchase or sale of a security. The men in the department went out of their way to explain things to me and to give me advice. In my spare time, they showed me the reports that they were making on various companies and their recommendations to buy or sell their stocks.

I stayed in this job for two great years until Earl Biggs, my former boss, showed concern about how long it was going to take me to get a college degree by attending only evening classes. He offered me an opportunity to return to my former job in his department working only from noon until 5:00 p.m. each weekday and on Saturday mornings so I could attend classes at the Western Reserve University campus during the morning and then go to the downtown campus in the evening. That way I could take a full load of college courses.

I told Bob Blythe, of course, that I was going to accept Earl's offer and thanked him for the opportunity to learn so much about the securities business. After I had talked with Blythe, just by chance I overheard him telling Bill Borse, another man in the department, "Let's replace Don Noble with someone who is not as ambitious as Don is, so we can keep him on the job longer and not have to train a new person so soon." The man who replaced me in the Securities Analysis Department did indeed stay on the job for about 20 years, so I guess they got their wish.

Since I referred to attending college full-time, I should break down the seven years of study that led to my graduation. A portion of my college education consisted of four years of part-time night school work at the downtown facility of Western Reserve University, which in those days was called Cleveland College and today is Case Western Reserve University. The four years that I attended on this basis ran from September 1933 to June of 1937. Cleveland College was located on the northeast corner of the Public Square, next door to the Society Savings Bank.

I attended classes five nights a week, Monday through Friday. There were two classes, one from 6:00 until 7:20 p.m. and the other from 7:40 to 9:00 p.m. I had two classes most nights, but some nights only one. As I have said elsewhere, I walked 2.2 miles to work each morning, reported in about 8:15 a.m. and worked till 5:15 p.m. with an hour off to eat the lunch I carried and play a little ping-pong in the basement of the bank. Between the end of work at 5:15 p.m. and class at 6:00 p.m., I would study and eat something I had left over from my lunch or occasionally stop in at a drugstore counter for a bowl of soup or chili.

Most of the classes I was taking were provided through the American Institute of Banking (A.I.B.). Because I only got two-thirds college credit for these classes, it was necessary for me to take 50 percent more classes to get one year's credit than it would if I had been taking the regular classes offered by Western Reserve University. It required 30 hours of regular classes to constitute one academic year so I had to have 45 hours of A.I.B. classes. This I accomplished over the four years from the fall of 1933 to the summer of 1937 – getting one year of college credit for four years of work. I would walk home at night after classes ended at 9:00 p.m., getting home about 9:45 p.m., and then I would study for a couple of hours before going to bed.

While I was taking night classes, I was also working Saturday mornings at the bank from 8:30 a.m. to about 1:00 p.m. – walking both ways to and from work. I also was attending Sunday school and church on Sunday morning and the young people's meeting at the church on Sunday night. This did not leave me much time for other extra-curricular activities and none related to the college.

I attended college on a full-time basis from September 1937 to June of 1940 when I graduated. During this three-year period, I rode the streetcar in the morning from home to the Adelbert College campus of Western Reserve University at East 107th and Euclid Avenue which required transferring from one streetcar to another in downtown Cleveland.

My classes would start on the Adelbert campus at 8:00 a.m. and go through until 11:30 a.m. at which time I would catch the streetcar to go to downtown Cleveland, arriving at five minutes till noon to go on duty at the bank at 12:00 noon, having eaten a sandwich on the streetcar. Then I would attend night classes from 6:00 p.m. until 9:00 p.m. and either take a streetcar or walk home after that. I often walked even though I had the fare because I had done it for so long and I was trying to save money. After arriving home at about 10:00 p.m., I would study for two or three hours before going to bed. All my papers were written by hand; I never did own a typewriter.

Along with my full-time college schedule, I worked at the bank five days a week from noon to 5:00 p.m. and on Saturdays from 8:30 a.m. until 1:00 p.m. I also attended Sunday school and church services on Sunday morning and often on Sunday night. Again, the demands of this full schedule did not leave much time for extra-curricular activities and certainly none related to college life. During my entire seven years of attending part-time and full-time classes at Western Reserve University, I never attended a single athletic or social event at the college. Looking back, I know that I was so thrilled to be getting the college education I once had thought was impossible, that I did not need anything other than my class work and the great satisfaction I got from working at the bank.

For much of the time I attended college, I also taught a Sunday school class for boys ages 12 to 14. Occasionally, I would be asked to speak to the young people's group at the church. Some of the thoughts I developed for those talks still linger with me. One example was talking about a decision-making process in which I visualized a balance scale, putting all of the advantages on one side and all of the disadvantages on the other, and then visualized a weighing of both sides of the scale to arrive at an informed decision. Another thought I developed was, "To become rich, don't add to your possessions, decrease your wants."

In addition to giving me a good work ethic, living through the Depression had another lasting effect on me, which in a way reflects that thought about decreasing wants, or at least controlling them. Working in the bank, I saw people almost every day who had borrowed money and simply could not pay it back. They were devastated and in real trouble. I decided then and there that I would much rather be collecting interest by saving some money in the bank instead of having to pay interest by borrowing money.

As a result of that experience, Alice and I have never, and I mean never, bought anything other than a house on credit. We simply would not borrow money to buy an appliance or a car, however much we wanted it or needed it. We preferred to do without and to save money before we made any purchase of furniture or a refrigerator or an automobile. We always saved and then bought what we wanted for cash rather than taking out a loan, buying the item right away, and then paying interest on the borrowed money.

The Depression affected people so dramatically because 16 million people – one third of the total work force – were out of work in this country alone. You could read stories in the newspapers about people who had frozen to death in their homes because they could not afford coal for heating. There were other stories about families who literally had starved to death because they could not afford to buy food of any kind. People today tend to forget how tough it really was during the Depression. After I started working at the bank, I saw unemployed bankers come into the bank trying to sell coal or office supplies, anything to eke out a meager living. Prior to the Bank Holiday, these men had held very good, high-paying jobs and now I saw them coming in with threadbare coats and worn-out trousers; it was a sad sight because they were in pretty bad shape.

I saw even worse things during the Depression. Shortly after I started working at the bank, I was doing some posting in ledgers with my back to a first floor window that faced out on East 6th Street. I heard a thud and I thought that somebody had thrown a pumpkin out onto the street, because it sounded just like a pumpkin squashing. When I stood up and looked out, I saw that a man had jumped out of one of the upstairs windows of the building. I assume that he jumped because he had lost all his money in the stock market crash. There were a lot of suicides as a result of the crash and whenever I see one of those cartoons with a stockbroker standing on a window ledge getting ready to jump, I remember the awful sound I heard that day.

When you actually live through a period like the Great Depression about which so much has been written, you tend to be somewhat critical of the conclusions reached by the writers, many of whom were not even born in the 1930s. For example, it has been part of the conventional wisdom for decades that Herbert Hoover, and by extension the Republican Party, somehow caused the Depression. That is not true. President Hoover was not responsible for causing the Depression.

In my opinion, the Depression was caused by excesses of various kinds. Speculation in the stock market was one of those excesses. Prior to the market crash, there was a saying that, "the boot blacks are investing in the stock market." I do not know about the boot blacks but, in the late 1920s, everybody who had a few dollars was investing in the stock market and it kept going up and up on what I call the "greater fool theory."

By the greater fool theory, I refer to people who bought stocks they knew were overvalued, in itself a foolish thing to do. They thought that someone who was an even greater fool would buy their overvalued stocks at a still higher price allowing them to make a profit. In many cases, these stock speculators were using borrowed money to buy stocks on margin, which meant they were putting up only 10 percent or so of the total price. They figured to pay off the balance they owed on the stocks when they sold them to greater fools for a higher price and pocket the difference. Of course, it did not turn out that way. When the stock market crashed, speculators had to sell their overvalued stocks at a great loss, not raising anywhere near enough to pay back their loans.

There was also a lot of real estate speculation. Office building construction far exceeded the demand for office space and most of the construction was funded with borrowed money. There was similar debt-financed speculation in the development of residential areas. The Van Sweringen brothers were big real estate speculators in the Cleveland area during the 1920s. They borrowed money to buy farm land in what is now Shaker Heights and they also borrowed money to build the first rapid transit system to link downtown Cleveland with what they visualized as being a great residential area. Shaker Heights, of course, did eventually become prime real estate but that was not until more than a decade later.

After the stock market crash and the Bank Holiday, the Van Sweringens and other real estate speculators could not borrow money to finance their developments nor could they pay the interest charges on money they already had borrowed. So real estate speculation, which was going on all over the country, came to an abrupt halt. The result was a rash of foreclosures, with banks ending up holding title to thousands of parcels of land and buildings that they could not possibly sell.

Many banks contributed to the onset of the Depression by making bad loans. They were bad loans because the banks made them based on the wild speculation that was taking place. Because of the general euphoria and the belief that the economy would keep getting better and better, the banks did not apply strict criteria in evaluating whether debtors could repay their loans and they often had accepted highly overvalued property as security. So lots of people were guilty of fantastic excesses motivated by mindless greed – stock speculators, real estate speculators, and the banks all contributed to the stock market crash.

Under those circumstances, there was not much that Hoover or any other president could have done to head off the Depression. Once we were in the Depression, Hoover's administration did not do much to try to correct the situation. In my opinion, however, there was not much that could be done until the economic excesses and imbalances of the late 1920s had drained out of the system. The economy would have picked up naturally as the effect of the excesses caused by speculation began to lessen. If the private sector had been allowed by the government to get back to work and begin producing things again, we could have come out of the Depression without sacrificing so much of our economic freedom. That might have been possible if more Americans had been able to understand what had caused the Depression in the first place.

Back in the 1930s, only a small percentage of the public had the educational background to comprehend the economic factors that had caused the Depression. Some knowledgeable people realized that the Depression had been caused in large part by excessive speculation financed by too much borrowing. A few were even aware that the Smoot-Hawley Tariff Act had dried up foreign markets for American-made goods and, therefore, contributed to the general business downturn that made the Depression inevitable and delayed economic recovery. Far more people, however, did not have the faintest idea what had caused the Depression. All they knew was that they were out of work, their neighbors were out of work, and they were frightened. They thought the federal government should do something to correct the problem, so they blamed Hoover for not taking action. This widespread sentiment was evident in the presidential election in the fall of 1932 when Franklin D. Roosevelt was elected with a massive majority.

I was only a high school senior when Roosevelt was elected, but after his administration began pushing through New Deal legislation I began to think that he was on the wrong track. The core of his programs was socialism which I did not think then was a good solution for the problems of a capitalist economy and now I know that it was not. As it turned out, of course, many of the actions that Roosevelt took actually prolonged the Depression rather than helping to end it. Some of those things included the Bank Holiday, when he closed a lot of banks that should not have been closed and thus made it difficult for businesses to get the money they needed. His policy of having the government hire people at wages higher than businesses could afford to pay also delayed the ability of the private sector to hire back workers and get the economy moving again. Those actions by Roosevelt's administration had the short-term effect of prolonging the Depression, but many of the New Deal policies were also to have far worse long-term effects on business and on American society as a whole.

I think Roosevelt himself was only mildly anti-business, largely because his family lived off inherited money from property and he himself did not know much about how business worked. Many of the New Dealers brought into the government by Roosevelt, however, were far more socialistic than he was, and they were determined to punish business and bring it under their absolute control. To accomplish their goals, the New Dealers imposed upon business many costly regulations, only a few of which were justified. They also created a bunch of new federal agencies – with so many three-letter acronyms they looked like alphabet soup – which required business to file mountains of paperwork that added even more costs without providing much value to the taxpayers. Even worse, the New Dealers initiated the well-intentioned programs which have taken away the incentive to work from so many people, leading to generation after generation living on welfare.

Although Roosevelt and his policies may have done some good, many historians believe that the Great Depression of the 1930s did not really end until the American economy was stimulated by the heavy defense spending that began in the early 1940s. In my opinion, the private sector would have brought the country out of the Depression much sooner if Roosevelt's administration had not enacted laws and imposed burdensome regulations that caused America's industries to incur many unnecessary costs. Domination of the national economy by a heavy-handed federal government is not the way this country achieved the highest living standard in the world, and it is a battle that we are still fighting with the crowd down in Washington, D.C. to this day.

CHAPTER TEN • WE GET MARRIED AND I JOIN RUBBERMAID

In January 1934, Alice Jackson invited my sister Grace to attend her West Tech High School commencement ceremony, which was to be held at the Music Hall in downtown Cleveland (in those days, Cleveland high schools had two full-scale commencements, one in June and one in January). Alice told Grace that if she liked she could also bring her brother. Grace accepted for both of us and we attended the ceremony. Alice was valedictorian of her graduating class of about 340 students, and I was very much impressed by her valedictorian address. Before we left the Music Hall that night, I asked Alice if she would go ice-skating with me the next night and she said yes. I took her ice-skating at the Brookside Park ice-skating pond, which did not cost anything. Our subsequent dating was very infrequent because I was still going to night school five nights a week, taking a full college course, and was working 30 hours a week at National City Bank. Nevertheless, our courtship did end up with my winning her hand.

Following Alice's graduation from high school, she went to work for the National Brick Association as a bookkeeper. That fall, she started taking evening classes at the Cleveland College of Western Reserve University. We frequently arranged to see each other for a few minutes before or after class, and we actually took a few accounting classes and one American History class together. As valedictorian of her class, Alice had won a four-year scholarship to attend Western Reserve University, which would have paid all of her tuition on a full-time basis, but she felt that she had to work and, therefore, gave up the scholarship except that it did pay her tuition for night classes at the Cleveland College. In the spring of 1938, Alice changed jobs and went to work at Fuller, Smith and Ross as an accountant. She found this a much more pleasant place to work than the National Brick Association.

We were married on July 8, 1939, and for two years we lived in the attic of a two-family house at 13517 Clifton Boulevard, with one family living on the first floor and another on the second floor. The attic had been finished to make an apartment which we rented for $35 a month. In summer, the apartment would get extremely hot during the day when the windows had to be kept closed because we were both at work. Alice had saved a good portion of her earnings which went to buy furniture when we got married.

For the first year of our marriage, I was still going full-time to morning and night classes at Western Reserve University and working five hours every weekday afternoon and Saturday mornings at National City Bank. In June 1940, I graduated from Western Reserve University. I continued working as an accountant at the National City Bank in Cleveland. By the time of my graduation, I had been working there for seven years while attending night classes at the University, and I had no intention of leaving because I intended to pursue a banking career.

Early in 1941, after Alice and I had been married for 18 months, we decided to build a house in Berea. I intended to commute by bus to downtown Cleveland because I expected to work at National City Bank for the rest of my life. We bought a lot on Fournier Street, less than a mile from the center of Berea, for $500 which was our down payment on a mortgage that we had arranged through Society Savings Bank located on Public Square in downtown Cleveland. We built what we thought was a very nice, little two-bedroom house with an attached garage, gas furnace, and an unfinished second floor all for $4,900. With the lot, our total investment was $5,400. We obtained a Federal Housing Administration (FHA) loan through Society Bank for $4,900. The monthly payment was to be $33 a month, which included the payment on principle and interest, taxes, and insurance.

In the meantime, The Wooster Rubber Company was looking for an accountant and had gone to Western Reserve University asking for the name of a recent graduate who had majored in accounting. The University gave them my name and Paul Willour, the Assistant

Treasurer of the Company, called and suggested that I come to Wooster for an interview. When we met, Willour offered me total compensation that was only 16 percent more than I was being paid at the bank. I was making $125 per month at National City Bank, and banks did not pay extra for overtime in those days. Willour said Rubbermaid would pay me $145 per month. It was not until I was already working in Wooster that I realized that my base salary was, in fact, the same. The only difference was that I was being paid for working overtime so my total compensation was higher.

In addition to being interviewed by Paul Willour, I also talked to Jim Caldwell, the Company's President and General Manager. Caldwell took me for a tour of the plant and said that if I decided to accept their job offer, he would want me to dress in overalls for the first two weeks and work out in the plant at different jobs so that I would know what went on in the factory. A few days before I actually came to Wooster, Paul Willour called and said that I should not come to work in overalls and that, although they wanted very much to have me learn what went on in the factory, he had some work in the office that needed to be done right away. He added that at some later date he would arrange to have me work in the factory, but that never happened.

I have a suspicion that Caldwell said that I was to work in the factory just to see whether it would scare me away. I think he wanted to be sure he was getting someone who was not afraid of getting their hands dirty doing a dirty job. It did not scare me away. As a matter of fact, I always have regretted that I did not get the experience of actually working in the plant. In any event, Alice and I decided to move to Wooster so that I could join The Wooster Rubber Company because I thought that three years of industrial accounting experience would help my career advancement at the bank. I fully intended to go back to National City Bank after I had finished my stint in Wooster.

Alice had worked at Fuller, Smith and Ross from 1938 to May 1941, when she quit for two reasons. First, because she was expecting our first child and, second, because we were moving to

Wooster. I accepted Willour's offer and joined The Wooster Rubber Company effective Thursday, June 1, 1941. I continued to work at the bank until 5:00 p.m. on Wednesday, May 31, 1941. The movers arrived at our house at about 6:00 p.m. that same evening; they loaded our furniture and took it to Wooster. We arrived very late that night and unloaded. I reported to work at eight o'clock. the following morning at The Wooster Rubber Company leaving Alice with all the unopened boxes strewn around the house. We paid our own moving expenses.

Our move to Wooster on June 1 took place just three weeks before Alice and I were scheduled to move into our nice, little new house in Berea. In Wooster, we moved into the upstairs portion of an old home that had been converted from a single-family house into a two-family house. We had a coal-fired furnace in the base-ment and paid rent of $35 a month. We were able to get someone to rent the house in Berea for $60 a month, so financially we made out all right. It was a great disappointment to Alice, however, not to move into her nice, new home but instead have to move into a converted upstairs flat of a very old home at 348-1/2 North Bever Street, across from Nold Avenue in Wooster.

After we moved into the upstairs flat of the house on North Bever Street, one of the first things I did was to ask the landlord for permission to dig up part of the back lawn to make a vegetable garden. I had never had a garden and had no experience in garden-ing, but Alice's mother had always had a vegetable garden. For the next several years, wherever we lived we had a vegetable garden and during World War II we had a big Victory garden located in a big back yard two houses from where we lived in which other peo-ple also had their gardens. After we moved to our present home on Morgan Street, I again spaded up a plot about 20 feet by 20 feet for a vegetable garden and had one each year until about three years ago when I finally gave it up.

At this point, I am going to depart from the chronological order of my memoirs to look back briefly at the 21-year history of The Wooster Rubber Company before I joined it in 1941. The history of this predecessor of today's Rubbermaid Incorporated begins with the stories of two related events that involved a cast of extraordinary individuals. Although I joined the Company long after those events took place, I was fortunate enough to have known and to have worked closely with almost all of those wonderful people.

The first event took place on May 19, 1920, when nine individuals pooled their resources of $26,800 to form The Wooster Rubber Company. They rented an old building that had been a piano factory at the corner of South Buckeye Street and South Street in Wooster, Ohio, and began manufacturing Sunshine brand rubber balloons and novelties. The second event happened more than a decade later in Massachusetts when a man named James R. Caldwell invented a rubber dustpan that was to be the forerunner of today's Rubbermaid products. Today, one of those original dustpans is framed and hangs on a corridor wall in the Company's headquarters office building in Wooster, symbolizing the way in which the stories of these two events merged.

For the first few years after it was formed, The Wooster Rubber Company did reasonably well but it began experiencing difficulties during the mid-1920s and the original incorporators began thinking about selling it. In 1926, Horatio B. Ebert and Errett M. Grable bought the Company from the former shareholders and founders. Many years later, I heard both Ebert and Grable reminisce about why they were seeking an outside investment at that particular point in their lives.

When they bought The Wooster Rubber Company, Ebert and Grable were successful executives at the Aluminum Cooking Utensil Company, a subsidiary of the Aluminum Company of America (ALCOA), that made Wear-Ever pots and pans in New

Kensington, Pennsylvania. They met when they were selling Wear-Ever products door to door during their college years and had started working for the company in 1911 selling pots and pans by putting on parties in homes. They sold the products by actually going into a home and cooking dinner for guests invited by the housewife. During the dinner, they demonstrated the advantages of Wear-Ever cookware and took orders for it. They did this full-time and were soon promoted into sales management positions. For eight years they had worked their way up through the organization with Ebert becoming the manager of the Kansas City sales region and Grable manager of the Chicago sales region.

But their confidence in the future was badly shaken when they attended a sales meeting of the Aluminum Cooking Utensil Company in 1919. At the meeting in Pittsburgh, Arthur Vining Davis, the dictatorial chairman of ALCOA, said flatly that none of the managers in the subsidiary were worth more than $10,000 a year and should never expect to be earning any more than that. Hardly an inspirational talk!

Ebert and Grable were only about 30 years old at the time they attended that meeting and, after hearing Davis' statement, they decided that they could never earn enough money to amount to anything in the aluminum business. They began looking for an opportunity to invest in and the chance to become involved in running some other business on a part-time basis.

While they looked for the right opportunity, they sent their spare cash to Grable's father, a retired Presbyterian minister who had become a successful investor in second mortgages. He invested their money for several years until each of them had quite a tidy sum for those days. But it was not until 1926, when Ebert was visiting his parents in Wooster, Ohio, that he heard about the problems at The Wooster Rubber Company.

I remember hearing Ebert say that he immediately told Grable that this seemed like the chance they had been looking for and so they bought 100 percent of The Wooster Rubber Company's stock and its equipment, but not the rented building of course, from the

Company's founders for only $16,000. They retained Clyde C. Gault,* one of the original nine founders, as the General Manager. Ebert and Grable and their new management team reorganized the operations and by the end of the first year of their ownership they had made $8,000 profit!

Along with the Sunshine brand balloons, the reorganized Wooster Rubber Company made small rubber toys and other novelties for children. Their initial success gave Ebert and Grable enough confidence in the future to consider putting up their own factory building. In 1928, they purchased one acre of land on the south side of Bowman Street in Wooster and built the original portion of a Rubbermaid building which is still there.

The many contributions of Horatio Ebert and Errett Grable are even more remarkable when you take into account that they could never devote their full time to managing The Wooster Rubber Company. Their participation in the management of The Wooster Rubber Company and later Rubbermaid Incorporated was always on a part-time basis – evenings, Saturday afternoons, and Sundays. Both of them continued to work full time for the Aluminum Cooking Utensil Company and they were successful in their careers at that company. Grable was eventually named President and Ebert was a Vice President in charge of National Sales when he retired. Besides being good managers and smart businessmen, both Ebert and Grable had fantastic energy.

The energetic new management team did fairly well until the stock market crash in October 1929 ushered in the Great Depression of the 1930s. Sales of The Wooster Rubber Company's balloons and other products decreased sharply, and the Company actually lost money from 1932 through 1934 – a three-year period considered by historians to be the depths of the Depression.

---

*Clyde C. Gault was the father of Stanley C. Gault, who replaced me as Chief Executive Officer of Rubbermaid Incorporated when I retired in 1980. For 15 years, Clyde served the Company as a Board member and as an officer, including nine years as Treasurer and General Manager, one year as Secretary and Treasurer, and five years as President.

This is the point where we pick up the story of James R. Caldwell and his rubber housewares business which eventually was joined with The Wooster Rubber Company. Born in 1896 as the son of a tobacco farmer in Hazardville, Connecticut, by 1915 Caldwell was a promising pre-medical student at Georgetown University in Washington, D.C.

A couple of years later, there was a tobacco crop failure on the family farm and Caldwell's father could no longer afford to continue sending his son to Georgetown. So the young man had to drop out of college and go to work for the Fisk Rubber Company in Massachusetts. Because of his prior studies in chemistry and biology, he was assigned to work in the laboratory at Fisk. He also played football on the Fisk company team.

Later, Caldwell left Fisk and went to work for the Seamless Rubber Company in New Haven, Connecticut, as vice president in charge of manufacturing. He supervised the building of a large new manufacturing plant in New Haven, which is still in use today. But with the coming of the Great Depression, the sales of the Seamless Rubber Company fell off sharply and Caldwell and other executives were given 10 percent pay cuts every three months. Because of the pay cuts, Caldwell resigned from the Seamless Rubber Company to join the Church Toilet Seat Company in Monson, Massachusetts. Hard times also hit that company and his pay was again being reduced regularly. After several pay cuts, he told his wife, Madeleine, "If we are going to starve to death working for some one else, we may as well starve to death working for ourselves on our own ideas." So he resigned from his job in Monson and they moved to Norton, Massachusetts.

During the late 1920s, the synthetic dye industry had begun making bright new colors which for the first time could be used in molded rubber products. Caldwell's background and training was in rubber chemistry, manufacturing, and management, and after he saw the new color ingredients, he was convinced that there was an opportunity to market a whole bunch of new rubber products. Every evening, Caldwell and his wife Madeleine spent hours discussing products for kitchen, bathroom, and general home use which could be made out of the brightly colored molded rubber. Eventually they had a list of 29 possible products, all of which they were sure would be best sellers. He and Madeleine decided that their first product to be manufactured would be a molded rubber dustpan on which they got a patent in May 1933. Up until then, all dustpans had been made of metal. A metal dustpan would get bent out of shape and the dirt would be swept under it instead of onto it. Caldwell thought a rubber dustpan would conform better to a floor surface and would be a big improvement in terms of durability.

Caldwell borrowed $400 on an insurance policy and gave the money to a toolmaker to make a dustpan mold which he took to the U.S. Royal Rubber Company to have the rubber dustpans made. Caldwell picked up the dustpans in his car and took them home where he and his wife and two daughters trimmed them in their basement. Then he went out to sell them. He went first to the Outlet Company department store in Providence, Rhode Island, where the store's housewares buyer dashed Caldwell's high hopes by saying that he did not have any calls for rubber dustpans. Caldwell asked the buyer, "How could you have any calls for rubber dustpans when nobody has ever seen one before?" In desperation, he went through his sales pitch, saying that because the dustpan was made of rubber it was flexible and would adjust to uneven floors, its molded legs would keep it tilted at the right angle, and it would not chip holes in the plaster when it was hung on a wall. The buyer was unmoved, saying that it was still only a dustpan and that the only kind of dustpan that would sell was a 39-cent metal pan, adding that one dollar, which was what Caldwell was hoping to sell them for at retail, was far too high.

To Caldwell's frustrated amazement, he got the same response from every department store buyer, including Al Porcelain at Jordan Marsh and Company of Boston, who was one of the country's most important housewares buyers. As he was driving home from Boston, he wondered what to try next. Then he remembered how well the Fuller Brush man was doing selling door to door to housewives and decided to try that approach. Because he and his wife had invested every penny they had in the world in their dustpan mold, he really did not have much choice. At that point, Caldwell was in Attleboro, Massachusetts. He stopped on a side street lined with two-family houses and rang the first convenient doorbell. I'll let Jim tell the rest of the story in his own words, which were recorded in an interview many years later:

"'My heavens! What have you there?' asked the pleasant woman who answered the door, pointing to the five colored dustpans under my arm. When I told her they were made of rubber she wanted to know why; so I told her that if I could come into her kitchen and use her broom I could explain better, and she invited me in. I showed her all of its features, even sweeping up the plaster on her closet floor caused by the chipping of the wall from her tin dustpan. 'I have been after my husband for months to fix those holes,' she told me. Then she asked me the price. 'Only one dollar,' I replied bravely. Then she said, 'Can I have the red one?' – and the very first Rubbermaid sale had been made!"

Within a short time after he returned from Attleboro, Caldwell had hired 25 salesmen to sell his dustpans house to house. He hired people he thought he could trust with his precious samples and offered them a 40 percent commission. From then on for nearly a year, most of Caldwell's marketing efforts were focused on door-to-door sales to homemakers. After six months, sales had reached a point that it was possible to add some other products to the Rubbermaid line. Caldwell had a mold made to make a rubber drainboard tray. Until that time, drainboard trays had been made of porcelain-covered steel and he thought that a rubber drainboard tray would be easier on the dishes and not chip them as the porcelain did. Then he added a sink mat to replace sink protectors made of wood. He also added a stovetop mat and later a three-cornered sink strainer to hold garbage in the sink. Prior to this, sink strainers were made of porcelain-covered steel which were noisy and unsightly when the porcelain chipped off.

About then, Caldwell received a letter from Al Porcelain at Jordan Marsh which stated, "Since we are getting calls from customers for Rubbermaid dustpans and other products, please have your representative call on us." Caldwell called on Porcelain the next day – a day he never forgot because he got his first retail store order, a dozen of each of his products in assorted colors. But Porcelain accompanied the order with a lecture on retail merchandising and advertising. He told Caldwell that they could sell a lot more of his new Rubbermaid products if they had a demonstrator. After Porcelain explained what a demonstrator did, Caldwell quickly said, "That's no problem. We've got the best demonstrator in the world for Rubbermaid products." And the very next morning, Madeleine Caldwell was busily demonstrating the advantages of the rubber dustpan to shoppers at Jordan Marsh. She showed women how the rubber conformed to the floor's surface as she swept dirt or sawdust into the dustpan. She did such a good job that they soon had a constant stream of new orders.

Caldwell had adopted the name Rubbermaid for his products shortly after developing them. He told the story of how he and his wife would sit around the kitchen table night after night trying to figure out the best name for their rubber products and making lists of potential names. Before the Depression hit, it had been common for many American homes to have full-time maids. But by 1933, most housewives had to do without their maids. Because their molded rubber products made it easier for a housewife to perform a maid's functions, the Caldwells came up with the name "Rubbermaid." The name was an inspired choice and quickly caught on with the public. For many years, the Company used a logo which actually had a silhouette of a maid wearing a maid's cap to symbolize the double meaning of Rubbermaid – products made of rubber which made life easier and more convenient for housewives; like having their own maid, in effect.

The Rubbermaid business was good and there were some signs of a slow economic recovery. It also was becoming increasingly clear to Caldwell that having his Rubbermaid products made by someone else was at best a short-term arrangement and that he eventually would have to do his own manufacturing. He believed that he and his wife would not truly be in business for themselves until they had their own factory where he could use his 14 years of experience in compounding rubber formulas and manufacturing processes to maximum advantage.

In late 1933, Caldwell decided to have his products made by the Goodyear Tire and Rubber Company in Akron, Ohio, then the center for rubber product manufacturing. He moved his family to Akron and made it the base for his Rubbermaid business, selling his products to department stores around Ohio while continuing to sell them through agents on the East Coast. Caldwell's move took place at a time when the Depression had created serious problems for the new owners of The Wooster Rubber Company, 35 miles from Akron. Sales of the Company's balloons were down sharply and the debt they had incurred for their new factory building was proving to be a burden. Ebert and Grable were on the lookout for some molded rubber products for use in the home. But both Ebert and Grable knew that what they really needed was an executive who knew the technical end of the molded rubber business.

Ebert was selling Wear-Ever pots and pans to the same department store housewares buyers to whom Caldwell was selling his Rubbermaid products. He saw Caldwell's products in the department stores and got the idea of having Caldwell use the almost idle plant in Wooster to manufacture his own product line. Through a buyer at the May Company in Cleveland, Ebert arranged to meet Caldwell at the Statler Hotel in downtown Cleveland on a Sunday in June 1934. They discussed the possibilities for much of the day and then drove 60 miles to Wooster to look over the factory. Caldwell was delighted and said it was just what he had been looking for; Ebert and Grable felt the same way about him. There was a minor snag, however, because their creditors were pressing the owners of The Wooster Rubber Company pretty hard for payment and the business was not generating enough money to pay Caldwell a salary. Caldwell said he needed a minimum of $400 a month, so Ebert and Grable agreed that they would pay him out of their own pockets until the business could afford to cover his salary. After they reached that agreement, Caldwell moved his family to Wooster and started work as President and General Manager of The Wooster Rubber Company on July 1, 1934.

That is how these two businesses, which began more than 700 miles and over a decade apart, were merged together through a series of fortunate circumstances to become today's Rubbermaid Incorporated, a major manufacturer of housewares and other products and one of America's most respected corporations. But a lot of work lay ahead for Caldwell and his new business associates.

When Caldwell came on board, The Wooster Rubber Company only had equipment for making rubber balloons. It had no mills for compounding rubber and no presses for making molded rubber products. Caldwell immediately went to Akron and bought used mills and used presses that were necessary for manufacturing his rubber products. As soon as he could do so in an orderly fashion, Caldwell closed out the manufacture of rubber toy balloons and the Company had to write off a large amount of obsolete inventory. Always technically innovative, Caldwell had forms made to manufacture rubber household gloves by dipping them in the same tanks used to make toy balloons. By 1936, he had begun using these same tanks to dip wire dish drainers to make rubber-covered dish drainers. Prior to this time, dish drainers had been made out of plain wire or paint-coated wire which often chipped dishes.

Caldwell continued to add other new products to the line. Many of the products that he introduced and manufactured at that time are still made of rubber and are still in the Rubbermaid line – bathtub mats, drainboard trays, and sink mats. But Caldwell was not the only product innovator. After Caldwell joined them, Ebert and Grable used their own experience with aluminum cooking utensils to develop some related rubber products for use by housewives. For example, women complained that the steel wool used for cleaning aluminum pots and pans scratched their fingers and nail polish. Ebert developed a small rubber handle with little wires projecting on the inside that held the steel wool and protected housewives' fingers and fingernails. They began making the steel wool holder in the Wooster plant. They also developed a rubber spatula that is still in the Rubbermaid line today. In addition, Ebert suggested products that he and his wife, Lyda, had been designing even before Caldwell came to Wooster. Along with the steel wool holder, they came up with such products as a table protector pad, which protected the edge of a table from being marred when a food grinder was clamped onto it. Ebert also developed a round, rubber mat about nine inches in diameter to be used under a Wear-Ever food press. So he and Caldwell worked very well together in creating the innovative new products that would eventually win Rubbermaid the nickname of "the new product machine" and which continue to be a major strength of the Company today.

Because of Caldwell's training as a chemist, he could do the laboratory work that was needed to develop formulas for making these rubber products by mixing together rubber, clay, whiting, sulfur, and other ingredients into rubber compounds. Having been a factory manager at the Seamless Rubber Company, Caldwell knew how to manage a factory and how to deal with employees. Because of his experience in selling products that had never before been in existence – both door to door and to department store buyers during a very difficult time – he had become quite an expert at marketing and merchandising. Both Ebert and Grable also used their Wear-Ever positions to help launch the new Rubbermaid line. They knew all the leading housewares buyers and after talking about their Wear-Ever products, they would casually mention that there was an interesting new line called Rubbermaid the buyers might want to look at – which helped a lot to boost the sales of their other company.

I want to make clear, however, that there was never any corporate connection whatsoever between Wear-Ever and The Wooster Rubber Company. Grable and Ebert's ownership of The Wooster Rubber Company was their own personal investment. They subsequently did invite some of their business associates at Wear-Ever to make personal investments in The Wooster Rubber Company. These men also became directors of the Company (see Chapter 39). Ebert made a tremendous contribution to the success of Rubbermaid on a part-time basis through his knowledge and skill in helping Caldwell develop a marketing strategy for the Company. Grable also contributed a great deal on a part-time basis in the management of the business, particularly in the area of finance. I doubt that The Wooster Rubber Company would have survived, let alone succeeded, without the talents and skills of all three of the men involved in the business during its formative years – Ebert, Grable, and Caldwell. Like a three-legged milking stool which cannot stand if any one of its legs were to be removed, The Wooster Rubber Company could not have made it without any one of these three extraordinary men.

Despite the conversion of the plant to the new Rubbermaid products and the success of those products in the market place, the Company continued to lose money from 1934 through 1937. For example, sales for the first fiscal year ending September 30, 1935, totaled only $79,858. Many times both Ebert and Grable had to lend their personal funds to the Company to meet payrolls during those lean years. Sometimes this was paid back, but sometimes it was accumulated and eventually put into preferred stock.

As a future inducement for Caldwell to join The Wooster Rubber Company, Ebert and Grable promised to give him a number of shares equal to the number of shares that each of them owned, which he would receive at the end of the first year that the Company made a profit. It was not until 1938, however, that the struggling new business turned its first profit. That same year, the decision was made to recapitalize the Company with an issue of seven percent preferred stock, most of which – along with some new common stock – was exchanged for the existing common stock. They also sold some preferred stock at $100 per share to their business friends at Wear-Ever. For each share of preferred stock, the buyers received one share of common stock free. Later all the preferred shares were redeemed. After the Company was recapitalized,

Caldwell was given the number of newly issued shares of common stock which Ebert and Grable had promised him.

In those early days, it was quite common for several members of a family to join the Company. This began a tradition which still continues today and there are a lot of families who have worked at Rubbermaid for a number of generations. The story of how the four Stefanski brothers became part of the Rubbermaid team is a good example of this family type of employment. Soon after Caldwell started at The Wooster Rubber Company, he sent for Frank Stefanski, who had worked with him at the Seamless Rubber Company. Frank started in supervision in the factory, worked his way up to superintendent of the factory, and later became our Vice President of Manufacturing. Frank Stefanski was not there long before he sent for his brother, Ted, to join the Company as a foreman in the plant. A short time later, Caldwell called yet a third Stefanski brother, John, who was an expert in maintenance, and asked him to join The Wooster Rubber Company. Caldwell told John that the Company, at this point, was in great need of a truck. He asked John to buy a used truck which he could use to move his furniture to Ohio. John bought an old International Harvester truck and drove it from Massachusetts to Wooster, Ohio, where it was used around the Company to do all kinds of hauling jobs for many years. Ed Stefanski, who was a half-brother to Frank, Ted, and John, also joined the Company. As a very young man, Ed started working in the factory and eventually became supervisor of all of the finishing operations at Rubbermaid. In later years, he was in charge of the Company's employee store and worked at Rubbermaid for a total of 42 years before he retired.

CHAPTER TWELVE • MY EARLY DAYS AT RUBBERMAID

The title that I was given to attract me to The Wooster Rubber Company was "Assistant Office Manager and Chief Accountant." The truth of the matter is that the job was that of an accountant. My first job assignment was to bring the Company's asset ledger up to date. This meant going back through invoices for purchases of equipment, preparing a ledger sheet for each new piece of equipment, recording on it the name of the vendor from whom the asset was purchased, the date of purchase, and the amount paid for the equipment. It also meant posting into the ledger for the last couple of years the depreciation on each piece of equipment. The totals in the asset ledger then had to balance with the accounts in the general ledger. The last I knew, this asset ledger was still in the archives of Rubbermaid Incorporated with postings in my handwriting on many of the pages.

The entire office space at the Company in those days was 900 square feet, which was the floor space in a room 30 feet by 30 feet square. All of the executives and office employees – a total of 26 people – worked in this tiny space. The area was so crowded that the table I was given to work on was only about 30 inches by 20 inches – not much bigger than the area a desktop computer sits on today. A big improvement in the offices that summer was putting screens on the windows. There was no such thing as air conditioning back then, so the windows had to be kept open in the summer. Prior to the screens being put on, I had to brush flies away from the ledgers as I posted in them; and, of course, even after the screens were put on, dust from the road continued to blow in. The road outside the office building was only paved the width of one-and-a-half cars and every time two cars met, one car would have to ride along with two wheels off the pavement on the soft shoulder throwing up clouds of dust.

When I came to Wooster in 1941, there were approximately 100 people working in the factory. Many of the factory jobs at that time were difficult and unpleasant, particularly in the rubber milling and press departments. In the milling area, the rubber compounds were "milled" or mixed in a Banbury, basically like a giant food mixer. The ingredients going into the Banbury consisted of rubber, clay, whiting, sulfur, and coloring agents. Except for the rubber, all those materials were loose, powdery substances making it dusty, dirty work. The press room was a basement room with a low ceiling and poor ventilation, which made it get very, very hot during the summertime from the heat of the presses that molded and vulcanized the finished rubber products. After each molding operation, the heavy molds had to be pulled out of the presses and opened up to take the products out. Then the molds had to be reloaded with compounded rubber and pushed back into the presses. This job was done with brute force by big husky fellows because some of those molds weighed 200 pounds.

The finishing department consisted primarily of women using scissors to trim the "flash" or rubber overflow off the mats. I used to joke that the biggest piece of capital equipment in the finishing department at that time consisted of the many pairs of scissors the ladies used. That was not quite correct, because there were two punch presses that were used to punch out the holes in the sink and the bathtub mats which allowed water to drain through them.

In those days, the maximum factory wage was 35 cents an hour. The factory worked three eight-hour shifts, six days a week, or a total of 48 hours for each employee. The office staff regularly worked five-and-a-half days a week. Every office employee worked Saturday mornings and no one even thought about taking a Saturday off; we figured we were lucky to have Saturday afternoons and Sunday free! The vacation policy was equally tough by today's standards. When employees completed a full year of employment on May 1, they were entitled to one week of vacation. A full year on May 1 meant that a person had to have put in a full 12 months as of that date. If an employee started work on May 15, he or she would have to work one year plus eleven-and-a-half months before being entitled to a vacation. After five full years of service on May 1, an employee was entitled to two weeks vacation, and two weeks was the maximum vacation to which anyone was entitled, regardless of their position or length of service time.

The factory and offices were closed for only six holidays: New Year's Day, Memorial Day, the Fourth of July, Labor Day, Thanksgiving, and Christmas Day. Factory workers would get the holiday off, but without pay. Office workers who were being paid overtime would be paid for the holiday, but they would not be paid anything beyond their base salary until their actual hours for the week exceeded 40 hours. This meant that during a week when a holiday fell, there would be no pay for the Saturday morning worked that week. If the holiday was on a Saturday, only that day could be taken off. There was no such thing as taking off the day before if a holiday happened to fall on a Saturday.

Today, those working conditions and personnel policies may sound like something out of Dickens, but we did not look at it that way. They were pretty standard in American industry in those days, so it did not bother us. Besides, the Company was very progressive in many ways. For example, when I joined the Company it already had an IBM Punch Card System, which was very forward-thinking for an organization of its size at that time. A card was punched for every line on an invoice showing the item number, the number of units, the price per unit, and the extension of the billing amount. These punch cards were sorted with an IBM Card Sort Machine and put into an IBM Tabulator (nicknamed "The Jeep"), which broke out the various factors making up the invoiced amounts, including sales by product type, by account type, and by the manufacturers' representatives in order to calculate their commissions. The results appeared on a dial and were recorded in hand writing by the lady operating the machine. She wrote it down because, of course, in those days there was no printer.

From the beginning of the business until as late as 1955, the accounts receivable were all posted by hand. There was one page in a ledger for each customer account. On that page was posted the amount of each invoice after shipment was made to that customer and each payment was posted when it was received. After each posting of either an invoice or a payment, a new balance due was calculated and posted.

I was fortunate enough to have excellent people as well as good equipment. Shortly after Caldwell came to Wooster, his wife Madeleine started working in the factory. About the same time, Marge McClelland, who graduated from Wooster High School in June 1934, started working in the factory alongside Mrs. Caldwell. Marge later transferred into the office and worked with me in the accounting function. By 1955, prior to the operation being mechanized on a Burroughs bookkeeping machine, there were 12 books of ledger sheets and each book was about five inches thick! For quite a few years, Marge McClelland posted the invoices and payments in those big ledgers. The ledgers stretched across the full 60-inch width of her desk. Each day, Marge would post a couple of hundred invoices and then she would post roughly 150 payments and calculate the balance due from each customer after the posting. At the end of the month, she ran a tape of the balances for all of the customer accounts creating an adding machine tape as much as 20 feet long! The total, of course, had to balance with the general ledger account for accounts receivable. Every day, that general ledger would have been posted with one figure for the total of the shipments made and one figure for the total of payments received.

Marge was so accurate that she usually balanced on the first run. If the run did not balance, she had to spend many hours checking the postings and calculations for the whole month to discover the error or errors that caused it to be out of balance. This was an unbelievably difficult task and one which I believe very few people other than Marge could have accomplished. She put in a total of 44 years at Rubbermaid and was a terrific worker.

Rubbermaid was not only one of the leaders in the use of punch card equipment, it was also one of the first companies to install computers. In 1963, Rubbermaid installed a General Electric 225 computer and a second one in 1968. Those two computers – each one three times as big as a large refrigerator – handled all of our order entries, invoicing, production scheduling, and inventory control, and also supplied us with marketing data. Back then, we thought they were absolutely marvelous, even though they were a bit temperamental at times. It makes you realize how far computer technology has advanced in only a little over three decades when you consider that those two very big computers had less capacity than a good lap top computer has today.

One thing I learned soon after joining the Company was that no office employee was to leave the office at night until all of the invoicing for the prior day's shipments had been completed and the invoices mailed. Caldwell would never go home at night before looking at every invoice for that day's billing. It did not matter how many times Madeleine called him and told him to come home. Even knowing that guests were waiting at the house for him to get there for dinner, he still took time to leaf through every invoice.

Every Thursday, commission checks were mailed to the manufacturers' representatives for the preceding week's shipments. Caldwell thought this was an important way to keep the manufacturers' representatives happy and working on getting new orders for Rubbermaid. The manufacturers' representatives worked for other companies as well as for us, and Caldwell shrewdly and correctly thought they would devote more of their attention to the manufacturer that paid their commissions most promptly.

Chapter Thirteen • Rubbermaid Goes to War

On December 7, 1941, the Japanese bombed Pearl Harbor and the next day the United States declared war on Japan and Germany. In early March 1942, the use of rubber was "frozen" to make it available only for use in making military products; not one ounce of rubber could be used for domestic purposes, including rubber tires. As a matter of fact, Caldwell was called to Washington to help write the executive order that froze rubber for civilian use. This meant that the Company was entirely out of the consumer products business. It also meant that the Company had to start laying off workers immediately and was soon down to only 16 factory employees. They were kept busy painting the shop and maintaining the building and equipment.

On August 15, 1942, I received a call in the afternoon from Dr. Clarence E. Josephson, the President of Heidelberg College in Tiffin, Ohio, who was calling from Cleveland. He said he wanted to talk with me and wondered if he could take me to dinner that evening. Over dinner, Dr. Josephson told me that Heidelberg College was in need of a full-time instructor in Economics, starting the first of September, and that Western Reserve University had recommended me for the position. I went to Caldwell the next morning and told him I knew how he could cut the Company's overhead further. Then I told him about the offer I had to become an instructor in Economics at Heidelberg College. He said he would hate to see me leave but, given the state of the Company, he was fearful that within three months I would wish I had taken the job. So he recommended that I accept the offer, but asked whether I would come back to Wooster one Saturday morning each month to close the books. I said I would.

Alice and I drove to Tiffin for further interviews and I accepted the position at Heidelberg College. On August 31, we moved our furniture and our 11-month-old son to an upstairs apartment we had rented in Tiffin. At 8:00 o'clock the very next morning, Dr. Josephson was at our door asking me to come to a faculty meeting. So once again, I left Alice surrounded by boxes and went off to start my teaching career. It turned out that I was to teach five different classes of three hours each, for a total of 15 hours. Today, most professors consider nine or ten hours to be a full load. Since only two of the classes were the same, I had four different preparations for four different subjects. I taught Principles of Economics, Principles of Accounting, the History of Economic Thought, Economic Geography, and Public Finance.

In late September 1942, three weeks after we moved to Tiffin, Caldwell was successful in having The Wooster Rubber Company become a subcontractor to Goodyear Tire and Rubber Company to make fittings that connected the fuel lines of bombers to self-sealing fuel cells. This war work made the Company very busy. So instead of coming back to Wooster one Saturday morning a month, I left Tiffin at noon every Friday and worked at the Company in Wooster on Friday afternoon and evening, all day Saturday, and then would head back to Tiffin Saturday night. Sometimes, I would even work all Saturday evening and Sunday morning and then return to Tiffin to prepare for Monday classes. On some of these trips, I went alone but sometimes Alice would go with me. She would drop me off in Wooster and drive to Cleveland to stay with her mother. She would then pick me up late Saturday afternoon or Sunday noon to go back to Tiffin. During the nine months of that school year, I also worked at The Wooster Rubber Company every day during every school vacation – Thanksgiving, Christmas, Spring Break, and Easter. The only holiday I took off was Christmas Day.

In September 1940 – more than a year before Pearl Harbor – the U.S. Congress had enacted the first peacetime draft law in U.S. history, which required all young men to register for military service, although at that time no one knew whether the United States was going to enter the war. I registered for the draft in Lakewood, Ohio, where we were still living in the spring of 1941. I was not called to report to the draft board during a period of time in which we made three moves: to Wooster in June 1941, to Tiffin in September 1942 to teach at Heidelburg College, and back to Wooster in June 1943. Later, I received word from the draft board that I had been reclassified into a classification based on doing essential war work. At that time I was one of three top management people at The Wooster Rubber Company managing a business that was engaged 100 percent in producing products to support the U.S. war effort and which employed some 500 people. It was not until much later – after I had become Chief Executive Officer of Rubbermaid – that I looked in our Personnel Department files and found copies of letters Caldwell had written to my draft board every six months outlining the essential nature of the war work the Company was doing and the importance of my job to the management of the Company. Up until then, I had not known what information the draft board had used to determine my classification as doing work that was essential to support the war effort.

In June 1943, Caldwell asked me to return from Tiffin to Wooster to become the Secretary and Treasurer of The Wooster Rubber Company. As an inducement, he offered me a salary of $4,500 a year plus a bonus estimated at $400. Since my starting salary two years earlier had been only $1,500 a year, his offer was too good to pass up so I resigned with some regret from Heidelberg College, and we moved back to Wooster where I took up my new duties at the Company.

Now I want to describe how we applied our expertise in working with rubber to make fittings for self-sealing fuel cells used in bombers. A self-sealing fuel cell was made of two sheets of Chemigum synthetic rubber with 3/8 of an inch of Chemigum synthetic rubber in a jellied state in between the two sheets. This made a gas tank that repaired itself. If a bullet ripped through the fuel cell, the jellied rubber would flow together and prevent gasoline from leaking out. The first war work the Company did as a subcontractor to Goodyear was to make rubber fittings to attach the fuel line hoses to the fuel cell. These fittings had a metal insert in them surrounded by Chemigum rubber which fitted onto the rubber liner of the tank. This was very precise work. If the seal of the rubber to the metal was not perfect, gasoline could leak out and cause an explosion. Although we were accustomed to working with rubber, the precise tolerances involved made the work a real learning experience for the Company personnel who manufactured the fittings. A totally new process was required to make the fittings so that the rubber adhered very firmly to the metal inserts. If they did not, they were rejected and the rubber had to be cut off the metal inserts and then buffed off in order to reuse the metal inserts, which were of considerable value because they were precisely made and because of the wartime metal shortage.

Soon after we started our war work, Goodyear placed Howard

Winget as a full-time inspector at the Company, and he later moved his family to Wooster. Winget also hired other inspectors, a staff which grew to 40 or 50 employees. They were on Goodyear's payroll, but they worked on-site at the Company in Wooster inspecting products before we could ship them to Goodyear.

We had to give Goodyear a price quote for each of the fitting parts. Caldwell told me that the husbands of his two daughters were serving in the military and that he did not want us to make any more dollars of profit on war work than we had made during the last year of civilian work. He said that even though we might take on more business or grow, he still wanted us to make only the same dollars of profit that we had made on civilian production. This was his patriotic decision to contribute in a big way to the war effort, but not to make even a normal profit level compared with the huge profits other companies were making from war work.

Over the course of the war, the Company actually grew to more than $5 million in annual sales, which was about 12 times the size of our sales in the last year of civilian production. But in each of the war years, we made just about the same number of profit dollars as we had during our last pre-war year. This meant that the percentage of profit to sales went down drastically. At the end of each year during the war, U.S. Army Air Force officers came in to re-negotiate our contracts. At the conclusion of each of these re-negotiating sessions, the officers involved said that we could have made several times as much profit as we did and they would not have taken back any of that profit.

We soon began manufacturing other products for Goodyear, including the entire self-sealing fuel cell, which involved insertion of some of the fittings we were making. We also sent the fittings we made to other companies making the self-sealing fuel cells. Then we began to make tourniquets and the "Mae West" life vest, which was a life vest that went over the head and was inflated in the front by carbon dioxide cylinders. The "Mae West" could hold a man's head and shoulders up out of the water for many hours until he was rescued. They were used by Navy personnel when ships were sunk and by Air Force crews when their aircraft crashed into the sea.

No new tires were made for civilian use during the war. So when tires wore out, they had to be retreaded. The government did allocate rubber for retreading tires, which took considerably less rubber than new tires. You could also buy retreaded tires, but most people took their own tires in for retreading and they bought retreaded tires only when a tire was damaged too badly to be retreaded. Gasoline, of course, was also rationed and the Company had to set up a system for allocating the necessary gasoline ration stamps to employees who had to drive to work. Before the war, Perry G. Peckham had been a manufacturers' representative for The Wooster Rubber Company responsible for covering the State of Ohio. When the war came along, he had nothing to do so Caldwell offered him the job of firing our coal-burning steam boiler and he took it. It was a dirty job so he wore coveralls because he would get covered with black coal dust. Caldwell also assigned him the job of disbursing gasoline ration stamps to employees who had to drive to work. These were available only to employees who lived too far away to walk or ride their bicycles to work. It was up to Peckham to calculate the number of miles employees had to drive each month to get to work and then give each of them the number of gasoline stamps needed to buy enough gasoline for that number of miles. He did this while still wearing his coal-dust-covered coveralls, but he washed his hands to avoid smudging the stamps.

Not long after the Company had subcontracted 100 percent of its manufacturing capacity to Goodyear for war work, we were asked by Goodyear to subcontract out additional work to the Pretty Products Rubber Company in Coshocton, Ohio. We did so and, just as we had to quote on each product we made for Goodyear, we had Pretty Products quote on each of the fittings they manufactured for us. That made us responsible not only for allocating the work to Pretty Products, but also for the quality of their finished products.

Our involvement in war work also meant that we had to hire new employees because the people we had been forced to lay off earlier when civilian production stopped had either been drafted or had found war work elsewhere – most of them outside Wooster. This was because Wooster had very little in the way of war work and most of the companies in the city had also laid off employees. The United Rubber Workers Union (URW) recognized this as an opportunity to come down from Akron to organize our new factory workers. If the Company had been able to maintain its former employees, who understood the Company and were happy on the job, there was no way the URW would have been able to organize our plant. But because the recently hired employees did not know or understand management, the URW organizers were able to talk them into voting for a union. This was a bitter disappointment for Caldwell, who had always been very thoughtful, kind, and considerate of his employees and considered them his friends.

During World War II, almost everyone working in civilian jobs also did part-time war work in addition to their regular jobs. We hired teachers, Post Office employees, mail carriers, college students, retail clerks, farmers, and people from many other occupations to work four-hour shifts after they finished their regular work. One of these part-time workers was Stanley Gault, who worked at The Wooster Rubber Company each evening while he was a student at The College of Wooster. His job was to buff the rubber off metal inserts from defective fittings and it was a very dirty and dusty job. Gault likes to tell the story that after he became Chairman of the Board and Chief Executive Officer (CEO) of Rubbermaid in 1980, he had someone look into the personnel files to find his file. In it was a termination slip on which there was a question: "Would you re-hire this person?" The answer was "Yes" and the slip was signed by Don Noble.

One afternoon, a group of college students came to the Company applying for part-time work. Among them were two Japanese-American or *Nisei* girls. After interviewing all of the college students, including the two Japanese-American girls, I told them to come to work the next afternoon. A few minutes later, I got word that the department in the factory where I was planning to assign them had heard that I was hiring two Japanese-Americans. The women in that department sent a message in to me that they refused to work with the girls because we were fighting the Japanese. They said they did not trust Japanese-Americans. I immediately went out and talked to the group of about 60 women and listened to their arguments. I told them that if they objected to working with the Japanese-Americans, they also should object to working with me because I was of German descent and that we were also fighting the Germans. They said, "No, that was different." I came back into the office feeling defeated, but about an hour later somebody came in from a department which had only eight women in it who said they were willing to work with the two Japanese-American girls. So, I re-assigned them to that department and they worked very effectively for the rest of the war.

During the war years, there were only three individuals on the top management team: Caldwell, as President and General Manager; Frank Stefanski, as Factory Manager; and me, as Secretary and Treasurer. Each of us wore many hats. Caldwell, in addition to handling the major contacts with Goodyear and with Pretty Products, also worked in the laboratory and with factory supervision trying to improve the adherence of rubber to the metal inserts. Frank managed the entire factory, including the receiving of materials and the shipment of finished products. He also spent a great deal of time trying to decrease the number of product defects.

In addition to accounting, cost accounting, and finance which would normally come under the Secretary and Treasurer, I did all the office personnel work and most of the factory personnel work, interviewing and hiring people to work in both office and factory jobs. I also supervised all purchasing and the payroll for both the office and factory. I personally prepared all price quotations for the new parts Goodyear asked us to make for them. Once a month, I drove to Akron to reconcile differences between the count of raw materials Goodyear had shipped to us and the count of finished products we had shipped to them. I also went to Pretty Products Rubber Company in Coshocton and did the same thing each month.

For the three years that the Company was engaged in war work, all of the management people worked 11- or 12-hour days, six days a week, taking only Sunday off. None of us took any vacation time whatsoever and observed only one or two holidays during the entire year. We always took off Christmas Day and sometimes half a day for Thanksgiving, but that was it. We worked New Year's Day, Memorial Day, the Fourth of July, and Labor Day.

In order to expand our capabilities for war-time production, the Company rented a large building in downtown Wooster that had been a Packard Automobile Dealership located on South Market Street, south of Henry Street. We used that building for producing self-sealing fuel cells. We also rented a building just east of the curve on Bowman Street, which had previously been occupied by the Steel Storage File Company. This was a building that had been built only a few years before World War II started and had good, clean floor space without pillars; we used it for additional production of self-sealing fuel cells. We rented another building on Liberty Street, east of Bever Street, which after our war-time occupancy became the location of Imhoff and Long Hardware. We also rented a warehouse on Spruce Street which, prior to that time, had been the Buckeye Pickle Works. At one point shortly after the war ended, the creek running alongside that warehouse rose to flood stage and we had three feet of water in the basement.

In 1944, we built a new press room which was three times the size of the old one. It was attached to the west side of the old building and had a high ceiling and forced-air ventilation – a big improvement over the old press room which was very hot and dirty. The Company went from having only 16 factory employees immediately prior to getting into war work to a total of approximately 500 employees a year and a half later.

On V-J Day, August 25, 1945, I spent the entire afternoon on the telephone with Goodyear procurement people who gave me cancellations for contract after contract. As each contract was canceled, I sent someone to the department involved telling them to stop work on whatever they were doing. At noon that day we had been going full blast, but by 5:00 p.m. war work contracts had been canceled for every department in the Company, so we closed down and had to lay people off.

We spent the next month packing up all of the finished fuel cells and tagging and packing up all of the work-in-process fuel cells. We also packed up all the inserts and identified and weighed all the other raw materials that we had in inventory. Everything was sent back to Goodyear with invoices covering it. At the same time that we were assembling all these items to go back to Goodyear, Pretty Products was assembling all their finished products and raw materials and their work-in-process inventory to send back to us, which we in turn had to re-tag and ship back to Goodyear. The invoices for the finished products were at the prices we had quoted to Goodyear. The price of raw materials was the price at which we had been billed when they were received. The work-in-process had to be costed and calculated and priced to Goodyear for the amount of material and labor we had put into them at the stage when the contracts were canceled.

In 30 days, this job was all completed and we were in an empty factory. A month later, Goodyear paid us for all our invoices on finished products, raw materials, and work-in-process inventory. At that point, The Wooster Rubber Company had the most liquid balance sheet any company could ever imagine. Our assets consisted of cash and the book values of our equipment and buildings. That was it – no accounts receivable and no inventory. Not a bad position to be in as we began getting ready to resume the production of our housewares lines.

Prior to World War II, we had used a numbering system consisting of only two digits for our consumer products. As the war drew to a close, I started thinking about our re-entry into the housewares business and it seemed to me that it would be a good idea for us to have a numbering system that would accommodate more than 99 products. I anticipated that we would quickly grow beyond that kind of limitation and I had always believed in planning ahead. To accommodate the higher post-war sales volumes I envisaged for consumer products, I worked out a four-digit numbering system in which the first digit represented a broad product category, such as bathroom products. The second digit designated a group of products within that broad category. The last two digits would be the number of a specific product within each category and group. That numbering system has served the Company well and is still in use today.

During the 30 days that we were assembling all of the material to send back to Goodyear, Caldwell was starting to work on getting us back into civilian production. He began placing orders for rubber, chemicals, and the other materials needed for making household rubber products. No coloring agents were available, however, to make colored rubber products because all the chemicals that were used in making coloring agents had been diverted to the war effort. It was going to take several months for the chemical companies to convert back to producing the coloring agents we needed to make our brightly colored rubber goods. Nevertheless, Caldwell decided to proceed with the manufacture of housewares products, but the products would all have to be all black because the only coloring agent immediately available was carbon black.

Because no rubber housewares of any kind had been produced for almost four years, the pent-up demand was so great that both retailers and consumers were willing to accept all-black housewares products. So when we received the raw materials about 60 days after V-J Day, we started to call employees back to produce housewares products, including rubber-covered wire dish drainers, but all in black rubber. After about five months of producing nothing but black products, coloring agents became available again and that made our entire inventory of black rubber products unsaleable. This was true not only for the black products we had in inventory at the plant, but also for those we already had shipped to department stores, hardware stores, and wholesalers throughout the country. We had to scrap our own inventory and negotiate a settlement with all our customers throughout the country under which we absorbed part of the loss they were taking on their inventory of black products. It was a costly conversion to resume making colored products, but it was just something we had to do – even Henry Ford was not able to get away with saying "you can have any color you want, so long as it is black."

Immediately after World War II, Caldwell hired two Goodyear employees. One was Forrest B. Shaw, who had been our liaison man at Goodyear. He joined us as Factory Manager replacing Frank Stefanski, who had been transferred to work on research and development projects. Caldwell also hired Howard Winget, who had been Goodyear's resident product inspector in Wooster in charge of all the Goodyear inspectors. He became Superintendent of the Rubber Mixing and Milling and Press Departments. The Company also hired many other veterans, including Lee Hart, who was hired as Chief Engineer; Clyde Breneman, who was hired to work on product development with Caldwell; and Grant Rose, who became our Factory Personnel Manager.

Sales in the first post-war year were $2.5 million and by 1949 had increased to $5 million. At this point, it became necessary to expand our plant floor space. An addition of 50,000 square feet was made to the building at the east end of the existing plant on the area that had been the employee parking space. We made a new parking lot on the north side of Bowman Street. Since the old building had 50,000 square feet, the addition gave us a total of 100,000 square feet of factory space on the south side of Bowman Street, all sitting on 3.8 acres of land.

Shortly after V-J Day, we purchased a building a half mile east of the existing plant on Bowman Street which had been owned by the Steel Storage File Company and which we had rented during the war for making self-sealing fuel cells. Our purpose in buying the building was to install equipment for making wire dish drainers. This was one of the products Caldwell developed soon after he joined the Company because he could use the same dip tanks that had been used to produce rubber toy balloons. Prior to and immediately after World War II, we were still using these tanks containing liquid rubber latex. The dish drainers were attached to a rack and dipped by hand into the rubber latex. It was crude but it worked and there was nothing better at the time.

Before we began operations in the newly acquired building, however, we designed and installed special new equipment to move the wire dish drainers on a conveyor. The conveyor carried the bare wire dish drainers up through an oven to be heated. Then they went down into a tank of liquid rubber. Because the dish drainers traveled through the tank, we put a false bottom in the tank with an agitator in it. This agitator moved the liquid rubber in the upper part of the tank at exactly the same speed that the dish drainers were moving on the conveyor. Therefore, the rubber did not "drag" on the dish drainers moving through it and they became coated evenly. After the dish drainers had been carried at the right speed through the tank of rubber, the conveyor took them out and up to another oven where the rubber coating was cured.

In 1947, we purchased the Midwest Metallic Products Company in Garfield Heights, Ohio, a suburb of Cleveland. They had been supplying about half of our wire dish drainers, while the other half came from Union Steel Products in Albion, Michigan. After purchasing Midwest Metallic Products, we expanded operations there to produce all our wire dish drainers. We bought land in Garfield Heights during 1953 and built an entirely new plant for Midwest Metallic Products to expand their manufacturing capacity. Midwest Metallic was also manufacturing the wire racks for Hobart's Kitchen Aid electric dish washers, which we were dipping for the Hobart Manufacturing Company in Troy, Ohio.

In 1948, plastic housewares products such as soap dishes, dish pans, buckets, and sink strainers began to appear on the market for the first time. Unfortunately, the development of plastic raw materials was still in its infancy and plastic lacked the durability and stability it has now. The early plastic housewares products tended to warp in hot water, crack in cold weather, and break in use.

We had talked frequently about Rubbermaid getting into the production of plastic products, but Caldwell was very firm in saying that Rubbermaid would not make any plastic products until raw materials were available that would make durable plastic products. He did not want the Rubbermaid name to be on any product that would not give satisfactory service. So it was not until 1955 that we purchased a plastic injection-molding machine and had our first injection molds made, one to make a plastic dish pan and another to make plastic handles for our rubber plate and bowl scrapers. We purchased the very best, highest-grade material available for the dish pans and the plastic handles. Then we tested the finished products repeatedly to be sure that Rubbermaid plastic products would stand up under hard use before we sold the first one on the open market. That was the beginning of Rubbermaid's entry into the plastic housewares business, which grew rapidly and soon surpassed the sales volume of our rubber products.

In 1967, our Research & Development Department developed a new dish drainer that all of us welcomed with great enthusiasm because it was made entirely of plastic on an injection-molding machine. The plastic dish drainer held more dishes and silverware in the same amount of space as the old wire dish drainer, and it was not only a better-looking product but also easier to make than the wire version which required the rather complex dipping process I described. And even more important, we were making far less than our normal profit on the wire dish drainers which by then were being coated with vinyl instead of rubber. On the new plastic dish drainers we were going to make more than our normal profit even with a retail price about 20 percent lower than the price of the vinyl-coated wire dish drainers. Because we thought the new plastic dish drainer would eventually force us to phase out of the wire dish drainer business, we decided to sell the Midwest Metallic Products Company but continued to buy our bare-wire dish drainers from them thinking we would soon drop the product line. After we sold Midwest Metallic Products in July 1968 and were debating whether to drop the vinyl-coated wire dish drainers, I said to the New Product Development Committee, "Why don't we let consumers decide which of the two dish drainers they want? Instead of dropping the wire dish drainers, let's raise the price to where we will make a normal profit on the product and let consumer purchases determine whether we should drop it." So we raised the price to a normal profit point and an amazing thing happened. We continued to sell as many wire dish drainers as we had sold before, and we sold about an equal number of plastic dish drainers. To this day, Rubbermaid still sells large volumes of both plastic and vinyl-covered wire dish drainers. After we found that the vinyl-coated wire dish drainers were continuing to sell so well, we regretted having sold the wire manufacturing company. Rubbermaid still buys its wire dish drainers from the new owners of the Midwest Metallic Products Company, but Rubbermaid recently contracted out the dipping operation to a supplier.

Rod Hazlett, who worked at Seiberling Rubber Company in Akron, came to Wooster in 1948 to discuss another new business opportunity with us. He told Caldwell that the rubber door mats we manufactured could be installed inside used automobiles to cover the worn spot in front of the accelerator pedal. Prior to this time, rubber door mats had never been used for this purpose. Although it seems hard to believe in hindsight, the car makers had never offered an automotive floor mat for either new or used cars. Hazlett asked whether he could start selling our door mats to the used car dealers in and around Akron. Caldwell told him he would pay him a commission on all the mats he sold and told him to go to it. Hazlett started selling the mats during evenings and on Saturday afternoons. He was so successful that he soon resigned from his job at Seiberling to sell our rubber mats full time. Sales of the mats increased so rapidly that Caldwell gave Hazlett a job as Sales Manager and asked him to hire other salesmen to sell the door mats. He gradually built a sales force and the volume became sufficient for Rubbermaid to design a floor mat specifically for use in automobiles. This was a totally new product because there had never before been a mat especially designed for automobile floors.

Sales of the automotive floor mats continued to grow and we soon had several different designs of mats in various shapes to fit the floor contours of different car makes and models. We changed from selling directly to used car dealers to selling to automotive supply wholesalers who warehoused the mats and sold them to both new and used car dealers throughout the country. This was a very profitable business for us for many years, but during the 1970s the business became very competitive. Bill Coulter, Vice President in charge of Automotive, thought we were a high-cost producer because we priced our mats higher than the competition. He, therefore, proposed that we move manufacture of the mats to Tennessee, where labor costs would be lower. A study showed that our costs were no higher than those of our competition; the price difference was all in the profit we were adding. So we did not move the operation, and a few years later we chose to go out of the business entirely. Today, car makers produce floor mats for their vehicles as a matter of course, but the product idea and design originated with us at Rubbermaid.

Because the majority of the Board members lived in the Pittsburgh area, most of Rubbermaid's Board meetings were held in Pittsburgh during the 18-year period from when I joined the Company in 1941 until Errett Grable's death in 1959. The meetings were usually held on a weekday evening, starting at about 5:30 at the Duquesne Club in Pittsburgh, or in the summer time at the Rolling Rock Club in Ligonier, Pennsylvania. They were scheduled at that time so the Pittsburgh-based Board members could continue working in their offices at the Aluminum Cooking Utensil Company until 5:00 p.m. and come straight to the meeting. The meeting would be held from 5:30 to 7:00 or 7:30 p.m., at which time we would have dinner, continuing our discussion during dinner on whatever major topics had come up during the meeting. Then Caldwell and I would stay overnight and drive back to Wooster the next morning.

My most vivid memories of our trips to Pittsburgh were those we made during winter, when we would drive through heavy snowstorms on U.S. Route 30 which went directly from Wooster to Pittsburgh. Route 30 was a two-lane road but it seemed pretty good back then. Two-lane roads were the only kind of road available before the four-lane interstate highways or turnpikes were built. I also say "directly" in a loose sense of the term, because Route 30 wound around the hills of eastern Ohio and West Virginia, and then on into the much more substantial hills and mountains of Pennsylvania. Therefore, the drive on a wintry night through a heavy snowstorm was a challenge to say the least.

Another memory I have of our Board meeting trips to Pittsburgh is of Leonard Park, who was a partner in the firm of Peat, Marwick, Mitchell and Company, our public accountants, and the head of the firm's Cleveland office. Park went with us at least once a year after the close of the books in early December. He drove to Wooster, left his car at the Company, rode over with us, and then came back with us in the morning. I remember driving while Caldwell and Park sat in the back seat with a suitcase between them making a tabletop to hold the cards for their gin rummy game. They started playing gin rummy the minute we got into the car and the game continued until we arrived at the Duquesne Club. Even when Caldwell and I would go alone, I was invariably the driver. Later on, after Bob Critchfield, the Company's outside counsel, became a member of the Board, he also accompanied us on the trips to Pittsburgh.

When I first went into the Duquesne Club, I thought I was walking into some kind of a palace. I had never been in a place that was so plush, so extravagantly built, or with such elaborate facilities as the Duquesne Club. After the first several trips, I would come back and tell Alice about the Club's luxurious furnishings and elegant appointments. I remember so well trying to describe to her the thickness of the doors. They were big solid oak doors two inches thick with heavy metal hardware that gleamed from frequent polishing. The club also had a beautiful billiard room with, I think, eight billiard tables. Down every hall of the Duquesne Club and on the walls of every room were hung beautiful, original paintings of fox hunts or horseback riding, all with a strong male orientation. The dining room carried out this exquisite decor scheme, all done in extremely good taste but very masculine. The Duquesne Club was a men's club and, except for what was called the "ladies' dining room," women were not allowed in the Club. The ladies' dining room was strictly for women as the guests of members and they had to use the "ladies' entrance" to enter the Club. This luxury was all the more awesome because of my having been brought up in very meager circumstances. I always was very impressed by the elegance of the Duquesne Club even after I had been there many times.

When Caldwell began talking about retiring, many people asked me whether I wanted to be President and General Manager of Rubbermaid. My answer always was, and very sincerely was, that I did not know whether I wanted to be President. But I always added that I felt it was necessary for me to do everything I knew to prepare myself to be President, even though I did not know whether I ever would be, or whether I even really wanted to be. I did not feel I could do my job properly as Chief Financial Officer, Secretary, and Treasurer unless I was working diligently to prepare myself to be President and General Manager, as though I knew that someday I would be appointed. I believed that to do my job as Chief Financial Officer it was necessary for me to learn as much as possible about every facet of the business. This, I thought, was the same thing I would have to do in preparing for the job of President and General Manager. I certainly did not know whether I would be competent to do the job. In addition, I also believed that having become Chief Financial Officer, Secretary, and Treasurer of the Company was in itself a very satisfactory career achievement.

In December 1958, Forrest B. Shaw was elected President and General Manager of Rubbermaid to take over the duties of Caldwell, who wanted to retire. A natural leader with an engaging personality, Caldwell had a unique combination of imaginative technical and manufacturing competence plus equal ability as a dynamic and creative marketing expert. I think Horatio Ebert summed up the feelings of all of us at Rubbermaid when he said, "Jim Caldwell did a magnificent job. I don't believe all this would have been possible without him."

After he replaced Caldwell as President, Shaw stated that although Rubbermaid had enjoyed a very good growth rate in recent years, he thought that in the future the Company would have to settle for a lower rate of growth. Shaw said he believed this because every department store in the country was selling Rubbermaid products and they already were giving our products as much shelf space as he thought they would give to any one product line. That was the thinking that made Shaw predict much slower sales growth than in the past. In August 1959, Shaw resigned because of a difference of opinion with Caldwell. On August 25, Caldwell, Bob Critchfield, and I went to Pittsburgh for an evening Board of Directors meeting at the Duquesne Club.

At one point during the meeting, Errett Grable, who was Chairman, asked me to leave the room. Ten minutes later, he called me back in and announced that the Board had elected me President and General Manager of Rubbermaid Incorporated. That came as a great surprise to me because I had no clue that they were even thinking of making me President.

Despite my surprise, I managed to respond by saying I wanted to tell the Board three things. "First, I want to thank you for your confidence in me. Second, unless you instruct me otherwise, I will not spend any more time during the next year looking for acquisitions because I believe we have so many growth opportunities in our own backyard that we can do better for the stockholders by concentrating on our own business. Third, I will not waste any more time listening to people who want to acquire Rubbermaid."

The reason I made these three points was that I thought the Company had just recently made a poor acquisition when it bought Jamestown Finishes in Jamestown, New York. I also thought we had wasted a lot of time listening to various offers being made for the purchase of Rubbermaid. Caldwell had let it be known that he was interested in selling the Company. Ebert and Grable were willing to listen to offers, but thought the Company was worth far more than any offers being made – at least twice as much. Therefore, I thought it was a waste of time to go through the exercise of letting people make offers for the Company because we would never reach agreement.

The next morning I called together what became my Operating Committee. This consisted of Tom Clark, who had replaced me as Secretary and Treasurer; Richard Raeder, who became Controller; Ed Fredericks, Vice President of Sales and Marketing; Bill Coulter, Manager of Automotive Product Sales; and Les Gigax, who became Vice President of Manufacturing and later Chief Operating Officer. I told them I thought it would be well for me to set out the way we were going to operate because we would be working together for many years – it turned out to be 20 years, which I consider something of a record in U.S. industry.

That morning I said, "On every issue that comes up in our group, I want each of you to express to me your opinion on the subject and I want you to make sure that I understand your point of view. If it is necessary in order to have me understand your position, I want you to pound the table, stand up, jump up and down, or shout, whatever it takes to be sure I understand your point. When I have heard and understood each person's views, I will consider what each of you has said and then I will make a decision, which might not be a majority opinion or may even be a minority opinion of only one. There will be no votes. I will make the decision. When the decision has been made, all of us are to go out of the room with locked arms, figuratively speaking of course, operating as though it were a unanimous decision. If one of you always agrees with me, one of the two of us will not be necessary." In other words, I did not want any "yes men" working for me.

As a group of executives work together over a period of time, they develop certain tacit understandings that make communication possible with fewer words. This became very evident when our Operating Committee had been operating for a couple of years without any change of personnel and we then added one executive to the Committee. We found that as we discussed a subject, we would have to stop and explain to the new member what we meant by certain phrases or concepts. This took extra time to bring him up to speed on the understood meanings of terms that we as a group had developed so that we could use shortcuts in communications. For the new participant, however, we had to stop and explain what we meant. As a result of this, I had Al Stark prepare a *Glossary of Terms* with explanations of what the terms meant to Rubbermaid executives. Examples of these terms are the definitions we used for the words "box" and "carton." In common usage, these two terms are basically interchangeable, but at Rubbermaid they had taken on specific meanings. The word "box" for Rubbermaid executives meant a light-weight chipboard box into which a certain number of our products were put and then several boxes were packed into a "carton" for shipping. A "carton" meant a container in which the products were placed when they were ready for shipment, or the container in which we shipped the products.

After becoming Chief Executive Officer, I also remember telling the members of my Operating Committee that I believed, "He rules best who rules least." That meant that I wanted managers to think for themselves, use their own initiative, develop their own strategies, and operate as if they were entrepreneurs. To achieve that goal, when I delegated responsibility and authority to the General Managers for the operation of their divisions, I used this non-restrictive language:

> *"I delegate to you the total responsibility and give to you the total authority to manage your business as you see fit to accomplish your objectives with only the following limitations.*
> * *You must sell your products in the markets assigned to your operation, such as housewares, commercial, or industrial products.*
> * *You must operate your business in accordance with the philosophies and principles set out in the Statement of Rubbermaid Philosophy and Fundamental Principles.*
> * *You must do your accounting in the manner set forth by the Corporate Controller.*
> * *You must purchase insurance for your operating unit through Corporate."*

This is the exact opposite of the way most companies delegate responsibility and give authority to their senior executives. Usually, general managers are given a defined set of responsibilities and their specific authority is set forth in detail. As a result, general managers are limited to the responsibilities and authority that are prescribed in this fashion; in short, such executives are not really in control of the operating business they head. It always seemed much more effective to me to delegate total responsibility and authority to manage the business, and then set forth in detail only the few restrictions on that responsibility and authority that are essential to maintaining good corporate oversight.

Another concept I used was saying that being a Chief Executive Officer was like being the conductor of a symphony orchestra. Although a conductor himself might know how to play only one or, at the most, only a few of the instruments in the orchestra, he could wave his baton and keep the musicians playing together and making beautiful music in harmony. My analogy, of course, was that as Chief Executive Officer, I did not know how to perform most of the jobs at Rubbermaid. Therefore, I expected each of the managers to do their own job well, just as a symphony conductor expects his musicians to play their own instruments well. My role was to set the goals for the Company and establish the strategies and business principles we would use to achieve those goals. In effect, I waved my baton and kept the music going.

When Caldwell retired as Chairman of the Board in March 1965, the Board approved establishment of the James R. Caldwell Scholarship to honor his contributions to Rubbermaid. This plan provided for the award of scholarships paying $500 per year (subsequently increased to $2,000) for four years to two children of Rubbermaid employees upon their graduation from high school. Scholarship awards were to be based on a combination of academic achievement and extracurricular activities that gave evidence of a student's potential leadership qualities. The scholarships were not to be based on need, because obviously the parents would be employed.

In setting up the Caldwell Scholarship, I had envisioned that at least half of the scholarships would go to the children of factory employees, which in some cases would be the difference between the kids being able to go to college and not being able to go to college. During the first several years, however, all the scholarship winners were the children of salaried employees. To correct this, I changed the plan so that one scholarship each year would go to a child of salaried employees and one to a child of factory employees. The judges who decided the scholarship winners were a panel made up of the President of The College of Wooster, the Superintendent of Wooster City Schools, and the Superintendent of Wayne County Schools. After the judging was over and the awards had been made, the winners got plenty of external publicity with photos and articles in the local and Cleveland newspapers. But we also made sure that all of the kids who had applied were given internal publicity in Rubbermaid publications, because in every case the applicants were outstanding youngsters who had excelled in their school work and had been natural leaders in their extracurricular activities. This visibility for their kids with their fellow workers pleased their proud parents very much and gave a great boost to everyone's morale.

CHAPTER SEVENTEEN • BUILDING A NEW HEADQUARTERS

Although Caldwell wanted the Company to prosper, he did not seem to have any desire for it to grow into a large corporation. As a matter of fact, I think he did not want to see it grow beyond a certain size. When Caldwell was interviewing me before I accepted the job in Wooster, he showed me a factory addition being made at that time and said, "We think this expansion will take care of our growth for many years to come, because we do not want to see the Company grow much larger than this addition will accommodate."

When I came to Wooster, the entire worldwide Rubbermaid operation was located on one acre of land and the 23,000-square-foot building was the same building that Horatio Ebert had built in 1928 on the south side of Bowman Street. The addition Caldwell showed me that day was the first one ever made to that building, and it expanded floor space by about 12,000 square feet.

The lot west of the plant on the southeast corner of Bowman Street and Palmer Street was a corn field. Across Bowman Street, the entire area east of Palmer Street, all the way to the curve of State Route 585, was also one gigantic cornfield. Shortly after I joined the Company, the cornfield adjacent to the plant on the southeast corner of Palmer Street and Bowman Street became available for purchase. Arthur Miller, a good friend of Caldwell and part owner of the Holmes Construction Company, told Caldwell that Holmes Construction owned the corner lot and was willing to sell it. They had another buyer, Delroy Franks, owner of the B & F Transfer Company, but Miller wanted to give The Wooster Rubber Company first chance at buying it. Caldwell told some of us that the land was available, but said he did not envision that the Company would ever need it. I argued that we might very likely grow into that space, but the decision was made not to buy it.

Other examples of Caldwell's reluctance to expand took place in 1946. The Wooster Board of Trade purchased the land on the north side of Bowman Street from Palmer Street east to the curve of Bowman and arranged it so that the industries owning land on the south side of Bowman Street could purchase the corresponding land across the street to the north. Again, Caldwell told us that he could not see any need for buying the land across the street, but this time we convinced him that we might someday build on the rest of the land we owned on the south side of Bowman Street and would need the additional land for parking. So it was agreed to buy it. Not long afterward, the B & F Transfer Company, which by this time had built on the corner lot west of the Company, decided they did not want their land on the north side of Bowman Street and offered it to Caldwell. Once more, he told us that he could see no need for the Company to own that land. Again, we convinced him that although we also could not see any immediate need, it would be a mistake to let someone else buy the land and build there, forever closing us out from owning it. So very reluctantly, he allowed the Company to purchase that land.

In 1952, a Rubbermaid building was built on the north side of Bowman Street to house our finishing department. A bridge was built across Bowman Street so people could walk back and forth between the plant on the south side and the new building. There was also a conveyor to carry molded goods from the press room on the south side to the finishing department on the north side. When the new building on the north side of Bowman Street was completed in the late fall of 1952, and before machinery had been moved in, Caldwell arranged for a caterer to serve dinner and invited all of the office and factory people to come and bring their spouses for a gala party on the building's second floor. There was a very large turnout because almost all of the factory and office people accepted the invitation and it was a great party. Several additions were made to this building over the next few years until 1958, when we had built to the edge of the land we owned.

North of the land we owned at that time was a building built by the Bauer Ladder Company which faced Palmer Street. We worked out an arrangement with Harold Arnold, who was owner of the Bauer Ladder Company, to buy his building and to sell him our building a half mile east on Bowman Street, which we were using for dipping wire dish drainers. We then built an addition to the building on the north side of Bowman Street that connected with the rear of the prior Bauer Ladder building. In 1957, we began to realize that it might soon be necessary to build on the parking lot at the corner of Bowman and Palmer Streets in Wooster. So we started buying lots on the west side of Palmer Street to use for parking. After we had bought several lots, we also began to buy houses as they came on the market. Our thinking was that if we were going to use the vacant lots for parking, the Company had better own the adjacent houses too so we would not run into complaints later from the property owners.

Prior to Forrest Shaw's resignation, he and Caldwell had obtained approval from the Board to construct an expansion of the building on the north side of Bowman Street. This expansion would extend out into the parking lot at the corner of Bowman and Palmer Streets and that would require moving some parking across Palmer Street to the lots the Company had purchased earlier. Shaw had engaged Constanzo Construction to bring in a bulldozer and a power shovel within ten days to dig a hole in the parking lot to start constructing the building expansion. One of the first things I did when I became President was to cancel the bulldozer and power shovel and postpone the date for starting the expansion, because it looked to me as though we were going to be building ourselves both figuratively and literally into a corner. I could not see how we could continue to expand at that location because to continue buying houses and lots on the west side of Palmer Street would be very expensive. Even if we transferred all of the parking to the lots across the street, we would soon reach the limit of the space at the corner of Palmer and Bowman Streets. It was during this period that I worked out the Company's growth formula which established an objective of doubling the business every six years (see Chapter 18). Adoption of that formula dramatically showed that within a short period of time – three or four years at most – we would outgrow the location at Palmer and Bowman Streets.

So we embarked on a search for land on which we could build to provide space for Rubbermaid's future growth. Our search was conducted within a 15-mile radius of Wooster. We thought we should stay inside 15 miles because there would be a great deal of transporting product and equipment between the existing plant and the new plant. We looked at sites in Apple Creek, Creston, Orrville, Smithville, and Wylersville, and west as far as Jeromesville. We actually took an option on a farm in Wylersville at the corner of the Back Orrville Road and Eby Road. Because we were going to need a substantial quantity of water, we began drilling a test well on the optioned farm property. While that was going on, I received a telephone call from the farmer who seemed very upset. He said, "My wife and I want to talk to you." So I drove over to the farm, went into the house, and found the farmer and his wife – a couple in their seventies – literally with tears streaming down their cheeks. "We've decided we don't want to sell our farm," they said. I tried to calm them down by telling them they were going to get a lot of money that would enable them to live comfortably wherever they wanted. "But we don't want to live anywhere else; we've lived here all our lives," they wailed. I returned to my office, feeling really bad about the situation. As it turned out, the problem was soon resolved. When we drew the quantity of water we would need from the test well, it lowered the water level in the wells of farmers for a mile around the proposed site. We realized we could not get the water we needed without damaging our neighbors, so I took a trip out to Wylersville and told the farmer and his wife that we were not going to buy their farm, much to their relief as well as my own!

From the start of our search, we had been considering the purchase of the 100-acre Steiner farm on Akron Road, just one mile east of our existing plant. It was very hilly terrain so it would cost what we originally considered to be a prohibitive amount to move enough dirt to create a level building site. But after looking at all the other sites, we came back to the Steiner farm, figuring that the earth-moving cost ultimately would be a smaller disadvantage than the disadvantages presented by the other sites.

We purchased an option to buy the Steiner farm, but I refused to exercise the option until we had ascertained for sure that the farm could be annexed to the City of Wooster. It was already adjacent to the border of the city limit of Wooster, so I thought that it could be done. I wanted to be sure that the property could be added to the City of Wooster for several reasons:

- I wanted to be able to get city water and sewers;
- I wanted the protection of the city's fire department;
- I wanted the taxes which we would pay to go to support the City of Wooster whose services we would be using, and
- I wanted our corporate taxes to support the Wooster City Schools which would be attended by most of the children of our employees.

The annexation went through and we exercised our option to buy the Steiner farm. Then we engaged the engineering firm of Dalton & Dalton in Cleveland to design a new factory and to establish a level for the factory that would enable us to build a factory of one million square feet, all on one floor level. They were to establish a level that would enable the dirt moved from the top of the hills to fill the valleys, resulting in a uniform level for the plant building. When that was underway, we had them design a building of 124,050 square feet – 107,600 square feet of factory space and 16,450 square feet of office space – which was to be built immediately. This, of course, is the site where our main plant and headquarter offices are located today, and we have now expanded beyond one million square feet of floor space.

Building the factory and office on the Steiner farm took more than one year from decision to completion. It took that long partly because of the tremendous amount of dirt that had to be moved to prepare the building site. In addition, the entire infrastructure to support the new building had to be installed. Water and sewer lines had to be brought in and roads, parking lots, and a railroad siding had to be built. Because we had to cut down the hills to fill the valleys, the solid ground of the site ended up in a horseshoe shape. So we designed the building in a horseshoe shape. The railroad siding also had to be in a similar horseshoe shape to serve the building. Because we were providing an infrastructure for a much larger facility, it was very expensive and took a great deal more cash and time to complete than if we had built the same amount of floor space at the corner of Bowman and Palmer Streets. It also adversely affected our expenses and earnings.

Our decision to buy the Steiner farm and build a plant on it had not been approved by a unanimous vote of the Board. Caldwell, in particular, thought we would have been better off building at the corner of Bowman and Palmer. During the three years that our earnings were adversely affected by the cost of the expansion on the Steiner farm, Caldwell reminded me several times that he had not been in favor of the project and had not voted for it. Toward the end of the three-year period, Dick Raeder, our controller, came to me and said, "Don, your idea of sacrificing the present earnings for greater future gains is great, but I'd like to be here to enjoy that future." What he was telling me was that he thought the Board of Directors were getting impatient with the reduced earnings caused by the expansion costs and by my repeatedly talking about "non-recurring expenses."

Despite the Steiner farm project's impact on earnings, I pressed on with it, solving various problems as they arose. For example, while they were designing the new office building, the architects brought in plans that showed the front of the office building made entirely of glass. I remember objecting to this because it would add to our heating and air conditioning costs.

The architects tried to convince me that the additional cost would not be much, but I insisted that whatever it was, it was wasteful and would be more than we would want to pay. I told them to take the plans back and work out a new design that provided windows comprising not more than 20 percent of the total wall surface. They came back with a design with which I was very pleased. It had long, narrow windows, comprising exactly 20 percent of the wall space. They then told me that they had reduced the cost of the heating and air conditioning equipment to half of the original estimate, and they admitted that using less glass had made possible the substantial reductions in the heating and air conditioning requirements. I'm afraid I said "I told you so!"

The new plant and office complex on the Steiner site was started in 1960 and we moved into it in 1961. In 1963, we decided that the next department to be moved to the new facility was the rubber mixing and rubber molding operations. There were several reasons for this decision. One, we were outgrowing our space on the south side of Bowman Street. Two, the equipment for both the mixing and the molding operations was old and much of it badly worn. Three, our R&D people had developed new and much improved processes for both mixing and molding rubber.

To describe the improved rubber mixing and molding processes, I need to describe the old methods, starting with the Banburys and mills. A bale of rubber weighing about 150 pounds was put into a Banbury along with chemicals, clay, whiting, sulfur, and color, making a total batch of 200 pounds. The rubber and other ingredients were mixed together, similar to mixing cake batter. After the batch was thoroughly mixed, it dropped out of a door at the bottom of the Banbury onto a rubber mixing mill located on the floor below. The rubber mixing mill had two rollers side by side, each roll 30 inches in diameter and 60 inches long. These rollers further mixed the rubber compound which then emerged in a sheet that was then taken off the rollers and fed into a calender with three chrome-plated steel rolls – each 24 inches in diameter and 50 inches long – stacked vertically. The rubber was fed through the rolls which were set so that it came out in an even thickness. As it emerged, the sheet of rubber was sliced into the correct width by two sharp knives and then cut into the proper lengths to be put into molds for making finished rubber products.

The new mixing process installed in the new building was totally different. All the ingredients, including rubber, clay, whiting, sulfur, and coloring agents, were in granular form and were mixed together into a 900-pound batch in a big mixer. The mixed ingredients, still in granular form, were put in a huge cloth bag and then dispensed slowly into a small extruder. The extruder further mixed the ingredients and the friction caused the rubber to become hot and soft absorbing the other ingredients. The compounded rubber emerged from the extruder in a continuous rectangular form which was cut by a knife into the shape of a brick. A conveyor carried the brick to a molder who put it into a mold while it was still hot from the mixing. If it was not used quickly, the brick cooled, became hard, and could not be molded because it would not spread out over the mold.

In the old rubber molding process, the molds were opened by sheer brute force because they were extremely heavy. The molder would then put a sheet of rubber, cut to the proper size, into the open mold. He closed the mold, shoved it into a press, and pushed a button to close the press. The press molded the rubber and cured it into a finished product that would hold its shape. The press opened automatically when the right time had elapsed. The molder pulled the mold out of the press and took out the finished product. Then he started the process all over again. The new molding process used what were called "clamshell presses." They opened on a hinge at the back and the mold stayed in the press attached to the top and bottom of the clamshell. The press opened automatically on a timed basis, the molder put in a piece of compounded rubber, and then pushed a button that closed the clamshell so the molding could take place. When the mold automatically opened, the molder took out the finished part, and the process started over again.

The building we constructed on the Steiner site in 1964 to

house the new rubber mixing and molding operations was built 1,100 feet from the building built in 1960. Our original master plan called for plastic production to be at the front end of the horseshoe layout and rubber production to be at the back end, with the finished goods warehouse in between. The two buildings were connected by a series of quontset huts to make a covered walkway from the plastic molding and warehouse to the rubber mixing and molding department. A conveyor running through this entire quontset hut walkway carried finished products in cartons from the rubber molding plant to the warehouse where they were shipped.

Every year we expanded our facilities to provide more production capacity as our business continued to grow. During the two-year period 1973 and 1974, however, an unusually large amount of building expansion took place and was described this way in the 1974 annual report:

> *"The Company completed a two-year major expansion program in 1974. A total of $30.0 million was spent to provide new capacity for further growth as follows:*
> * *a new 202,000-square-foot plant in Chillicothe, Ohio*
> * *a new 210,000-square-foot plant in LaGrange, Georgia*
> * *a 97,000-square-foot expansion in Canada, increasing the size of the plant by 40 percent*
> * *a 241,000-square-foot addition to the factory and warehouse in Wooster, Ohio*
> * *a 117,000-square-foot addition to the factory, warehouse, and office of the Commercial Products business in Winchester, Virginia*
> * *construction of 37,000 square feet of manufacturing and office space at Fusion Rubbermaid B.V. in Deventer, Holland, doubling production floor space, and*
> * *new molds and equipment at all operations."*

Although we were making additions to plants and equipment every year, the major investments in 1973 and 1974 were significant for several reasons. First, their magnitude. The new investment in 1974, for example, of $15.5 million was 44 percent greater than

1972, the highest annual expenditure prior to the 1973-1974 period, and was almost twice as much as any year before 1972. Second, the 1974 investment was significant because it was made during a recession year for the United States and the entire world. Our investment, however, was typical of what we did in recessionary periods. We had confidence that the recession would end and that when it ended, we would be expanding our business to a new level. Because of that anticipated growth, we believed we would need new buildings and equipment. This gave us the confidence to go ahead with expansion investments during even major recessions. Our investments during recessionary periods were beneficial to the Company in several ways. One was that we could have plant expansions built for less cost because building contractors were eager to keep their crews busy during the downturn. Second, we were able to negotiate much better prices for machinery and equipment from suppliers who were eager for sales. Third, we would be ready to expand our business to a new level as soon as the recession was over.

One of our Board members was James M. Dawson, Vice President and Chief Economist at the National City Bank of Cleveland. Jim provided support for our recession investment philosophy because he would predict that the recession was going to end and that business would increase. His optimistic but expert opinion helped our management team go ahead with expansion programs during recessions which ultimately saved us significant amounts of money and provided us with the enlarged capacity to grow as soon as the recession ended. This, in turn, gave us a market advantage over more timid competitors who had retrenched during a recession and had not made the investments necessary to be ready for the subsequent recovery.

CHAPTER EIGHTEEN • A FORMULA FOR GROWTH

As I covered in the last chapter, one of my first acts only ten days after I became Chief Executive Officer in 1959 was to postpone the bulldozer and power shovel which had been scheduled to start working on a building expansion at the corner of Bowman and Palmer Street. The expansion plan had greatly disturbed me because I felt that we would be, both figuratively and literally, building ourselves into a tight corner, one where we would run out of space in only a few years.

To show how quickly we would be running out of space at that location, I started making projections of our sales growth. After studying our recent history of sales growth, I saw no reason why sales could not continue growing at about the same rate they had over the prior years. I wanted to set a growth rate, however, that could be financed by plowed-back earnings (the difference between after-tax earnings and paid-out dividends).

These ideas led me to develop the following Growth Formula:

Growth Formula

The following basic objectives were set to support an annual compounded growth rate of 12-1/4 percent (to double the business every six years) and to pay out 33-1/3 percent of net earnings as dividends each year:

	Percent Required
Earn on beginning Gross Assets (assets before deducting Allowances for Receivables and Depreciation)	<u>10%</u>
Assuming the Allowances for Receivables & Depreciation equal 20% of Gross Assets–it will be necessary to earn on beginning Total Net Assets	<u>12-1/2%</u>
Assuming Net Worth equals 68% of Total Net Assets–it will be necessary to earn on beginning Net Worth	18-3/8%
Pay out each year one-third of earnings or pay out as a percent of beginning Net Worth	<u>(6-1/8)%</u>
Plow back each year two-thirds of earnings or increase Net Worth as a percent of beginning Net Worth	<u>12-1/4%</u>

As you can see, this Growth Formula would provide each year two-thirds of net earnings to be retained or plowed-back into the business. This would increase net worth 12-1/4 percent each year which would finance a sales growth of 12-1/4 percent per year compounded, which was equivalent to doubling the business every six years. This increase in net worth would finance the necessary growth in accounts receivable, inventory, machinery and equipment and buildings – in other words, all the assets on the balance sheet as illustrated in the following model:

Growth Formula Model
Growth from Plowed-Back Earnings

This model will work to have a Net Worth that doubles in six years to support a business that doubles in six years and to have a balance sheet that will stay as strong as it was in the beginning period without adding any new equity financing except the plowed-back earnings.

	Beginning of Year 1	During Year 1	Beginning of Year 2	During Year 2	Beginning of Year 3	During Year 3	
Gross Assets	$125,000		$140,318		$157,515		
Allowances*	25,000		28,064		31,503		
Net Assets	100,000		112,254		126,012		
Liabilities	32,000		35,921		40,324		
Net Worth	$ 68,000		$ 76,333		$ 85,688		$96,185
Earnings		$12,500		$14,032		$15,745	
Pay Out		4,167		4,677		5,248	
Plow Back		$ 8,333		$ 9,355		$10,497	

* Allowances for Receivables and Depreciation

Note: Net Worth for one year plus plowed-back earnings for that year equals Net Worth for the next year.

Since it may be necessary in any given year to spend more for capital expenditures than can be provided by available cash, it may be necessary to finance through long-term borrowing but this model will provide plowed-back earnings to repay the long-term financing.

I thought that this model would be easy to communicate because an average 12-1/4 percent annual compounded rate of sales growth would double sales every six years. In communicating this, I said that everything about the business would have to double every six years – sales, buildings, machinery and equipment, accounts receivable, inventory – in short, all the assets on the asset side of the balance sheet. Likewise, all liabilities, both current and fixed, would have to grow at the rate of doubling every six years, and, in order to balance the balance sheet, the net worth would also have to double every six years. This growth formula would provide plowed-back earnings sufficient to do that. Using the formula, the balance sheet would continue to be as strong as it was in the beginning period. All the critical ratios dealing with the balance sheet would remain the same, such as the ratio of current assets to current liabilities and the ratio of liabilities to net worth.

When I presented the formula to the Operating Committee, they thought it was a very difficult growth objective, but they agreed that it was worth trying. They were unanimous, however, in feeling very strongly that we should keep the objective and the growth formula quietly to ourselves, because they thought it would be very embarrassing if we let the entire organization know about it and then failed to meet it. On the other hand, I took the position with the Operating Committee members that we *should* let the entire organization know about the new goal, because it would help everyone in management, including foremen, to do their jobs more effectively if they knew what our growth objective was. I argued that the engineers could do a better job of planning for the growth of buildings and machinery and equipment if they knew that in only six years we were going to need twice as many buildings, twice as much floor space, and twice as much machinery and equipment as we currently had. I further argued that the Research and Development Department could plan their new product development efforts better if they knew they were responsible for providing enough new products to double our sales in six years. I also argued that Human Resources could do their manpower planning better if they knew we would need approximately twice as many employees within six years. Finally, I said that I thought the Board, if they agreed with our growth objective, would see what folly it would be to erect a building on our present parking lot because, in a matter of only three or four years, we would have outgrown the space even if we had built on the entire parking lot area. Within a few years, we would inevitably run out of space, even if we built on the city lots that we had bought across the street. To make things worse, only a few years out, it would be almost impossible to buy enough city lots and houses to meet our requirements, to say nothing of the horrendous cost of tearing down existing houses to provide space.

After my discussion with the Operating Committee, we showed the growth formula to the Board of Directors. With this information in front of them, the Board agreed with my cancellation of the building on the parking lot at the corner of Bowman and Palmer Streets. They also agreed with our proposal to find another site within 15 miles of Wooster on which we could start construction of a new building complex. Somehow, I had prevailed and we publicized the growth formula to the entire management organization, including foremen and department managers. As soon as possible, we also let the financial community know what our growth objective was. I argued that the fear of embarrassment at not meeting an announced goal would actually spur us on and make it more likely that we would succeed in achieving our objective.

During the 1970s, the country was going through a period of excessive inflation, with inflation rates reaching double-digit numbers. We felt that the 12-1/4 percent growth rate for sales under those circumstances was no longer sufficient because hyperinflation was providing a major portion of our sales growth. Therefore, in 1977, we changed our sales growth rate objective from 12-1/4 percent per year compounded to a 15 percent compounded annual growth rate. We then revised the entire growth formula to fit the new rate of growth in sales. The 15 percent growth rate was one that would double sales and all of the other critical business factors involved every five years instead of every six years. Because the formula I originated back in 1959 has been used so consistently all of these years, it has come to be known at Rubbermaid as the "Noble Formula."

Operating with this kind of consistent growth philosophy benefits all of the people who have a stake in a company's ongoing success – the shareholders, customers, employees, suppliers, governments and residents in host communities, and ultimately consumers in general. At Rubbermaid, our thinking quickly became imbued with the growth philosophy as our annual financial results validated the effectiveness of the formula year-after-year. So much so, that I began to believe that every business should have as one of its prime objectives the desire to grow at a rate that could be financed by plowed-back earnings.

Given my deep commitment to growth, it came as quite a shock to me when a businessman told me at a dinner I attended years ago while I was Chief Executive Officer that he and his partner had been working for more than 30 years to keep their business at a size not larger than 150 employees. He went on to say proudly that as long as their business did not grow larger than that arbitrary level, either he or his partner could manage the business alone. That approach allowed each of them to take a vacation of four to eight weeks in duration every year. Apparently, both the businessman and his partner valued their time off more than the long-term success of their enterprise because their operating philosophy, which I would describe as purposeful stagnation, almost guaranteed that they would be leapfrogged by more aggressive competitors.

I want to cite some of the major benefits that Rubbermaid has derived from our growth philosophy over the years and which the Company is still realizing today.

- The first benefit is the positive effect of growth on a company's work force. It is my opinion that a consistently growing company attracts better management people than one which is not growing. Capable, energetic young managers want to join a company where they see many opportunities for advancement being created by the expansion resulting from strong, dynamic growth. It is easier to recruit such effective managers when they know their performance will be highly valued and that they will not have to wait until someone retires or dies to get a promotion.

- A second benefit is that a dynamic, growing company tends to retain superior management personnel better than one that is not growing. This involves a kind of reinforcing process – a growing company is able to hire capable managers who generate the additional growth that makes them want to stay on themselves and also periodically attracts a new batch of effective management people, who in their turn generate more growth. Conversely, a company suffering from stagnation is not likely to get its fair share of the best and brightest managers, and the few good managers a stagnant company is able to hire tend to leave quickly for other opportunities. So a growing company enjoys an upward spiral while a stagnant company suffers from a downward spiral – and these positive and negative spirals both tend to accelerate over time.

- A third benefit is that a growing company has a better opportunity to keep up to date with rapidly developing new technologies and to acquire the most modern and efficient plant and equipment. As new machinery and equipment are added to accommodate the increased market demand generated by a growth philosophy, management has a strong incentive to identify, evaluate, and invest in the most efficient equipment available. In this kind of growth environment, senior management is much more likely to be aware of old equipment becoming obsolete. This encourages management to analyze whether it would be advantageous for the business to junk the old equipment in a timely fashion and replace it with new, state-of-the-art equipment that will provide a competitive advantage.

- A fourth benefit for a company with a growth philosophy is the opportunity it presents for management to study and evaluate a wide range of new products and new market opportunities, and then select those opportunities that will generate the greatest return on investment. A company which is not growing is more apt to continue making its existing product lines and selling them into its traditional markets. That makes a stagnant company more vulnerable to growth-oriented competitors, because it lacks the capacity to develop new products with higher rates of return and to enter new markets where it might enjoy a competitive advantage.

- A fifth benefit for a growth company is an opportunity to diversify. Highly selective diversification provides growth companies with the kind of stability that a non-growth company is unlikely to achieve. A company that puts all of its eggs in one basket is much more vulnerable to economic fluctuations and competitive pressures than a company which continually expands its product and marketing scope. Rubbermaid's growth philosophy permitted us to diversify in many different directions over the years, broadening our opportunities to generate even more growth. For example, Rubbermaid was solely in the housewares business until 1947. Over the next two decades, the financial strength resulting from our consistent growth enabled us to diversify into automotive accessories as well as commercial and industrial products. We also diversified by going into business in Canada, Germany, and Holland, providing the international experience base for the Company's current global expansion program.

The growth formula has served as a guide for Rubbermaid management ever since it was established in 1959, and it has worked to provide the necessary plowed-back earnings to finance our objective growth rate.

Each year when I addressed shareholders at the Rubbermaid Annual Meeting, I reported on performance during the preceding year against our growth objective of doubling the business every six years. Graphs were prepared to show how the business had grown in comparison with the average 12-1/4 percent annual increase which the formula required to meet that objective. Although sales for any given year might not increase by 12-1/4 percent, sales in preceding years typically would have exceeded that objective to such an extent that, on average, we would still be meeting our growth target over a six-year period. And during most of the time in which I was Chief Executive Officer, earnings grew at a rate in excess of doubling every six years. That enabled us to meet our commitment to pay out one-third of earnings in dividends and plow back two-thirds of earnings into the business, averaging the 12-1/4 percent necessary to double our net worth every six years.

I viewed the increase in shareholders' equity as being fundamental to Rubbermaid's growth because everything else involved in the business is built on this foundation. To achieve our target of doubling the business every six years, all facets of the business – accounts receivable, inventories, machinery and equipment, and buildings – had to grow at the same rate. It was necessary for net worth to increase in order to finance the growth of all of these.

Two of the most significant graphs in the series were the graph showing net sales and the graph showing earnings per share, which are shown on the facing page.

The vertical scale on these graphs is logarithmic so that a constant rate of annual percentage increase is shown as a straight line; therefore, the objective increase of 12-1/4 percent per year compounded is shown as a straight line. These graphs show that both sales and earnings per share increased at a compounded rate in excess of the objective of 12-1/4 percent per year meaning that they more than doubled every six years.

At each Annual Stockholder Meeting, I showed a series of other graphs to illustrate the progress of the Company in a very effective visual way. Some of the graphs used at the 1980 Annual Stockholder Meeting included the following:

- A graph showing the value each year of 1,000 shares of Rubbermaid stock for the past 18 years. It showed that in the first six years, the value of the stock had more than doubled; over the 12-year period it had more than quadrupled; and at the end of the 18-year period, the value of the stock was worth

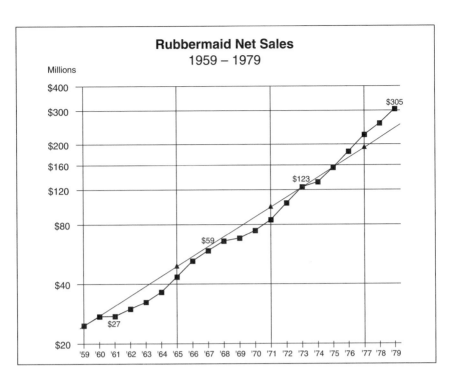

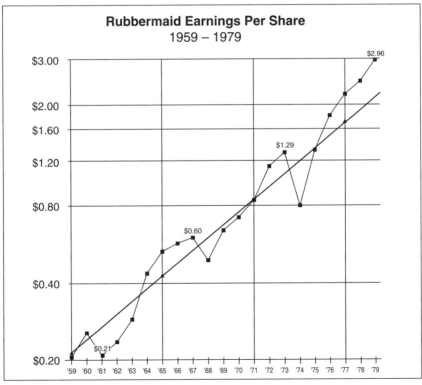

eight times as much as it had been at the beginning, a rate of increase of more than doubling every six years.

- A second graph showing an increase in dividends per share from $.06 per share paid in 1961 to $.84 per share in 1979. This far exceeded doubling every six years.
- A third graph showing Rubbermaid's earnings as a percent of net worth to be usually 30 to 50 percent higher than the average return on net worth for all U.S. manufacturers.
- A fourth graph showing Rubbermaid's long-term debt for the last nine years had been less than 20 percent of share-holders' equity, whereas the average percentage of long-term debt to equity for all U.S. manufacturers was more than 30 percent.

As those graphs demonstrated, the growth formula which was adopted in 1959 served Rubbermaid extremely well over the years, and it is still working very effectively. Today, consistent growth is continuing to fuel the Company's development of innovative new products, improvements in existing product lines, and the exploration of completely new markets.

Chapter Nineteen • ROAE as a Measure of Performance

In 1950, I sent away for a book written by a man named Oliver which described the benefits of using the concept of Return On Assets Employed (ROAE) for analyzing business results. I liked what I read so much that I decided we should use ROAE as a management tool at Rubbermaid. Prior to 1950, we had measured our profit on the basis of "return on sales," as most American businesses did then and many still do. We used return on sales to measure our success in several different aspects of the business. For example, we measured the profitability of each class of trade such as department stores, wholesalers, and private label customers. Beginning in 1950, we began measuring the profit of these various categories based on ROAE.

The following formula is used for calculating ROAE:

Rubbermaid's Return on Assets Employed Formula

Return on Sales	X	Asset Turns	=	ROAE

$\dfrac{\text{Net Earnings}}{\text{Net Sales}}$	X	$\dfrac{\text{Net Sales}}{\text{Assets Employed}}$	=	ROAE

Example:

$\dfrac{1,200}{20,000}$	X	$\dfrac{20,000}{10,000}$	=	ROAE

6% Return on Sales	X	2 Turns	=	12% ROAE

Note: Sales can be canceled out:

$\dfrac{\text{Net Earnings}}{\text{Net Sales}}$	X	$\dfrac{\text{Net Sales}}{\text{Assets Employed}}$	=	ROAE

To abbreviate this:

$\dfrac{\text{Net Earnings}}{\text{Assets Employed}}$	=	ROAE

Example:

$\dfrac{1,200}{10,000}$	=	12% ROAE

At that time, we were making a private label product line for Sears. Based on a return on sales analysis, we showed a 10 percent return on sales of this Sears line while the average return on sales of our regular Rubbermaid line was only seven percent. So we thought that making the private label line for Sears was a very profitable operation and we were working hard to increase this kind of business. But when we calculated the profit on our Sears business based on ROAE, we found that the return on assets for the Sears line was only five percent compared with a 10 percent return on assets for our own Rubbermaid line. This was because the asset turns on the Sears business were only 1/2 times, whereas the asset turns on the Rubbermaid business were 1-1/2 times. The 1-1/2 times asset turns meant that annual sales were 1-1/2 times as much as the assets employed to manufacture Rubbermaid items, but the Sears annual sales were only 1/2 as much as the assets being used to make their private label line. The reason was that we had to make a separate mold for the relatively small volume on each Sears product, whereas we needed only one mold for the higher volume of each Rubbermaid product. We also needed to carry an inventory of products, cartons, and boxes for Sears, much larger in proportion to their annual sales volume than we needed to support the much higher Rubbermaid annual sales volume.

So we found that the Sears business based on return on assets was actually unsatisfactory, whereas an analysis based on the return on sales had made it appear very attractive. This led us to re-negotiate with Sears for a higher price on their private label line. Eventually, we convinced Sears to drop their private label products and begin carrying the regular Rubbermaid line.

Our experience with using the measurement of Return On Assets Employed to determine the profitability of the Sears business resulted in our adopting, as a policy, that we would no longer solicit or engage in the manufacture of a private label line for any customer. We went on to develop the use of the ROAE analysis as a management tool to calculate the true profitability for each of our products, for each department in our manufacturing operations, for each class of trade in which we participated, and even for our business with each of our large customers.

Each product that we manufactured was analyzed on an ROAE basis at the end of each year. If a product's ROAE fell below what had been established as an acceptable minimum goal, it was designated to be dropped from the line. If marketing, manufacturing, or research and development (R&D) wanted to work on improving a product's ROAE, the product would be put on probation for six months. Marketing, manufacturing, and R&D would then work together to achieve the necessary improvement. If they succeeded, the item stayed in the line; if they did not, the item was dropped.

For each new product being developed, an ROAE was calculated based on estimated sales volume, costs, and an expected selling price. Unless a new product's ROAE met the minimum threshold ROAE established for new products, it would not be approved for market launch. Since its inception in 1950, ROAE analysis has served the Company well over the years and is still used today.

In 1950, Caldwell set up the Company's first management incentive plan. This simple plan calculated a management bonus using a formula based on five percent of the pre-tax profit above a certain threshold. The amount accumulated under this formula was distributed to executives based on their salaries with a higher percentage for executives at higher levels than those at lower levels. The threshold amount that had to be earned before the executives received any bonus at all was an amount that would give the shareholders a respectable return on their investment.

In 1968, we revised the Short-Range Incentive Plan based on one year's ROAE. We set up a threshold of ROAE below which no incentive would be paid. Just above the threshold, a small percent of profit would go into the incentive plan. The greater the ROAE for the year, the higher the percent of profit going into the incentive plan. The amount in the incentive plan was then distributed to the executives in proportion to their salaries – partly based on the ROAE of their operations and partly based on a subjective appraisal of how each executive had performed in accomplishing goals set up and agreed to at the beginning of the year.

In 1975, we set up a Long-Range Incentive Plan on a five-year basis as a restricted stock incentive plan. Under this plan, each executive was granted a certain number of shares of Rubbermaid stock based on grade level and base salary. This stock was held in trust by the Company for five years during which time the executive collected dividends and voted the shares.

An average threshold ROAE objective was set up for the five years. If the threshold ROAE had not been achieved at the end of the five-year period, all of the stock was forfeited back to the Company. A scale was set up so that the greater the average ROAE attained for the five years, the greater the number of shares the executive would keep and the fewer would be forfeited until at a high level of ROAE, none of the stock would be forfeited. The threshold was set at the average ROAE achieved by the Fortune 500 companies so that unless the Company exceeded the average ROAE of the Fortune 500, the executives received nothing.

Each year a new five-year Restricted Stock Incentive Plan was started. Because Rubbermaid did so well, there was always a pay-off on the plan. I am inclined, however, to believe the reverse was true – it was because we had such an effective incentive plan that Rubbermaid did very well.

CHAPTER TWENTY • PLANNING FOR SUCCESS

One great benefit of our ROAE analysis was its application to the business planning process, which I always liked to think of as being in the form of a continuous circle. The arcs making up that planning circle consisted of the economic outlook together with the Sales, Research and Development, Advertising and Sales Promotion, Manufacturing, Finance, and Administrative Departments of the business. The final arc in the circle consisted of senior management's strategic objectives.

The problem is that in most companies, the planning process is limited to going around the planning circle only once. Based on an analysis of the economic outlook, the Sales Department estimates how much the market for its products will grow and sets sales objectives for each product line. Then the other areas of the business are expected to develop plans that support achievement of those objectives. But in too many cases, the only planning passed on to the other functions are the Sales Department's financial figures – the sales dollar objectives – rather than the underlying planning assumptions that are represented in those figures.

In order to have effective business planning, I believe it is necessary to go around the circle at least twice – regardless of where you start on the circle. It is essential for each function to see the input of all the other departments before they can finalize their own planning in a meaningful way and establish realistic objectives that are based on the capabilities of the entire business.

Every spring, each of our Rubbermaid operating units prepared a rolling five-year strategic business plan covering the current year plus four additional years. The fifth year was the operating unit's first look at that year while the current year was an updating of unit plans prepared the previous fall. The plan for the year immediately following the current year was done in considerable detail and represented the first go around the circle in an intensive fashion for the business plan the operating unit would use in the year ahead. This five-year plan was far more than just a projection of past trends. It was prepared by each department in the operating unit and set out not only what the objectives were but how the various departments proposed to accomplish them:

- The operating unit's Sales Department identified product categories and estimated sales volumes for each of those categories and each class of trade for the upcoming year. The Sales Department also identified new products that it already had been promised by the Research and Development Department and estimated the sales volumes from each of those products over the year. For the subsequent four years, the Sales Department estimated the volumes anticipated from products which were not yet completely developed and identified the markets in which it expected to sell them. The Sales Department also was responsible for providing cost estimates on the advertising and sales promotion programs it would do each year for the entire five-year cycle.

- The operating unit's Manufacturing Department then had to estimate the new equipment expenditures which would be necessary to produce the Sales Department's estimated volumes and the amount of new building needed to house that equipment and increased inventory.

- Each Department in the operating unit, including the Staff, had to estimate the number of hourly and salaried employees it expected to have at the end of each planning year.

We considered this five-year planning cycle to be extremely important from many different aspects. It provided excellent communications among the various Departments of the operating units. These improved communications enabled each department to know what the others were planning for the next five years, so they could all be pulling together in the same direction. At the same time, the five-year plan gave the general manager of each operating unit the information he needed to provide the leadership that would help his employees achieve the objectives established for his part of Rubbermaid's business. And it enabled corporate management to coordinate the long-range direction of the entire Company because it identified new products and new markets as well as the capital investments in plant and equipment that would be needed to support the overall corporate sales and marketing effort.

Because each five-year plan was prepared on the basis of Return On Assets Employed, proposals that did not measure up to Rubbermaid's ROAE criteria were simply not included in the business plan, which saved a lot of time and avoided a lot of trouble downstream. The ROAE estimates were also used to evaluate which of the operating units presented the best opportunities for additional investments at a point when changes could still be made with a minimum of cost and before people became committed to their "pet projects." Consolidation of all the five-year plans permitted the Corporate Controller to see what long-term financing was necessary. When more projects were submitted than the Company could finance realistically, those projects which were least likely to succeed or those with the lowest ROAE were pruned.

In the fall, each of Rubbermaid's operating units again looked at the coming year, this time in greater detail. This involved going around the planning circle completely at least two more times. The first cycle started with a letter from me setting forth strategic management objectives and the economic outlook as we saw it at the time. I spelled out our ROAE objectives and specified what our short-term tactical objectives were compared with our long-term strategic goals. There was a distinct advantage in having all the operating units prepare their plans based on the same set of assumptions about the economic outlook. It certainly made it easier for us to compare the potential pluses and minuses of all their plans.

When I was Chief Executive Officer, we did our long-range planning as though there would never be a recession. Of course, we would pull in our horns when the evidence of an economic downturn was unmistakable, but countless opportunities have been lost by companies that "played it safe" and were too timid to see beyond a possible downturn to the recovery that was sure to follow. A Director, who was an economist, provided valuable support for this approach (see Chapter 17).

Our fine tuning of plans for the coming year began with the Research and Development Department which reported on the products that it expected to have ready for market launch and on the long-term projects it would be developing over the period. Then the Sales, Manufacturing, and Administrative Departments addressed the overall plan from their perspective. Each of these Departments prepared a base projection describing what the business would be like if no new action were taken – that is, if the business continued exactly as it had during the current year.

The Departments then identified any major improvement opportunities – new products, new markets, new sales promotions, or new equipment – which they saw as having the potential to expand sales volumes or increase profits. These improvement opportunities were outlined in detail, describing what was to be accomplished, how much it would cost in terms of capital investment, how much it would cost in terms of expense, what the benefits would be in the year being planned, and an estimate of what the benefits would be on a long-term basis.

We would then discuss each improvement opportunity with the general manager of the operating unit involved and, if approved, it would become part of the preliminary planning package that was put together by each operating unit. This preliminary package was summarized in the form of a profit and loss statement, a balance sheet, a capital expenditures estimate, and a cash flow statement for each of the five planning years. The package also included manpower planning and a calculation of the Return On Assets Employed for all the proposed products.

Corporate management then reviewed each operating unit's preliminary planning package, with particular attention to proposed improvement opportunities, since at that point they still could be approved or rejected. The approved package was sent back to the operating unit where each improvement opportunity was turned into an action plan. These action plans were prepared to reach as far down into the organization as possible – ideally to the level of the employees who were responsible for accomplishing specific planned actions. That meant the action plans had to include detailed descriptions of exactly what was to be accomplished, who was responsible for implementing each plan facet, and when the plan was to be completed. The action plan was the basis for creation of a final goal-setting package which was communicated to the employees responsible for implementing the action plan – that way everyone knew what they were expected to accomplish and how.

Our planning process never lost sight of the responsibility of corporate officers to run the business to create value for our share-holders, but it also provided a great deal of autonomy to the oper-ating units. Each of our operating units was a totally integrated business and it was the responsibility of the unit's general manager to run the whole thing. The general manager was free to run his business within the marketing franchise assigned to him and in accordance with the principles and policies of Rubbermaid Incorporated. Only a small number of functions were reserved for corporate management, those that made sense for the entire Company to do. This reflected my philosophy on delegating responsibility and authority (see Chapter 16).

For example, an operating unit general manager was required to buy his insurance coverage through the corporation. That made sense because we could negotiate better rates than the operating unit could on its own. He was also required to follow our guide-lines on accounting and to use the corporate computers with compatible language. Barring things of that kind, each general manager was really in control of his own business, but always in accordance with the *Statement of Rubbermaid Philosophy and Fundamental Principles*. We allowed our operating units to exer-cise a high level of local autonomy to preserve the entrepreneurial spirit that we knew was vital to fostering innovation and growth – a spirit that withers when a general manager is constantly constrained by too much top-down direction. We also believed that spirit was affected by the size of an operating unit.

Whenever possible, we tried to keep any single profit center no larger than 500 employees. We spun off four U.S. operating units to keep our operations at a manageable size. This reflected our conviction that an individual can manage only what he can get his arms around. He needs to know his people, and they need to know him and be close enough to him to look to him for leadership. The key is having a work force big enough to get the job done without becoming so big that you lose that kind of relationship.

One great benefit of our emphasis upon planning was the stabil-ity it gave not only to the individual operating units but also to the

Company as a whole. Our reliance on long-term planning meant that we could build into each unit's plan concepts such as continuous cost control. Les Gigax, both as Vice President, Manufacturing and later as President of the Company, said over and over again, "Don, let's not have crash cost-cutting programs. Let's control costs every day. Let's have cost-cutting efforts every day." This I thought was good counsel and I think we did a good job of implementing it. So many businesses let costs get out of control and then institute a major cost-cutting program where people are laid off and non-essential costs are eliminated, all of which is painful and disruptive to people's lives. Les thought, and I wholeheartedly agreed, that it is much better for the business and for the people employed in the business to be vigilant on controlling costs on a daily basis. As a result, we built cost-cutting into each operating unit's long-term and short-term plans and, therefore, we did not have major crash cost-cutting programs.

During the 21 years I was Chief Executive Officer, we never laid off any salaried employees. We fired some salaried employees who were not performing adequately in their job for one reason or another, but there were no layoffs. Over that same period, we had only one layoff of hourly workers. That was in 1974 when business fell off because of raw material price increases and we had to lay off 242 people temporarily.

CHAPTER TWENTY-ONE • PHILOSOPHY AND PRINCIPLES

When I became Chief Executive Officer, I inherited from Jim Caldwell an unwritten, but very well-developed philosophy, and set of principles for operating the business. Because I thought that they were important concepts that should be communicated very broadly, I had the philosophy and principles published as a printed statement which was distributed to all our employees, suppliers, and customers. Over the years, the printed statement has been updated a number of times, but the same basic concepts are in each update, including the latest version which is prominently displayed today in our headquarters lobby in Wooster. The original printed statement has been duplicated in Appendix 2.

I think one of the important sections in the *Statement of Rubbermaid Philosophy and Fundamental Principles* is the one that says, "For our employees we will strive to recognize the intrinsic value of each employee as an individual. We will strive to recognize the value and potential of self-motivation of people who thoroughly understand their jobs, not only what they are supposed to do, but the reason why, so that individual initiative and thought will be encouraged in the accomplishment of their tasks." It is that emphasis on respecting the value and dignity of our employees and encouraging them to take initiative which has fostered the innovation that has contributed so mightily to Rubbermaid's success and growth over the years.

In the letter to our shareholders in the 1962 Annual Report, I wrote, "The loyalty and dedication of this Company's employees to doing their individual jobs to the very best of their ability is a continuing inspiration. I recently asked all Rubbermaid employees to dedicate themselves to the 'Pursuit of Excellence' in every phase of their work in 1963. Their overwhelming response is assurance to our shareholders that Rubbermaid's reputation for integrity, leadership and highest quality products will be maintained and enhanced in the years ahead." It is interesting to me that the employee pursuit of excellence I described in that statement parallels the same ideas found many years later in the highly successful companies profiled in the book *In Search of Excellence* written by Thomas J. Peters and Robert H. Waterman, Jr.

Another vital operating principle set out in our *Statement of Rubbermaid Philosophy and Fundamental Principles* is the establishment and maintenance of long-term alliances with suppliers. While I was Chief Executive Officer, I characterized these long-term supplier relationships as being, in effect, partnerships in which both partners benefited from cooperating with one another in everything from cost control to new product development. We frequently re-affirmed our policy of not changing suppliers to achieve only a fraction of a cent reduction in the per-pound price of raw materials. This was because we believed that a long-term relationship was ultimately more beneficial than the short-term price reduction advantage we might gain from changing suppliers. By staying with a supplier company over a period of years, we knew that they would learn our requirements and would be planning ahead and thinking about ways in which they could better serve Rubbermaid's needs.

Another advantage of cultivating long-term supplier relationships was that when materials were in short supply, Rubbermaid would be placed at the top of their list to supply our requirements. Our long-term alliance approach also encouraged our suppliers to use their technological capabilities for developing materials and processes that would help us make the innovative new products that were the key to Rubbermaid's continued growth and profitability. A few of the supplier companies with which we developed this type of long-term alliance are:

- Corrugated Container Corporation of America
- Dow Chemical Company
- E. I. du Pont de Nemours and Company
- Goodyear Tire & Rubber Company
- International Paper Company, and
- Union Carbide Corporation

These, of course, are suppliers of manufacturing materials but we also developed similar alliances with the suppliers of various services—relationships which have lasted for many years. The ones that come most readily to mind are:

- Peat, Marwick, Mitchell, which became our auditing firm back in 1926 when Horatio Ebert and Errett Grable bought out the original stockholders. Peat, Marwick, Mitchell have continued to be our auditors from that time up to the present day, a period of 70 years.
- Critchfield, Critchfield, Critchfield & Johnston, a Wooster law firm in which Robert Critchfield was a partner. Bob became counsel to Rubbermaid when Caldwell joined the Company in

1934. With the able help of John Johnston and Lincoln Oviatt, who also were principals in the firm, Bob actively represented Rubbermaid until his death in 1981. He also served as a member of Rubbermaid's Board of Directors from 1959 to 1981. The firm is still used extensively by the Company.

- Ketchum MacLeod & Grove, which became our advertising and public relations agency immediately after World War II and continued to serve us until 1984, a period of almost 40 years. This kind of long-term relationship with an advertising agency is almost unheard of in business today when businesses change their advertising agencies all too frequently.

- McDaniel Fisher and Spellman Company, an advertising firm in Akron, which was represented by Robert W. Loos. Bob handled our advertising for the automotive division from the first advertising we ever did on the car mats in 1948 to when we went out of the business in 1977, a period of 29 years.

- Wayne County National Bank, which has been Rubbermaid's bank from the time the Company was founded in 1920 to the present day, a period of 76 years.

- National City Bank of Cleveland, my previous employer, to which we went in 1947 when we first needed banking services that could not be handled by the Wayne County National Bank. Our relationship has continued for a period of 49 years.

- Equitable Life Assurance Company of New York, with which we have done all our long-term borrowing starting in 1947 and continuing until recently.

- Wooster Office Equipment, a home town operation that has served Rubbermaid's needs with great efficiency and dedication since 1945.

In our *Statement of Rubbermaid Philosophy and Fundamental Principles*, we also said that "for our communities, we will strive to promote the general community welfare" by encouraging officers and employees to participate in community affairs. This we did. Almost every civic and charitable organization in communities where we had facilities had at least one and sometimes several

Rubbermaid representatives on their Board of Directors or Board of Trustees. I had another motive for encouraging young executives to participate in community activities. I told them that when they took positions of responsibility in civic and charitable organizations it would be necessary for them to get people to do things on a voluntary basis. By doing this, they would learn the best way to supervise and direct their own employees. I told them that in such organizations they would not have the kind of authority they did at the Company. As a result, they would have to persuade other volunteers to get something done by convincing them that it was the right thing to do. Similarly, in business it is always best to convince employees that what you are asking them to do is indeed the right thing. When you persuade employees to take action because they want to, it is infinitely better than forcing them to act simply because you have the authority to dictate that they must. In my opinion, that is misuse of authority in any setting.

Along the same lines, I always encouraged executives to tell their employees *why* they were doing something rather than just commanding them to do it. By making sure that employees knew why they were doing something, both the executive and the employees could be sure that what they were planning to do was worthwhile. I told our executives that if the only reason they were doing something was because it had always been done that way, they should find out *why* it needed to be done, and that would help determine whether it was still necessary to do it at all.

In the *Statement of Rubbermaid Philosophy and Fundamental Principles*, the text goes on to say that "For our communities we will strive to be a good neighbor by being mindful of the Company's ecological responsibilities." There are several examples of this good neighbor policy in action.

Shortly after World War II, on a Monday morning, I received a telephone call from a woman who lived not too far from the plant. She said that soot from the Company's smoke stack was soiling her clean wash that she had just hung out to dry on the clothes line in her back yard. Later, I went over this call with Jim Caldwell. He asked me to look into what it would cost to change from coal to gas-fired boilers. When we looked at the numbers, we found it would involve a considerable cost to make the change; nevertheless, he decided to do it in order to avoid soiling the laundry of families living near our facilities—taking action that was necessary to be a good neighbor.

Another example occurred shortly after we moved to our new factory site on State Route 585. We were using water to chill the molds in the Plastics Department and then disposing of the water directly into a nearby creek, which slightly raised the temperature of the creek water. There was some thought that this elevated water temperature might affect the fish and other marine life downstream, so we spent the money to install a closed system and a chiller. That way we could chill the water and recirculate it without discharging warm water into the creek. Again the cost was worth it to assure that the Company would continue to be a good corporate citizen.

The first set of principles in the printed *Statement of Rubbermaid Philosophy and Fundamental Principles* includes these words: "For our customers, we will strive to price our goods to provide a reasonable profit to wholesalers, retailers, and others selling our products." That reflected Caldwell's desire for all of Rubbermaid's customers – both wholesalers and retailers – to make a profit. He was convinced that a reasonable profit level would provide wholesalers with an incentive to maintain an adequate inventory of Rubbermaid products and motivate retailers to allot adequate shelf space for displaying them. To assure that both wholesalers and retailers made an adequate profit, he set a minimum retail price for each product and then sold it to wholesalers at a discount of 50 percent off the retail price and sold it to large retailers at 40 percent off the retail price. This gave them a pre-determined profit margin.

This method of pricing was protected by statutes in 45 states which were collectively called the "Fair Trade Laws." These laws permitted manufacturers to specify a minimum retail price for their products and said that if a manufacturer chose to set such a price, retailers were obligated to charge no less than that price for the manufacturer's product. As an example, when Rubbermaid set a price of $1.00 for a product, it would be sold to wholesalers for 50 cents and to department stores, such as the May Company or Macy's, for 60 cents. The wholesalers could then re-sell the item to hardware stores at 60 cents or maybe a little more than that to cover the added cost of selling in smaller quantities. But the retailers, including hardware stores and big department stores, would be obligated to sell the product to consumers at no less than $1.00. They could not try to get a competitive advantage by selling it at 95 cents or 90 cents to attract customers.

The theory of the Fair Trade Laws was that a trade name such as Rubbermaid belonged to the manufacturer which had spent large sums of money on advertising and sales promotion to build goodwill for the name. It was, therefore, considered improper for retailers to use that trade name to attract customers into their stores by putting a lower price on the manufacturer's products. The Company's practical concern, of course, was that if retail stores sold Rubbermaid products at a price lower than our minimum, they would make a lower profit margin and that would discourage them from carrying an adequate inventory or from giving us adequate shelf space – maybe both!

Although a retail store might benefit by attracting customers with a lower advertised price for our products, Rubbermaid would lose out over the long term because the store might not stock enough of our products. Or the store might put our products way in the back in a location where customers might not ever get to them. Such a retailer would be misusing the Rubbermaid name to attract customers and would hurt the Company in the process because we would sell fewer products. We believed that the retailer also would lose out ultimately because he would not be able to meet the strong demand for our products. It was a lose-lose situation.

Because we believed so strongly in the importance of maintaining the retail price to enable retailers to make a profit, we reluctantly sued those of our customers who violated the Fair Trade Laws by discounting the prices of Rubbermaid products. While I was still Chief Financial Officer of the Company, I made many trips to call on customers who were discounting to try to convince them of the merits of maintaining prices before we initiated a law suit. In some cases, I was successful and in some cases I was unsuccessful.

In 1968, after I had become Chief Executive Officer, I called Harry Cunningham, the Chairman of the Board and Chief Executive Officer of Kmart in Michigan, and set up an appointment to see him because his company refused to carry Rubbermaid products at all. We had been told that the big discount chain had a policy of not carrying any products that were price-maintained in accordance with the Fair Trade Laws. I drove from Wooster to Detroit to see Cunningham and spent 45 minutes trying to convince him that it would be a good idea for Kmart to carry Rubbermaid products at fixed retail prices because they would be assured of a consistent profit. He told me kindly but in no uncertain terms that he himself had set the policy of not carrying any price-maintained products and that he was not about to make an exception for Rubbermaid!

Other discount stores either followed Kmart's practice of not carrying price-maintained goods, or they carried the goods but periodically violated the law by discounting them. Since discount stores were a growing factor in the retail market and department stores were not, we were faced with the dilemma of not having our products displayed at many growing retail outlets where we felt we should be represented. This caused us to reconsider whether we should continue to insist on our retail customers maintaining our minimum prices. Rubbermaid had defended the practice of maintaining retail prices for many years and we were convinced that it was the right way to go. As a result, it was very hard for some of us to re-adjust our thinking to accept the idea of dropping our efforts to protect customer profits through the Fair Trade practices which typically had been followed by many U.S.

manufacturers. On the other hand, some of our management, particularly in sales and marketing, argued strongly that market trends dictated abandoning the Fair Trade Laws and letting all our customers sell at whatever prices they wanted to set. Finally, we made the decision to abandon the Fair Trade pricing policy; it was a very traumatic time and a very traumatic decision, but it turned out to be the right one. Because the discount houses were growing so fast, going to the more flexible pricing policy was very beneficial for Rubbermaid. Our business with discount houses grew rapidly while department stores became a less and less important factor in our sales.

In 1975, shortly after we decided to abandon Fair Trade pricing, Congress repealed all Fair Trade Laws across the United States. We had read the trend and took action on it, which has always been the basis of our success in developing new products and new business opportunities.

CHAPTER TWENTY-TWO • SHOW TIME

Displaying our products at the Housewares Shows has always been an important part of Rubbermaid's sales and marketing effort. In the early years, the Housewares Shows were put on by a profit-making organization under the leadership of Flo English. These shows were held at different times of the year and rotated around from city to city, including Atlantic City, Chicago, New York, and Philadelphia.

In 1948, the National Housewares Manufacturers Association (NHMA) was formed by the housewares manufacturing companies with the primary purpose of putting on their own shows. They agreed to have the summer Housewares Show start on the first Monday following the Fourth of July and run through the following Friday. The summer show was held at the Atlantic City Convention Center in Atlantic City, New Jersey. All the hotels up and down the Boardwalk were used by companies participating in the show. Rubbermaid's executives, employees, salesmen, and many of our manufacturers' representatives stayed at the Dennis Hotel. The five days of the show were usually the hottest week of the summer. In the early years, we took a Pennsylvania Railroad train from Wooster to Philadelphia where we got a shuttle bus to Atlantic City. Later, we flew into the Philadelphia airport and took a shuttle bus to Atlantic City. We used buses because it saved money. A Rubbermaid sales meeting was always held on the Sunday afternoon prior to the regularly scheduled Monday opening of each Housewares Show. The Show gave the Company's manufacturers' representatives a chance to become familiar with our new products and our new marketing and merchandising programs.

The NHMA settled on Chicago as the site for the winter show, which was always held starting the first Monday after New Year's Day and going through the following Friday. Of course, this usually turned out to be the coldest week of the winter. For many years, the Chicago show was held at the Navy Pier, a cold, drafty building. Rubbermaid's booth always seemed to be right next to an outside door that kept opening and closing, which caused a draft of frigid air to go whistling through our booth. By Tuesday or Wednesday, Caldwell often came down with a severe cold or flu and spent the last two or three days of the show ill in his hotel room. When the City of Chicago built McCormick Place, the Housewares Show was moved from the Navy Pier into the new facility which was more satisfactory. It certainly was warmer in the wintertime!

For many years, Caldwell was a member of the Board of Directors of the NHMA and worked his way up the ladder of executive positions of Treasurer, Vice President, and President, holding each of them for one year. Later, I became a member of the Board of Directors of the Association and ascended the same ladder of executive positions. In 1955, the NHMA decided to discontinue holding the summer show in Atlantic City. Both the summer and winter shows were then held at McCormick Place in Chicago.

The Shows underscored the fact that Rubbermaid had a lot of competition, even when we made only housewares. In the early Housewares Show directories, there were always 30 to 35 companies listed in the rubber housewares category. The Show directories for later years have a similar number of entries in the plastic housewares category.

The Housewares Shows were extremely important because they gave us a chance to talk directly with the buyers from the wholesale hardware companies and the department stores. It was also important for Rubbermaid executives to meet the top executives from those same companies and stores who would accompany their buyers to see what the housewares business was all about.

After I became Chief Executive Officer, I found the shows to be extremely important for me personally because it was usually there that I would first hear from our customers about their complaints – complaints about our products, service, programs, or people. In 1959, the year I became Chief Executive Officer, I was deluged with complaints at the Housewares Shows because our product quality and customer service had slipped badly. Also, changes in some of our policies had made our customers very unhappy. I took these complaints very seriously and met with our executives in meeting after meeting to deal with each one of them.

Starting in 1950, Rubbermaid hosted a luncheon on Tuesday for the magazine and newspaper editors and reporters who attended the Housewares Show. This was a very valuable practice because it enabled the executives of Rubbermaid to become acquainted with the people of the press and vice versa. We never put on a big product pitch at these press luncheons, but instead had some light-hearted entertainment. While we wanted the media to be aware of and write articles about our products, we knew that they would get most of that from simply attending the show. The purpose of the luncheons was to allow our executives to talk one-on-one with the press people and gain their respect. I believe that as a result of the press luncheons we gained more publicity for our products than our competitors did and the publicity was more favorable.

Starting in 1964, we held the summer show press luncheon aboard a boat. The boat would dock at McCormick Place to pick up the press people and take them out onto the lake to relax and chat with our executives. We always served them a boxed lunch. This event turned into an annual affair that became very popular with the press people.

At the last press party before I retired from being Chief Executive Officer, the press corps presented me with a scroll which all of them had signed and on which was lettered in a beautiful flowing calligraphy the following words:

"We, the fourth estate, salute Donald E. Noble, in recognition of his outstanding leadership in the housewares industry, 1941 to 1980, on this day, January 15, 1980. We honor him, in particular, for his fortitude in surviving 57 press parties, 24 of which were at high seas and 23 during January blizzards. From his many friends in the media, we wish Don success for a joyful and prosperous retirement."

Along with the scroll, the press people presented me with a beautiful piece of Steuben glassware which I prize very highly and still keep in my office today.

On January 16, 1967, the Sunday night before the Housewares Show was to open the following morning, McCormick Place caught fire and burned to the ground. I was Vice President of the NHMA at the time. At 3:00 a.m. my phone rang in the Blackstone Hotel. It was Dolph Zapfel, Managing Director of the NHMA, who told me that McCormick Place was burning and there would be no show. He said that he was calling a meeting of the NHMA Board of Directors at 9:00 the next morning in his office, and he asked me to call all the board members to invite them to attend. My hotel room looked out toward McCormick Place, and from the window I saw the flashing lights of fire engines and could actually see the flames so I knew it was "for real."

I had quite a time calling the board members. The reaction of each one was the same – "You've got to be kidding!" It took some time and convincing to make them realize that McCormick Place was really on fire. Someone had been playing a prank on one board member, calling him once an hour during the night. When I called this board member, he thought it was the prankster and hung up on me. I had to call another executive of his company and ask him to tell the board member that there actually was a fire!

Les Gigax was my roommate. We sat on the edge of our beds discussing what we should do with the many Rubbermaid executives and employees who were in Chicago for the show. We decided a few of the top Rubbermaid executives could meet with customers in our hotel suite and we would send the rest of the employees back to Wooster. Les got on the phone to make airline reservations for these people, because we knew there would be a great out-flow of people and later in the morning reservations would be difficult or impossible to get. We placed announcements on local radio stations to inform our customers that we would be available to meet with them in our suite at the Blackstone Hotel. Most of our customers came and we accomplished a great deal with them despite the fire and the show being canceled.

Following the fire, the NHMA Board of Directors had to find a place to hold the next summer show. Consideration was given to having it in Atlantic City, Dallas, Miami, or New York City, but the decision was finally made to hold it at the Chicago stockyards. The primary reason was that there were just not enough hotels in the other cities to handle the number of people who came to the Housewares Shows. The stockyards was a very unsatisfactory facility for holding the show, but it served the purpose after a fashion. Some of the Rubbermaid executives felt that Rubbermaid did not have as good a location at the stockyards for our booth as we should have had considering our importance in the industry. They felt that because I was on the NHMA board and also an officer, the Association did not dare to give Rubbermaid a good spot for fear that it would look like preferential treatment. Three years later, McCormick Place was rebuilt, and all of us were happy to bid farewell to the stockyards and get back into a decent facility for the Housewares Show.

Caldwell's strong marketing and sales skills made him very conscious of the need to extend the marketing reach of The Wooster Rubber Company beyond Ohio and the northeast. Soon after he came to Wooster, Caldwell hired seven manufacturers' representatives to sell Rubbermaid products throughout the United States east of the Rocky Mountains. In 1936, while attending a Housewares Show, Caldwell met Arthur Clark, who was a manufacturers' representative in Los Angeles, and engaged him to sell Rubbermaid products in California. But it was five years before Caldwell could make his first trip to the West Coast because the Company could not afford the travel expenses to California and he rarely called Clark because the phone calls were also too expensive. So almost all their contact was done through the mail and by Caldwell meeting Clark once a year at the Housewares Shows.

Sales at that time were primarily to department stores. But Caldwell soon moved into new distribution channels by starting to sell to wholesalers, who in turn sold to hardware stores. The new rubber products being added – such as bathtub mats, soap dishes, floor mats, and stovetop mats – could be sold equally well in both types of retail outlets.

In 1938, The Wooster Rubber Company started its first national advertising by putting a small one-inch ad in *Better Homes & Gardens* magazine. The ad invited people to send in $1.95 for a Toilet Top Tray. I have a strong suspicion that Errett Grable had something to do with the running of that first advertisement because he was always interested in assuring that Rubbermaid had a strong national advertising program. A major part of Rubbermaid's sales success was the constant national advertising that grew out of that first small ad. Many years after it ran, Rubbermaid began advertising nationally on daytime television. Guil Johnson was once asked by someone, "How do you create a recognizable trade name like Rubbermaid?" He began his reply by saying, "Well, you start about 35 years ago." We advertised not only to sell our product lines but also, and equally important, to enhance our trade name and brand. We tried to have our advertising always done in good taste so it would reflect the high quality of our products and would promote a positive image of the Company itself.

It was also in 1938 that Caldwell re-established the demonstrator program, which Madeleine Caldwell had started by demonstrating products at the Jordan Marsh Department Store in Boston. This program continued until 1970, when it involved a total of 250 demonstrators who gained a great deal of visibility for Rubbermaid products with consumers. We also set up a program to build recognition for the Rubbermaid name among young consumers by giving high school teachers of home economics courses teacher's aids on which our Rubbermaid logo was subtly positioned. We also gave these teachers advice on how and where Rubbermaid products could be used to best advantage in the kitchen.

It did not take me long after I began working at Rubbermaid to realize how critically important it was for every employee to be involved in the Company's marketing and merchandising efforts. While I was still Treasurer and Chief Financial Officer of the Company, I often said that "Rubbermaid is first and foremost a marketing and merchandising organization." After I became Chief Executive Officer, when I made that statement I could sense that the heads of other disciplines in the Company felt that it relegated them to the category of second-class citizens. When I realized this, I changed my statement to say, "Rubbermaid is first and foremost a marketing and merchandising organization which means that all executives in every discipline must be marketing and merchandising people." By that I meant that no matter what their principal functions were, our executives must understand marketing. So they could learn marketing skills on a practical rather than theoretical basis, I insisted on all our executives attending the Housewares and Hardware Shows as well as making calls on customers.

Prior to this time, we had always paid our marketing and merchandising executives salaries that were about 10 percent higher than those paid to executives at comparable levels in other disciplines. I then decided that in order to compensate executives in other disciplines for learning marketing concepts and supporting the day-to-day marketing and sales of our products, we would pay them comparable salaries. This was not only good for morale, it also showed them that we meant business when we said that they had to be marketing and merchandising people.

By sending our executives to the various shows and having them call on customers, I wanted them to become aware of our competition. At the shows, they learned that we were in competition with every company that had a display, not with just our direct competitors. This was because we competed with all of the displaying companies for shelf space in the department stores, hardware stores, and discount stores to which we sold Rubbermaid products. I felt that I had been successful in this educational effort when Joe Biafore, our Vice President of Manufacturing, said to me, "Don, I now realize that my job isn't done until the merchandise is on the retail shelves of our customers."

But just being oriented to serving our customers was not enough. Our products played a unique role in the lives of the consumers who bought them and we had to be aware of and take advantage of that fact. So when I became Chief Executive Officer, we began putting very heavy emphasis upon responding promptly and fully to all consumer questions and complaints. We had always responded promptly to our direct customers, but now we began to focus on the handling of contacts with consumers because we recognized that they were our ultimate customers. Chuck Snyder, our Vice President of Marketing, took a great interest in this initiative and strengthened it by setting up a department staffed by employees who were specifically responsible for handling consumer questions and complaints. We made an effort to get our responses out to consumers within 24 hours. We also established a very liberal policy of providing replacement products when consumers indicated that they had experienced unsatisfactory quality or service problems with any of our products. We even sent out replacement products when consumers sent us unsatisfactory competitive products which they had mistakenly thought were made by Rubbermaid. In the cover letters accompanying such replacements, we, of course, pointed out that the faulty product was made by a competitor but, since the consumer had bought it believing that it was ours, we were replacing it. This liberal replacement policy was a terrific goodwill builder and a good sales tool. When replacing a competitive product, we told the consumer that our products always carried the name Rubbermaid and suggested that, to avoid similar mistakes in the future, the consumer should look for that name. This subtly conveyed the idea that by looking for the Rubbermaid brand, the consumer would get a product with consistently higher quality than a competitive product. Since the competitive product had proved to be defective, this approach inclined consumers to favor our products over competitive lines and was well worth the cost involved.

CHAPTER TWENTY-FOUR • NEW PRODUCTS FUEL GROWTH

One of the major factors in Rubbermaid's successful growth from the beginning has been our R&D investments to support a constant stream of innovative new products into the market – in some cases, creating a demand for products that had never before existed, such as the automotive mats. Under Caldwell's creative leadership, new products with great consumer appeal were added to the Rubbermaid line every year. In the early days of the Company, Caldwell himself was the entire Product Development Department. His approach to designing products was not very sophisticated. He would take a piece of brown wrapping paper and draw the product he had in mind; put in some rough dimensions; take it to a mold maker and ask him to make a mold.

Caldwell was always handy around the kitchen, and so he was constantly thinking of some product that Rubbermaid could make which would make life easier for the housewife. Frequently on Monday mornings during my early days with the Company, he would come into my office and say to me, "Don, over the weekend I was doing a job in the kitchen and I thought of a product that would really help." About three weeks later, he would come to my office and say, "Do you remember the idea for a new product I told you about some time ago? I have talked to my friends about it and they all think it would be a terrific product." Back in the 1930s and 1940s, he would test a new product idea out on his friends and if they thought it was a great idea, it normally was a successful product. Years later when he would come up with an idea and bounce it off his friends, the product was often unsuccessful. The difference was that in the 1930s and 1940s he and his friends were not wealthy. In later years, he became well-to-do and he associated mostly with affluent people. In the early years, he and his friends represented the mass market. Later on they did not. I am not sure that he ever understood the change which had occurred.

This unsophisticated approach went on until 1948, when Caldwell chose Clyde Breneman to help him with new product development. Soon after that, Caldwell created the Product Review Committee, consisting of Caldwell, Clyde Breneman from Research and Development, Jim Buckwalter from Marketing, Forrest Shaw from Manufacturing, and me, from Finance. It is significant that for product development, Caldwell included all disciplines of the business. Today, some businesses are adopting transdiscipline product planning as if it were a new concept, but we did it all along. It saves time and encourages innovation and cooperation because everyone is involved from the beginning.

After I became Chief Executive Officer, we had an iron-clad rule that we would not bring out any new product that did not have some new feature. To qualify as "new," a product had to be totally new or had to have an improvement making it demonstrably better than anything currently being sold. Another way of stating this rule was that we would not introduce any "me-too" products; we refused to copy a product already on the market and claim that it was new. I believe this policy was very important to Rubbermaid's sales success, because our wholesalers and retailers knew that when we introduced a new product it actually would have a new feature that consumers would want.

The Product Review Committee met monthly, but the selection of ideas for further development was made at semi-annual reviews. Twice a year, we would review the product suggestions that had come in since the last semi-annual review. These product suggestions came from many sources: from consumers, buyers, clerks in department stores, salesmen, and people in the Rubbermaid office and factory. We put the suggestions on a list, which we called the "Laundry List." There would often be as many as 300 suggestions on the list to be considered at our semi-annual review. We would go over the list and pick out approximately 20 product ideas for consideration. From this selection of potential items, maybe three would actually be developed into products that would be manufactured and brought to market approximately three years later. Between the semi-annual reviews, the Committee members would meet once a month to review the progress on products that were under development. Each of us would make comments on the items from our own point of view and based on our own expertise. Sometimes, these monthly meetings would go on for two or three days, and occasionally late into the night.

When a product was developed far enough to ask the opinions of others, it would be taken to our wives and to the women in the office to get their opinion on whether it would be successful. We would also ask for their suggestions for design improvements. Later on, starting in 1955, we would take the product to groups of church women and band mothers and pay their organizations a small amount for the members to give us their opinions on new product concepts. Later, we went to organizations and asked them to set up consumer panel groups so we could get their opinions on new products. Today, such consumer panels are called "focus groups." Dolores Marthey supervised these consumer panels, and sometimes she would take a product to the panels as many as five times before a mold was cut. In setting up consumer panels, we tried to get women who were economically in the middle class. In earlier years, we had taken products in the development stage to our wives for their opinions. Later, when they ceased being truly representative of the middle class, we stopped taking products to them because they did not represent our consumers in the mass market, anymore than Caldwell and his wealthy friends did.

After I became Chief Executive Officer of Rubbermaid, I became the head of the Product Review Committee so I usually opened our meetings by saying, "While I am in this meeting, I want to be considered as only one member of the Committee with only one vote on the decisions that are made here." The reason I said that was because I was much more interested in what a consumer panel of 300 women would say about a product than I was in my own opinion and I also wanted to be sure that my position did not unduly influence the opinions of the other Committee members.

New product development became increasingly important to achieving our growth goals. In my letter to shareholders in the 1960 Annual Report, when I had been Chief Executive Officer only one-and-a-half years, I wrote, "Some months ago the decision was made to perpetuate and accelerate Rubbermaid's rate of profitable growth through a major emphasis on new product and new market development. The first step in this expansion program has been the establishment of an entirely new activity and staff to be responsible for product planning and market development. The Product Development Department has already been expanded to approximately double its former size with some further expansion planned. Rubbermaid now has a separate staff of Product Development Engineers and Designers for each of our product categories."

We established an objective that 30 percent of our annual sales would be derived from products that had been introduced within the past five years. For our five-year planning cycle, that meant that we were setting a sales goal for some products that had not yet even been developed! Although it was an ambitious target, I was confident that the people in our expanded Product Development Department were up to the challenge and they did not disappoint me. Today, the goal is for a full 33 percent of annual sales to come from products introduced over the previous five years.

Along with our policy of no "me-too" products, we had another new product policy that served us well over the years. That policy said we could manufacture a new product if we knew either the manufacturing processes or the marketing requirements involved. In other words, we were willing to develop a product if we knew how to manufacture it but were not up to speed on marketing it. By the same token, we would develop a product if we knew how to market it but did not yet have the necessary manufacturing expertise. Although we could overcome one hurdle, two would constitute unacceptable risk. So we never entered into a new product development project where we neither knew how to manufacture the product nor how to market it.

Our project to develop water and winter play products was a violation of that sensible policy and its failure validated it. In 1968, we began looking at the possibility of producing a small boat made of plastic. We visualized such a boat being purchased for use as a dinghy with a small engine mounted on it or as a recreational boat which could be used either with a small engine or oars. We planned to balance this summer water play product line with a line of winter play products. To develop these products, we assigned two of our bright, young executives – Wolfgang Schmitt and Hank Lippisch. These young men worked diligently and did a fine job of producing sample boats and then taking them to nearby lakes for tests. They also developed snow sleds, small children's skis, and a snow bob (a vehicle like a bicycle with skis in place of wheels).

The development work, however, went slower than they had anticipated and they also ran into more problems than expected. As a result, they came back to the Operating Committee periodically saying that if they could just have $20,000 more they felt they would have successful product lines. This happened several times until we had a total of $275,000 invested in the project and Schmitt and Lippisch thought they were close to having developed a boat, sleds, and a ski bob that looked marketable. For a variety of reasons, the Operating Committee members decided that we did not have the distribution capability to market these products nor did we know how to manufacture them profitably. Therefore, we decided that we did not want to put any more money into developing them. For two years, Wolf Schmitt and Hank Lippisch had put much of their life and efforts into developing the plastic boat and other products and were enthusiastic about consumers having a positive reaction to the new lines. When we announced that we were not going to pursue the project any further, they were crestfallen. They felt their hopes for future career advancement had been dashed to pieces and that their business life was ruined.

I called Wolf and Hank into my office separately to talk to them. I told each of them what a fine job they had done and that our cancellation of the project was not a reflection on their abilities. I told them that its cancellation would in no way retard or restrict their future career advancement at Rubbermaid. I said that as an innovative business Rubbermaid had to try various avenues, some of which would fail, in order to find the projects that would succeed. I made it clear that I thought they had done the Company a great service by pursuing this project because their work had helped us determine that we did not belong in those markets. Without their hard work and dedication, we would never have known whether we were missing a great opportunity. One reason I spent considerable time with these young men was because I wanted them to go on to their next project at Rubbermaid with enthusiasm. I also remembered Caldwell asking me whether I had learned from a mistake I had made (see Chapter 32). So I told them that the only way not to have any failures was to not try anything new and that if we wanted to continue exploring new avenues of endeavor, we had to expect some failures. The important thing was to learn from the failures because that was the only way to find the successes. Both Wolf and Hank were successful in their next assignments. Hank left Rubbermaid a few years later, but Wolf went on to promotion after promotion until today he is Chairman of the Board and Chief Executive Officer of the Company.

To support our product development programs, we were very aggressive in acquiring new technology. We believed in analyzing all new equipment coming on the market so we could be up-to-speed on the new technological developments that seemed to apply to the manufacture of our products. That way we could make an informed decision as to whether we could justify buying the new equipment even though our existing equipment was not worn out. This analysis was made on the basis of Return On Assets Employed (see Chapter 19). If there were sufficient labor and overhead savings to provide more than an adequate return on the new investment involved in buying new equipment, we did it even though our present equipment was not worn out.

In addition to keeping our own technology up-to-date, we frequently asked our suppliers to use their research and technological capabilities to help us develop innovative new products. Manufacturers of plastic raw materials, such as Dow Chemical, Union Carbide, Phillips Petroleum, and Gulf Oil, worked with us continually to make raw materials that would make our products increasingly more durable and to develop new materials that would permit the manufacture of Rubbermaid products which had not previously been possible. An example of the latter case is our work with suppliers to develop a plastic garbage can.

In 1970, we began thinking it would be great if we could make a plastic garbage can* to replace the metal ones which in those days were the only kind on the market. It would be a great addition to our housewares line. At that time, however, no plastic material was available for making a product as large as a garbage can that was even minimally durable let alone capable of standing up to the rough treatment of refuse haulers and cold winter weather.

---

*In 1970, we still used the term "garbage can." Rubbermaid actually introduced and popularized the term "refuse container" after we had developed the plastic version.

We asked two of our suppliers, Dow Chemical and Union Carbide, to start developing raw materials for use in making a plastic garbage can with satisfactory durability. After many tries, they did, but the first materials they developed were so expensive that the plastic container would have to be sold at four or five times the price of a metal one. Nevertheless, we went ahead with experimental testing and also encouraged our suppliers to continue working on raw materials in an effort to develop a plastic that would give us both durability and good appearance, but at a lower price than those they had first developed.

I remember talking at that time about my confident belief that the day would come when we would make a plastic garbage can that would have the quality to stand up against both abuse and cold weather and which we could sell at a price competitive with metal containers. Most of the management team did not believe that this would ever be possible. They were nice about it, but they just did not share my confidence. Sure enough, when we first started manufacturing plastic garbage cans for sale, the retail price was substantially higher than that for metal ones and we sold only a few. But as our raw material suppliers developed new materials on which they could gradually lower their price, we continually lowered the price of our plastic garbage cans and sales volumes increased. When the price of plastic garbage cans got close to the price of metal ones, the sales volume of the plastic ones increased dramatically. The plastic containers were much more attractive than metal containers and they ultimately stood up better in use, which we highlighted in some very successful TV advertising.

Early on, Rubbermaid established a reputation in the retail trade for having a very good batting average on new products. Because of this reputation, department stores and later discount stores would buy our new products in volume without waiting to market test them. This, of course, made it even more important for us to be sure that a product would be successful before we invested in cutting a mold and starting to make the product. But we were never able to market test a product before we had started full-blown production and shipping. There were several reasons why we could not do market testing. First, the mold to produce a few dozen products for a marketing test would cost as much as the mold to produce hundreds of thousands of products for actual sale. The second and more important reason was that if we produced a few products and market tested them, we knew that our competitors would inevitably see the new products we were testing. They could then take advantage of our investment in innovation and beat us to market with a copycat version which they could sell at a lower price because they had incurred no research and development costs.

Part of the secret of our success was to maintain a six-month lead on the competition in bringing out a new product. As soon as our competitors saw one of our new products, they would take it to a mold maker and have a mold made for a similar product to compete with us. It was amusing that sometimes when we made a mistake in the design of a product or there was a flaw in the mold, our competitors would even copy the mistake or the flaw. Because we could not market test a new product, we would have as much as one or two million dollars invested in molds and inventory before we would know whether the product was going to be successful. That inventory would be stored not only in Rubbermaid's warehouses, but also in the warehouses of our wholesalers and retailers so there was a lot at stake. Fortunately, the success rate of our new products was very high, with nine out of ten of them meeting their marketing objectives.

Our inability to market test new products helped support my conviction that decisions should be made as far down the line in the Company as possible. That way, the employees closest to a new product during its developmental stage and then in the manufacturing stage are able to participate in the "go" or "no go" decision on whether the product was ready to be marketed. Over the years, the input of knowledgeable employees has enabled us to launch new products that have met their marketing objectives nine out of ten times without exposing our ideas in market tests to our competitors who are only too willing to benefit from our R&D

expenditures. This idea of pushing decision-making down to the lowest possible level in the organization is given lip service at most American companies, but at Rubbermaid we had procedures and policies in place that actually made it possible. The things enabling such decisions to be made included:

- The fact that we had a written *Statement of Rubbermaid Philosophy and Fundamental Principles* which was widely distributed to all employees. In that *Statement* there were so many descriptions of the way we wanted Rubbermaid business to be conducted that quite often guidance leading to the correct decision could be found in the printed pamphlet.

- The fact that we had a five-year plan which was redone every year meant that many directions for the business were spelled out in the plan. If a decision fitted within the plan, the person making the decision could do so with confidence that it would move the Company forward and help achieve plan objectives.

- The fact that we published a one-year plan in great detail also made it possible to make decisions with confidence.

- The fact that we had an announced growth objective of doubling the business every six years also made it possible for decisions to be made at a lower level. If a decision fitted within that growth formula, it could be made with confidence.

- The fact that we used Return On Assets Employed (ROAE) as a measurement and that we had set parameters for an acceptable ROAE for various operations made decisions possible at a lower level. An example was the acceptable ROAE threshold for new products. If employees developing a new product found that it was not going to reach the acceptable ROAE threshold, they knew that it was a waste of time to continue working on it unless there was some compelling marketing reason that it should be introduced at an ROAE below the threshold level. Likewise, there was a trigger point for dropping an older product whose ROAE had slipped below the level required to stay in the line. Employees knew that such a product had to be dropped unless there was a compelling marketing reason for continuing to carry it in the line. If either manufacturing or marketing people felt that they could bring the product's ROAE above the trigger point within six months, they could decide to keep it in the line.

- The fact that management worked very hard to create an atmosphere that reassured employees they would not be penalized for making mistakes made it possible for decisions to be made at lower levels. That same atmosphere encouraged innovation because people could try new things without fear of being penalized even if their new ideas did not work.

- And the fact that we believed the people closest to the action know best what needs to be done to improve an operation made decisions possible at the shop floor level.

I often said that I seldom had to say no to a proposal. That was because our decision-making and procedures were aimed at encouraging new ideas and fitting them into our overall plans. Even when someone proposed an idea in the five-year plan which I believed was not in the Company's best interest, I did not say no. Instead, I asked a lot of questions about the proposal. If it appeared in the next five-year plan, I asked even harder questions about it and usually it did not appear in the plan again (see Chapter 28). I felt that it was much better for an executive to withdraw a proposal than to have me or someone else in senior management say no to the project. If a supervisor gets his people all excited about a new project and it is then turned down by top management, it is difficult for him to go back and tell his people that it had been killed. He loses face. Whereas if he himself decides to pull the project and explains his reasons for doing so, he maintains a better position with his subordinates.

Pushing decision-making responsibility as far down in organizations as possible is viewed today by many business writers as a new concept. Actually, I think it has always been the case in successful companies and it certainly is a concept that we used for many years at Rubbermaid, particularly in new product development, because it fostered innovation rather than stifling it.

Another benefit of giving people authority to make decisions was that it helped guarantee the high product quality that Caldwell demanded. We told all factory employees that each of them was a quality inspector. Employees were told to throw out any product that they would not want to buy at full retail price. Employees knew that if they saw products with blemishes they had the authority to close down the line – shut down the machines and stop production until the problem was corrected. Sometimes, employees would throw out a product with a blemish so small that it was hard for an untrained eye to detect, but we never complained because we wanted to keep our quality standards high. After I became Chief Executive Officer, I went even further to assure quality because I believed that to produce a high quality product, you must have quality in every aspect of the business. I was convinced we needed quality people, quality employee relations, quality plants and equipment, quality offices, even quality landscaping. And, above all else, you must have consistent quality standards. You could not tell one group of employees to cut corners and make a cheaper, lower quality product while another group was striving to make the highest quality possible. All this emphasis on quality is the reason Rubbermaid enjoys the outstanding reputation it has today for manufacturing innovative, high quality products.

CHAPTER TWENTY-FIVE • A HIGH TECHNOLOGY COMPANY

As I said earlier, Rubbermaid has always been on the leading edge in the use of computers dating back to when I first came to The Wooster Rubber Company and the office staff was using an IBM Card Sort System. That system was quite advanced for a company of that size in 1941. Two decades later, in 1963, we purchased a General Electric 225 computer which was the most advanced technology available at the time. The unit was about three times the size of a large refrigerator and required a separate room with air conditioning and humidity control. We also had to build a false floor in the room to accommodate all of the wiring that was involved. At the 1965 Annual Meeting, I reported to shareholders about the installation of our new computer system in these words:

"Our new computer is already doing a fine job for us on order entry and shipping. We expect even greater things from it on production control and inventory management. The programming for production control and inventory management has been going on for the past eighteen months and just went 'on stream' on April 1."

More than 30 years ago, I already had some inkling of what a momentous role this advanced technology would play in the future. As I told the shareholders:

"The computer has undoubtedly done more to change the way of life for business in general than any other single development for many, many years – possibly it has done more than any single development ever before."

In addition, I said in my remarks to the shareholders that "any merchandising company which has not already installed a computer may find that it is now too late to do so, because of the tremendous head start and other competitive advantages that merchandising companies which have installed them already have."

In 1968, we purchased another GE 225. Although back in the 1960s, these two computers were state-of-the-art technology, today a laptop computer has more computing power than the two of them together. We always tried to stay abreast of the latest developments in computers, because we believed that advanced technology was necessary to stay ahead of our competition.

In 1975, we built a high-bay automated warehouse in which a driverless, computer-controlled "stacker" placed two pallets of products in a space on shelving that extended up to 57 feet from the floor. The "address" of the space was recorded by a computer, and later, the computer told the equipment exactly where to go to bring the two pallets out for order picking and shipping. Today, Rubbermaid's computers receive information directly from the Company's large customers that shows the withdrawal of Rubbermaid products from their warehouses. The computers then calculate an order of products to be shipped automatically to each customer to replenish their inventory. If we had not taken steps early on to obtain the latest computer technology, this kind of customer replenishment system would not have been possible.

In 1977, three years before I retired, computer-aided design, or CAD, was already enabling Rubbermaid designers to develop every aspect of a new product concept from dimensions to materials and colors. A much more sophisticated CAD system is used today to achieve substantial reductions in new product development cycle time and costs, providing significant competitive advantages for Rubbermaid. We also tried to stay current with state-of-the-art technology on our factory equipment.

The best example was in our Injection-Molding Department. When properly maintained, injection-molding machines will last for 25 years or more, but the average age of our injection molding machines was seldom more than four and a half years. There were two reasons for this. One was that we were constantly growing and, therefore, we were adding new machines on a regular basis. Second, and more important, the injection-molding machine manufacturers were constantly coming up with new technological improvements on their machines which required less labor and, therefore, made them more efficient. So when one of our injection-molding machines got to be eight to 12 years old, we found that buying a new machine could be justified on the basis of a Return On Assets Employed analysis, even though it might mean trading in the old machine and getting a very small trade-in value for it. I said that I hoped our competitors would buy the old machines we had traded in and use them. I thought that even though they would pay a very small amount for the older machines, we would have a competitive advantage over them with our new machines and the new technology built into them, even though our new equipment required a much larger investment than our competitors would be making.

Our staff always included very competent industrial engineers who greatly enhanced our plant technologies. I told Les Gigax when he was Vice President of Manufacturing that I never turned down his requests to hire industrial engineers because I was so convinced that they all more than paid for their salaries in the cost savings they generated by designing labor-saving equipment. Out of hundreds of examples, I will cite only two. One of the most visible examples was the manufacture of plastic buckets. A plastic bucket drops out of an injection-molding machine onto a conveyor that carries it in exactly the right position to a station. Above the station, a straight wire of the proper length drops down and is threaded through a plastic grip. With the plastic grip in the center of it, the wire is bent into a curved shape with loops on both ends. The wire then drops down and the loops are attached automatically to the ears on the bucket to make the "bail" or handle. A label is automatically slapped on the side of the bucket and a label carrying a bar code is placed on its bottom. The completed buckets then move on to another station where they are stacked 12 buckets high. When 12 buckets are accumulated, the whole stack moves to a packer who drops it into a shipping carton. The packer is the first human being involved in manufacturing plastic buckets – every other step is automated, including the feeding of raw materials and coloring agents into the injection-molding machines.

Another example of a labor-saving device developed by our industrial engineers was a driverless train that ran from the plastic department to the finished goods warehouse, a distance of an eighth of a mile, and carried pallets stacked with cartons of finished goods ready for shipment. The "tracks" on which the driverless train ran was a copper wire in the floor. When the train had been unloaded and returned empty to one of the stations in the plastics department, it stopped automatically alongside a tilted roller rack where pallets already loaded with finished goods in cartons were ready to be rolled onto the train. All a worker had to do was to flip a switch and the pallets would roll automatically from the rack onto the train. Another switch was flipped and the train started on its journey. The train had sensors, or block signals, just like a regular train so that if there was another train ahead of it, it would automatically stop and wait until the track was cleared. The train also had a bumper – a double piece of thin metal wired to a switch – on the front of it which reacted if the train did run into something on the track and put the brakes on immediately. That way even if a person were standing on the track, the train would merely touch the person and then stop immediately. When the train reached its destination in the finished goods warehouse, it automatically stopped beside racks with rollers on the bottom. A big arm came out to push the pallets automatically onto the roller racks, where they would wait until a lift truck came to take them to the finished goods storage area. This automatic, driverless train saved many man hours which otherwise would have been required for lift trucks to carry the goods that distance and the train was much cheaper to operate than lift trucks would have been.

All the labor-saving devices developed by our engineers were evaluated based on a Return On Assets Employed (ROAE) analysis before they were built. Only when the ROAE calculation showed that the proposed new equipment would generate a labor cost savings adequate to provide a satisfactory return was the project allowed to go forward.

I believe Rubbermaid was able to begin its program of mechanization and automation of its production processes as early as it did because the Company's management had created an environment that encouraged innovation and experimentation with new procedures, new materials, and new technologies. We never had any trouble with the production workers objecting to the installation of labor-saving devices. I think the workers knew that in order to afford the high wages we paid, it was absolutely necessary for as much of the work as possible to be done by machinery. Another important factor in not having any complaints was the fact that we never had a layoff in the factory resulting from the introduction of new labor-saving devices. This was made possible by the fact that we were continually growing and, therefore, any workers that might not be needed in one area as a result of labor-saving devices could be transferred to other jobs created by our rapid and sustained growth.

In 1955, Caldwell started talking about the possibility of selling regular housewares items to hotels, motels, and restaurants. He asked John Gans to start traveling east from Wooster on U.S. Route 30, stopping at every motel on the road to try to sell them bathtub and door mats, and, if they had a restaurant, to try to sell them dish drainers, drainboard trays, and sink mats. Gans took on his new assignment with enthusiasm and succeeded in getting enough orders to make his time worthwhile, so Caldwell sent out another man traveling west to do the same thing. Caldwell soon added other housewares items to be sold in this new market, including dustpans, plate and bowl scrapers, and floor mats. They all sold so well that we started making larger, heavy-duty items designed for use in hotels, motels, and restaurants. Caldwell put Gans in charge and he hired manufacturers' representatives to sell the new line to dealers specializing in this market.

The new line developed into what we called our Commercial Products business. This business grew and prospered to the point that, in 1968, we decided to build a new plant dedicated to manufacturing only commercial products. After we made this decision, I asked the Operating Committee to prepare a list of all the important criteria we should consider in identifying a city where we could best locate the new plant. After I had read their list, I said, "You have just described Wooster, Ohio" (see Appendix 3). So we focused our search for a new plant site on communities closely resembling Wooster. When we became seriously interested in four potential sites, we asked our accounting firm, Peat, Marwick, and Mitchell, to subscribe to newspapers in each of the four communities and then send them to us. We had the papers go to the accounting firm to maintain our anonymity and not get the local governments and citizens all excited about the prospect of a new employer coming to town. Each week the firm bundled up the papers and mailed them to Rubbermaid where a secretary would clip articles about schools, hospitals, parks and recreational facilities, water systems, local governments, labor relations, and anything else that would help us appraise a community's quality of life and business attitudes. We ended up selecting a site in Winchester, Virginia, for our Commercial Products plant because it was the best match for our site-selection criteria.

We were planning to build 75,000 square feet of factory and office space for the Commercial Products business. Five acres of land would have been ample to accommodate a facility of that size. But to provide for growth, the management team thought we should have 20 acres of land. I insisted on purchasing 40 acres of land in Winchester for the Commercial Products operation and we built the facility and began operations there in 1968. My operating policy that guided all of our facility expansion was to buy eight times as much land as would meet our immediate needs or twice as much land as we could possibly visualize needing in the future, whichever was greater. We followed that policy in purchasing land whenever we established a new location and we found that we soon grew into the entire space. A good example of the success of this policy is our Commercial Products business in Winchester, Virginia, where we have now built to the maximum extent possible on the 40 acres we originally purchased.

In 1958, Forrest Shaw and Bob Ebert learned of a new manufacturing process known as "rotational casting" – a process for making large plastic products such as 55-gallon garbage cans. This involved putting powdered plastic into a large mold, closing the mold, and putting it into an oven hot enough to melt the powdered plastic into a liquid. The mold was then rotated in several directions, making the liquid plastic flow into all the inside contours of the mold. The mold was then quickly transferred into a spray booth where cold water was sprayed over the outside of it as it continued to rotate. This solidified the liquid plastic into a "skin" adhering to all the inside contours of the mold. When the mold was opened, the container was extracted and the top of it was cut off and used to make the container's lid. We rented a small building in Wooster away from our main plant where we could experiment with this promising new production method. When the rotational molding process was developed far enough to give us confidence in it, we went to Statesville, North Carolina, and rented a small building to start production. Our first products were garbage cans in a 55-gallon size and a couple of larger sizes. At this time, there were no injection-molding machines big enough to make even a 55-gallon garbage can. We also expanded our rotational casting production by adding a line of large plastic push trucks for handling refuse and transporting merchandise in department stores and industrial settings. In addition, we made some big garbage cans in unusual shapes for use in department stores.

Bob Ebert, who had been in charge of the experimentation and development of rotational casting products in Wooster, moved to Statesville to manage the business there. After he had developed the process and product lines, we formed a new subsidiary – Fusion, Inc. The new business grew and prospered so much that it soon outgrew the original rented building. Two years later, we bought 29 acres of land on the edge of town in Statesville and built a facility with 57,000 square feet of office and manufacturing space and installed rotational casting machines in it. Our new business required a whole new marketing and sales approach because the plant's output was a line of industrial products. This grew into a very significant business for Rubbermaid, supplying large containers to industry and large material-handling push carts for industry, hospitals, and retail establishments.

CHAPTER TWENTY-SEVEN • SUGGESTIONS FOR NEW CEOS

I have said elsewhere that becoming a Chief Executive Officer is the second most difficult career change a person ever makes in corporate life (see Chapter 29). There, I said that a major adjustment a new Chief Executive Officer has to make is suddenly being responsible for supervising all the disciplines in the organization after having been an expert in his own function and knowing how to do the work of everyone in that function. It is a daunting prospect for someone with, say, a finance background to realize that he is now in charge of directing the heads of manufacturing, human resources, purchasing, and other disciplines in which he has not worked personally, which he has not studied, and cannot know whether work is being done efficiently.

Looking back at my own experience, I think that a new Chief Executive Officer is confronted with another and broader problem – the absence of any reliable guidelines for performing his critical function. The leading business schools do a fair job of giving their MBA graduates the *technical* skills that will allow them to pursue a general business career which may eventually lead to their election as a Chief Executive Officer. The business schools, however, cannot provide the guidelines on leadership that their graduates sorely need after they are elected to the top post.

One major problem confronting the beginning Chief Executive Officer is knowing exactly what his responsibilities are. This is extremely important because unless you know what is required, how can you be expected to discharge your responsibilities effectively? Some of my thoughts on this subject developed during the period from 1959 to 1980 when I served as Rubbermaid's Chief Executive Officer; others are the result of my reflections on the position since then. I will start by outlining ten suggestions which I consider important for performing the Chief Executive Officer's function effectively:

1. A Chief Executive Officer should establish his operating style as early as possible. Shortly after his election, a new Chief Executive Officer should sit down with his top management team and let them know clearly how he intends to operate. In my own case, I met with my Operating Committee the morning after my election and told them how we would proceed (see Chapter 16). I wanted to make clear to them that while I welcomed their opinions and counsel, responsibility for the final decision would be mine alone. My point was that on one hand, I did not plan on being an authoritarian but, on the other hand, I was not going to run Rubbermaid on the basis of consensus. Business is not a democracy and cannot be one. A related aspect of my operating style which I conveyed to my Operating Committee members was that I did not intend to interfere in the management of their own functional areas. For example, I told the Treasurer and the Controller that I did not intend to spend any time at all on financial matters because I was confident in their ability to handle those functions. This was a great relief to them because I had been the Company's Chief Financial Officer and they were naturally a bit concerned that I would not be able to relinquish control over their area. Similarly I told our Vice President of Manufacturing that I had no intention of learning the nuts and bolts of the manufacturing operation. I told him, "As Charles Schwab of General Motors once said, 'I think I am smart enough to hire someone to manage manufacturing.'" Then I said, "I hope you are that person." He was. He did a terrific job and I am glad that I gave him the freedom to do it.

2. A Chief Executive Officer should take action to set the "tone" for his entire organization. An important part of the Chief Executive Officer's responsibilities is to set the tone for the entire organization he heads. I think this is best achieved by creating an atmosphere of teamwork (see Chapter 33). At Rubbermaid, I made it clear that I favored cooperative harmony in which there was a minimum of political maneuvering. I also let everyone know that I did not look with favor on people who try to advance by stepping on others or by deriding the accomplishments of others. Having established these broad ground rules, I tried to live by them myself. For example, the Chief Executive Officer can set the proper tone for the organization by giving credit to others when there are significant accomplishments and by personally taking responsibility for the shortcomings and failures of the organization. Doing the first is a matter of generosity; doing the second is a matter of accountability. I also believe that the Chief Executive Officer must set a positive example by giving compliments when a good job is done instead of ranting and raving when there is poor performance. Sincere compliments spur employees on to even greater efforts; constant or overly harsh criticism discourages employees rather than motivating them and makes them afraid to use any initiative or try anything innovative. Whenever possible, I followed these concepts in dealing with employees throughout Rubbermaid.

3. A Chief Executive Officer should define the mission of his organization in writing. The Chief Executive Officer must spearhead the writing of a mission statement for the organization he heads. His personal involvement is necessary to avoid the development of a mission statement that recites a lot of pious platitudes but is ignored by employees in their day-to-day activities. Although he must be deeply involved, the Chief Executive Officer also has to avoid developing a mission statement by fiat. Instead, he should consult with the members of his top management team, who in turn solicit input from their direct reports. When the mission statement is sufficiently developed, the Chief Executive Officer should take responsibility for clearing a draft of it with his Board of Directors. With the Board's approval in hand, the Chief Executive Officer should publish the mission statement over his signature and make sure that it is distributed throughout the organization, ideally with every employee receiving a copy.

4. A Chief Executive Officer should publish his organization's philosophy and principles. A mission statement establishes the broad major objectives of the organization. The Chief Executive Officer is responsible for providing a "road map" for realizing those objectives in the form of a written statement of the philosophy and fundamental principles that are to guide the operations of the organization. The procedure for developing this statement is similar to that used to create the mission statement. A critical element, however, is the publication of the statement in written form along with a clear message from top management that these are real guidelines that everyone is expected to follow. In my opinion, the fact that we had a written *Statement of Rubbermaid Philosophy and Fundamental Principles* which was published and distributed to all employees, to customers, and to suppliers, was a major factor in the Company's success (see Chapter 21 and

Appendix 1). It told employees, especially younger employees and new hires, exactly what would be rewarded and what would not be tolerated. It told our customers that the Company was dedicated to providing them with quality products and superior services. It reassured our suppliers that they would be treated as partners in our business and that, if they also treated us as partners in turn, they could trust us to stay with them over the long haul. Many companies have similar operating philosophies and principles, but they often fail to publish and distribute them. Most important, senior management does not refer to them frequently enough so that everyone will realize that they are real and not window dressing. I believe our *Statement of Rubbermaid Philosophy and Fundamental Principles* contributed so much to Rubbermaid's success because the top management team made it clear that we ourselves subscribed to the tenets it contained and expected everyone else to do the same.

5. A Chief Executive Officer should establish and announce specific achievable goals. As we move through these suggested guidelines, it strikes me that we are dealing with a pyramid, the base of which is the mission statement. As we move up to the statement of philosophy and principles, we are establishing broad general objectives. Then we come to the apex of the pyramid which requires the Chief Executive Officer to articulate and refine a very specific set of objectives for growing the business. I have covered the growth formula I developed in some detail elsewhere (see Chapter 18). Suffice it to say here that there were two key factors which made that growth formula a success. First, it was easy to understand the concept of doubling the business every six years by achieving an average 12-1/4 percent annual compounded rate of growth. Second, publishing the growth objective throughout the Company made every Rubbermaid employee aware of what was expected, and publishing it to the financial community motivated our senior management group to put forward their very best efforts to achieve the annual growth objective.

6. A Chief Executive Officer should establish a measure for gauging performance. The Chief Executive Officer should establish a measure for gauging performance and communicate it to all employees. Using the analytical tool of Return On Assets Employed (ROAE) as a measure of performance and executive achievement (see Chapter 19) further strengthened our ability to achieve the growth objectives we had established. We calculated the ROAE for every product in our line, for each operating unit, for each class of trade, and for each of our large customers. This ROAE analysis focused the attention of managers not only on the amount of sales revenue and the costs associated with getting a return on sales, but also on the use of every asset of the business. In addition, they knew they were being measured on the turns of the assets they were using. Again, the critical point is making sure that everyone in the organization knows what they are expected to accomplish and giving them the tools to do it.

7. A Chief Executive Officer should develop sound plans to accomplish major goals. A key tool for assuring that everyone knows what they have to do in order to accomplish the organization's major goals is sound planning. The Chief Executive Officer should take the lead in setting up a comprehensive long-term strategic planning process accompanied by a short-term tactical planning process. At Rubbermaid, each spring we prepared an elaborate five-year plan for each operating unit and for Corporate (see Chapter 20). This was a "rolling" five-year plan because every spring we dropped the past year and added a year. To a major extent, I managed the business through this five-year planning process and, more importantly, so did everyone else in the organization. The plan provided a clear road map for employees at every level; they knew where we wanted the Company to go and the plan provided the information they could use to make the right decisions to get us there. Each fall, we prepared a one-year plan and budget derived from the five-year plan but, of course, in much greater detail. The Operating Committee seldom had to turn down any proposal in the one-year plan because we had eliminated undesirable proposals in the previous year's planning process.

8. A Chief Executive Officer should design short-term and long-term incentive plans. Since smart managers will always find a way to make any incentive plan pay off for themselves, it is vital to a company's success that all incentive plans be properly designed. If such plans are improperly conceived, managers will place their emphasis on the wrong things in order to maximize their bonuses but they will not take the actions that are best for the business. The Chief Executive Officer must take responsibility for proper plan design. At Rubbermaid, I was directly involved in designing our Short-Range Incentive Plan using Return On Assets Employed (ROAE) as the measure of achievement. Similarly, we found that our long-range incentive plan functioned best when managers' accomplishments were measured on the basis of ROAE and was structured in the form of a Restricted Stock Incentive Plan (see Chapter 19). This encouraged executives to pay attention to the long-term effects of their actions rather than just focusing on the immediate short-term needs of their operations.

9. A Chief Executive Officer should delegate almost total authority to operating unit heads. I have described elsewhere the importance of delegating almost total authority to the Presidents and General Managers of operating units so they could feel that they were in charge of their own businesses, subject only to necessary corporate oversight (see Chapter 16). It takes a substantial amount of self-confidence to grant such a delegation, but I believe it is far superior to delegating authority that is hemmed in and qualified by all sorts of restrictions. By delegating what amounts to autonomous authority, the Chief Executive Officer avoids having to respond to constant questions from his operating heads that boil down to, "Do I have the authority to do so and so?" In addition, I believe good professional managers respond to a looser rein with greater effort.

10. A Chief Executive Officer should make the long-range decisions that affect profitability. Because the Chief Executive Officer is the only company officer who really has an overall perspective on the business, he is uniquely qualified to make those long-range decisions which affect the organization's profitability. He alone can really see how much current profit needs to be sacrificed to produce greater future rewards. I have outlined in some detail how I pushed for a facility expansion program that had an adverse impact on profits for three consecutive years (see Chapter 17). If I had not resisted the concerns expressed by some of my senior management team and the pressures exerted by some Board members, we would not have had the expanded facilities we needed to achieve growth and future profitability far in excess of the profits we sacrificed in that three-year period.

These ten points are suggestions for someone tackling the position of Chief Executive Officer for the first time. As with any "doer" who becomes a supervisor of "doers," the new Chief Executive Officer quickly discovers that he no longer belongs to his former peer group. The group to which a new Chief Executive Officer actually belongs is outside his own organization. That group can consist of the Chief Executive Officers of other corporations; it can also include the Chief Executive Officers of trade groups to which his or her company belongs and the Chief Executive Officers who are members of other boards on which he or she serves or may serve in the future. Elsewhere I describe the value of associating with other executives who share a Chief Executive Officer's responsibilities and challenges (see Chapter 29) and the very real benefits of serving on different boards (see Chapter 31). It is in these groups of people who share the Chief Executive Officer's experiences that the best advice will be found.

CHAPTER TWENTY-EIGHT • SUPERVISION BY ASKING QUESTIONS

In the last chapter, I outlined ten suggestions that might be of help to a new Chief Executive Officer. Now, I want to provide some practical advice for young executives who aspire – as I think most bright and ambitious executives do – to becoming the head of their own organizations.

I will start with some thoughts on how to ask pertinent, penetrating, and perceptive questions. This is an especially critical skill for a new Chief Executive Officer who finds himself or herself supervising unfamiliar disciplines, but it is also a skill that is extremely valuable at any point during an executive's business career. One reason it is so important is that I think it is always better for a supervisor to challenge his or her subordinates by asking questions rather than by making direct statements of disbelief. Asking intelligent questions shows a genuine interest in the person making a presentation and an appreciation of all the work that has gone into the presentation. On the other hand, statements of disbelief can come across as being belittling, demeaning, and unappreciative of the work that has been performed. In addition, a supervisor who makes statements of disbelief runs the risk of later being proven wrong. That is not a risk in asking questions in accordance with these simple guidelines:

I. Start by questioning things in the presentation that look improbable, such as:
   A. Improbable statements presented as facts,
   B. Improbable statements presented as opinions, and
   C. Improbable estimates, such as optimistic target dates for delivery or project completion, and an unrealistic estimate of the work force required.

II. Next, question the assumptions made in the presentation:
   A. If assumptions are not listed, ask what they are.
   B. If assumptions are listed, ask if there are any others.
   C. Then question each assumption as to
      1. The information on which it is based and the reasonableness of that information.
      2. Presuming that the assumption is in the middle of the range of possibilities, ask what is the minimum possible assumption and what is the maximum possible assumption. This will give you some idea of the possible margin of error.

D. Often this series of probing questions will bring to light assumptions which were not listed or mentioned.
   1. Question these newly discovered assumptions.
E. Ask these questions, "If all the minimum (or poorest) assumptions were used, what is the worst possible scenario?" and "If all the maximum (or best) assumptions were used, what is the best possible scenario?"

III. A proposal is often a study of risk versus reward. If it is, ask questions about the risk or risks and the rewards, such as:
A. What are the risks?
   1. Ask that risks be listed in order of their seriousness, listing the worst first.
   2. What are the consequences of each risk?
   3. What is the probability of each risk becoming a reality?
B. What are the rewards?
   1. Monetary rewards (ask for them to be quantified).
   2. Non-monetary rewards – how do we evaluate them?
   3. What is the probability of each reward being realized?

IV. What are the alternatives?
A. Have you considered any alternatives?
   1. If not, why not?
   2. If yes, what alternatives did you consider?
   3. For each alternative that you considered, what are the advantages and what are the disadvantages?
   4. Which are the alternatives closest to the course of action being proposed?
   5. For each of these alternatives, why was this alternative not chosen?
B. Asking for alternatives gives you a chance to gauge the depth of thinking that has gone into the proposal. It also gives you an opportunity to ask that one of the alternatives be pursued in more depth. This is particularly true if you are not convinced that the proposal being made is the best one possible or if you have serious doubts about the entire concept embodied in the proposal.

By the time you and the presenter have run through this gauntlet of questions, you may have become convinced that the proposal is well thought out, that it is factual, and that it contains the right assumptions, in which case you can agree with the proposal and approve it. Conversely, by this time, the presenter may see the proposal as a bad idea and "throw in the towel." What is more likely is that the presenter at this stage will suggest going back to the drawing board to come up with new facts or improved assumptions as the basis for another course of action. If any of those conclusions are reached, that is the end of the questioning for that session.

If, however, you are still not convinced that everything has been done that should be done to arrive at the correct conclusion, rather than saying "No" to the proposal, it is better to take on the role of a skeptic and begin asking skeptical questions. That requires you to go back through the listed questions again, but in each instance you add a tone of skepticism to your questions and show that you are incredulous or unwilling to accept the points in the presentation at face value. Note that you still are not giving the presenter a flat "No," but asking skeptical questions should convey to the presenter that he needs to go back to the drawing board. If the presenter does not quickly come to that realization, I believe you should take the initiative by asking the presenter to rethink the proposal and come back with answers to your questions.

A young, impatient executive may think that it would be more efficient just to turn down a clearly flawed proposal. In most cases, however, it is better management style to direct the presenter to go back to the drawing board. While this may seem like a waste of time, taking the extra time is better than a total deflation of the presenter's ego – making him look small in the eyes of his subordinates. In other words, it is often better to allow the presenter to save face by rethinking the proposal and coming up with the conclusion on his own that it is not such a great idea. It is also possible that as a result of the rethinking process, a valuable proposal may emerge.

Part of my emphasis on using questioning rather than a flat turndown on proposals is an outgrowth of the important need for courtesy in dealing with others in a business situation, a need which is always present but becomes heightened in the case of a Chief Executive Officer. For example, when a supervisor is asking a subordinate to perform some task, there are several ways to communicate this request to the subordinate.

- It can be a simple request, "Please do so and so."
- It can be in the form of a directive, "I want you to do so and so."
- It can be a straightforward command, "Do so and so."
- Or, and I find this approach best, it can be posed as a question, "Do you think it would be a good idea to do so and so?"

When the question is properly asked and the subordinate agrees to do the task, he or she will have a feeling of ownership in the project. The subordinate is apt to give more thought to doing the project and is likely to do a better job than when he or she thinks he is merely carrying out a directive or command to do something. If the question is correctly asked and the subordinate is given an opportunity to disagree, it also can result in the project being reconsidered to the point where it produces a far better outcome. All as the result of asking a courteous question!

A corollary to the courteous question format for getting assignments performed well is the importance I think all executives should place on the spoken word, not only *what* you say but *how* you say it. For example, I found that when I became Chief Executive Officer it was necessary for me to be much more guarded with every word that I uttered than I had ever been before. I found that what I said and how I said it would be analyzed much more carefully and that much more weight would be given to whatever comments I made. When I was Treasurer I had done some kidding with subordinates and I would make light of certain subjects. I am afraid that I even used sarcasm at times. After I became Chief Executive Officer, I found that my kidding might not be taken as a joke and that people would start looking for some serious implication in my comments. The same was true of making light of subjects. Sarcasm became totally off limits because people would be deeply hurt by a sarcastic statement and take great offense at it because they placed so much more serious-ness on whatever I said. In Chapter 23, I noted that when I was Chief Financial Officer it was all right for me to say that Rubbermaid was first and foremost a marketing and merchandis-ing company. After I had become Chief Executive Officer and I said the same thing, the other departments of the Company felt I regarded them as being second class citizens.

In addition to being an important part of what you say and how you say it, executive courtesy is also an important part of what you *do*. Very early in my career I developed a habit of trying to be punctual. My extraordinary concern for punctuality may have started with my feeling that it was necessary for me to work more than my peers in order to be on an even playing field with them. It also may have developed because I remembered feeling that peo-ple who were late for meetings were being discourteous to those with whom they were meeting, whether it was a meeting one on one, or with a group. It rudely says to the other people, in effect, "I am more important than you are."

When I started working at the soda fountain in the drug store, it was imperative that I not only be on time but that I actually be early because I was replacing my boss who could not go home until I arrived. At the bank I always wanted to be there well ahead of the starting time so that I was ready to start work at that time. In order to do this, and since I was walking to work, I always tried to allow at least ten or 15 minutes of extra time to take care of any delays that might occur and so that even with a ten-minute delay I would still be there before starting time. My desire for being punc-tual stayed with me. When I was Treasurer of Rubbermaid, I always tried to be at meetings several minutes ahead of the starting time. When I called a meeting, I started the meeting precisely at the appointed time, even if there was only one other person there, and then I am afraid I frowned at people who came in late. I expected everyone to be there on time so that we could start the meeting with everyone present. It always seemed to me that if late-ness is tolerated when a meeting starts, the definition of what is late is questionable. If a person is five minutes late or ten minutes late, are they too late? But there is no question that being late wastes the time of other members of the group who are on time. If you establish a practice of starting meetings "on time" there is no uncertainty as to what is required and so everyone schedules himself to be there on time and no one wastes time waiting for others.

After I became Chief Executive Officer, the Operating Committee set a pattern of punctuality with all meetings starting precisely when scheduled and it saved a lot of time for everyone. When I was meeting with someone away from the office, I would always try to include an extra five to 15 minutes, depending upon distance, to allow for any travel delays so that I could still be there on time. To me, this emphasis on being punctual was a matter of courtesy. I always carried reading material with me so I could use the minutes productively until the meeting began.

Although it may seem like a very picayunish point for a freshly minted MBA graduate, I placed a great deal of emphasis on the dating of documents, whether they were my own or were presented to me. Part of that was my training as an accountant which emphasizes the need to date all work papers as well as ledger entries. When I became Chief Executive Officer, I insisted that every written document be dated, including a note from one person to another, a letter, minutes of a meeting, or any other written paper. I insisted that everything be dated for a very good reason. I think correct dating saves a lot of time in the long run because so often when a document is undated, a lot of time is wasted trying to determine when it was written and whether it preceded or followed some other document to fit it into the proper sequence. That sequence can have legal significance, so it is important.

In closing this chapter of advice for young executives who aspire to become Chief Executive Officers, I would pose this question: Do people become adept at asking the right questions and showing the proper courtesy to others after they have been elected Chief Executive Officer, or do they qualify for election to that position by having developed those characteristics early in their careers? I believe that the latter is the case and I would recommend that all young executives – regardless of what their eventual career goals may be – practice these techniques in their day-to-day relationships with their business associates. I sincerely believe they will realize big dividends from doing so.

Chapter Twenty-Nine • A CEO Seminar

After I became Chief Executive Officer, I encouraged each member of my Operating Committee to take a course entitled "General Management" which was offered by the American Management Association (AMA) in New York. This was a four-week course, one week to be taken at a time with a lapse of roughly three months in between each week of course work. I was impressed with the description of the course and felt that it would be beneficial for all members of the Operating Committee.

The members of the Committee came back to me and said they thought taking such a course would be beneficial, but it would be even more beneficial for them if I would take the course first. This seemed like a good idea to me because we would then have a common base of reference. I found that the AMA offered a special version of its General Management course for Chief Executive Officers only. It condensed the four-week curriculum into one week of intensive study. I enrolled in this course and found it to be very worthwhile. AMA permitted only a few chief executives to take this course at one time so all of the attendees became quite well acquainted. I met two men in particular who became lifelong business friends. One was Richard Tullis, who was Chief Executive Officer of International Intertype, which was located originally in Cleveland but later moved to Florida. Richard and I have stayed in touch and we still see other occasionally. The other person was John Gushman, who was Chief Executive Officer of Anchor Hocking Glass in Lancaster, Ohio. About two years after we took the AMA General Management Course for Chief Executive Officers, John and I were discussing the fact that we could not find additional training courses that would be as beneficial for us as that one had been. From this conversation, we developed the idea that we might be able to get a group of Chief Executive Officers together who could help each other and that would be better than any training course we could find. We invited five other Chief Executive Officers and set up what we called a Chief Executive Officer Seminar. This group met twice a year from about 1963 until we all reached retirement age at about the same time in 1980. The seminar group was made up of seven Chief Executive Officers: George J. Grabner, The Lamson & Sessions Company in Cleveland; John Gushman, Anchor Hocking Corporation in Lancaster, Ohio; Paul H. Smucker, The J.M. Smucker Company in Orrville, Ohio; Rene McPherson, Dana Corporation in Toledo, Ohio; John Suerth, Gerber Products Company in Fremont, Michigan; Bob Wingerter, Libbey-Owens-Ford Company in Toledo, Ohio; and me.

The format of our seminar was a simple one. We rotated acting as hosts. The host would entertain the rest of us, usually in the city where his plant was located. We would stay at a nearby hotel, or in a couple of cases, at the host corporation's guest house. About three weeks prior to the meeting, the host would send out a request for subjects for the agenda. Each of the members would send back three or four topics on which he thought he had some information that would be beneficial to the group or, more often, a problem on which he wanted to get the opinion of the members of the group. From the list of subjects the host would prepare an agenda, putting the various items into the order which he thought best and showing the name of the member who had submitted each item. The host would act as chairman for that meeting. We would arrive in time for cocktails and dinner and start the agenda after dinner. The following morning we would meet for an early breakfast with the discussion going through the entire morning and then through a late lunch. After lunch we would play golf or tennis, after which we would leave for home.

We were in totally non-competitive businesses, so it was possible for us to be free and open with all information about our businesses. Because we got to know each other very well, and because we built up a mutual respect for each other and total confidence in our abilities to keep the seminar subject matter completely confidential, it was possible for us to "let down our hair" and really get into the nitty-gritty of the subjects on the agenda. While we usually agreed on solutions to problems, the process of arriving at the solutions brought out many differences of opinion, often extreme differences of opinion. In each case, however, something was learned by the defense of the various opinions and the reasons why each person believed what he believed.

It was a great learning experience for each of us and extremely beneficial in running our respective businesses. My Operating Committee said they hated to see me to go the Chief Executive Officer Seminars because I would come back with a list of things to have them do or change. On the other hand, they did believe the ideas I brought back were worthwhile. We met twice a year, and I cannot remember any of us ever being absent from one of these sessions, which I think in itself indicates the value that we placed on the discussions and meeting together.

Since Paul Smucker, Chairman and Chief Executive Officer of The J. M. Smucker Company, lived in Orrville and I lived in nearby Wooster, we usually traveled together to wherever the meeting was held. This was a very rewarding experience for me because I respected Paul so highly and enjoyed and profited so much from my many discussions with him.

CHAPTER THIRTY • THE NOBLE FAMILY TAKES TIME OUT

When I looked over an early draft of these memoirs, I decided that I had concentrated so much on my business life that it presented a very unbalanced picture of the way my family and I actually lived. Although I got a great deal of satisfaction out of my work, Alice and I enjoyed what little leisure time we had together. We especially enjoyed things we could do as a family, bringing our two sons and two daughters along for the fun. One form of family entertainment was skiing, a sport which we discovered later than most people do but have enjoyed immensely for many years.

In January 1955, when Alice and I had both just turned 40 years old, we were at a party with Dr. Mo Dixon and his wife, Jill (Mo was a pediatrician with the Beeson Clinic in Wooster). Mo and Jill told us that in ten days they were going to go skiing at Boyne Mountain in Michigan and said, "We'd love to have you go along." They told us how much fun it was and that Boyne Mountain was a family-oriented place where everyone in the ski week program took ski lessons in the morning, skied in the afternoon, and then went swimming in the outdoor heated swimming pool. We decided to go and take our four children – ages four to 13 – with us.

The ski week was scheduled to go from Sunday afternoon through Friday afternoon. We drove to Detroit on Saturday and arrived in time to shop at the J.L. Hudson Department Store, where we bought ski clothes for the entire family, except for Nancy who was only four years old. On Sunday, we drove the rest of the way up to Boyne Mountain. We checked in and then went to the Boyne Mountain Ski Shop where we bought skis, ski boots, and poles for Alice and me and rented equipment for the week for our three oldest children – Jeanne, eight years old; Dick, 11 years old; and Dave, 13 years old. The next morning we all went out on the slopes in our classes. I remember thinking that I was going to learn the sport quickly so I could keep up with my two boys. As a result, I tried too hard and cracked an ankle bone. I was on crutches for the rest of the week and for five weeks beyond that. My youngest daughter Nancy and I spent the rest of the week together.

Wednesday night, following dinner, there was ice fishing on Lake Charlevoix. The boys and I went ice fishing, with me going on crutches about 150 feet out on the slick ice to the place where a hole had been dug in the ice for us to fish. We caught many smelt, a small good-tasting fish, which we ate at lunch the next day.

Alice, Dave, Dick, and Jeanne progressed very well and became pretty good skiers by the end of the week. Every afternoon we had a riotous time in the outdoor heated pool, swimming in ten degrees above zero temperatures and sometimes in a snowstorm.

For six years we went back to Boyne Mountain for a ski week in February. We would leave home about four o'clock on Sunday morning for the 11-hour drive to Boyne. At that time there was not a single mile of four-lane highway. It was all two-lane country roads which went right through the center of every little town on the route and made it necessary to watch our speed.

After making seven trips to Boyne Mountain we started going West to ski, starting with Vail, Colorado. When we first went skiing at Vail in March of 1962, there was only one lift going up the mountain and that was the gondola. There was only one place to stay, which was a motel out on the two-lane road. There was no tunnel through the mountain, which meant that we had to drive all of the way to the top of Loveland Pass, which sometimes was a very challenging experience, especially when driving through a snowstorm. In later years, we skied at Aspen, Steamboat Springs, Alta, Snowbird, Deer Valley, and other western resorts, including one in the Canadian Rockies.

In the summer of 1955, we bought a boat for water skiing. On Saturday afternoons and Sunday afternoons, we would go to Pleasant Hill Dam, about 35 miles west of Wooster, where we would all water ski. We all started water skiing using two skis but gradually progressed to where, after we used two skis to get up out of the water, we could drop one ski and ski on only one. We then progressed to skiing on a slalom ski, which has footholds for both feet and we would get up out of the water using only the one ski. Over the years we were water skiing, we progressed through three boats, each one with a slightly larger engine that enabled us to get up out of the water better and to go a little faster. We started water skiing when Nancy was only five years old and soon even she was getting up on the skis. We would bring a little grill with us to the lake and would often have grilled hamburgers or grilled wieners for lunch or supper. Because we usually skied from the same location on shore, we became acquainted with some of the other skiers. One family we enjoyed in particular was Bonnie and Dwight McKee and their children. Dwight was at the time a foreman in the factory at Rubbermaid. As we progressed to larger boats and larger engines, Dwight was always one step ahead of us with an even larger boat and more powerful engine and was always one step ahead of us on skiing skill, but we had great times together. We did this for quite a few summers until the children became involved in work and other activities that made our water skiing trips impossible.

Our entire family enjoyed ice-skating. Each child started out at about four years of age on double-runner ice skates and then moved on rather quickly to single-runner ice skates. We would go to wherever the ice-skating was best in town – usually a natural pond or lake, where often we would have to take along shovels to scrape the snow from the frozen surface to make a place for ice-skating. One of our favorite skating places was Miller Lakes, which was at the end of our street, only a five-minute walk from our house on Oakley Road. As the children got older, they divided up into sides and played hockey or crack-the-whip. Alice and I never missed one winter without getting in some ice-skating until she had a stroke in 1989. She and I always tried to go ice-skating on January 24th, the anniversary of our first date when I took her ice-skating at the pond in Brookside Park after her high school graduation in 1934.

We enjoyed quite a few family trips. One of the early ones was in 1949, before Nancy was born and when Jeanne was only three years old. We drove from Wooster to New York City to see Macy's spectacular Thanksgiving Day parade. We stayed at the Statler Hotel and were out bright and early Thanksgiving morning to watch the parade and its gigantic balloons and floats with Jeanne sitting on my shoulders to see over the crowd.

We also took a vacation trip to the New England area to see the historic sights around Boston when the boys were about 10 and 12 years old – old enough to absorb some of the colonial history of Concord and Lexington and Boston. We stayed at the Parker

House in downtown Boston and took trips from there each day. Another vacation excursion was a week at the shore in Rehoboth Beach, Delaware, in a cottage right on the ocean where Nancy, then three years old, declared that it was "her ocean."

One of our most memorable trips was taken in 1957, after I had been at Rubbermaid 15 years and, therefore, was entitled to my first three-week vacation. We drove out west in a four-door Oldsmobile with no air conditioning (air conditioning was just starting to be available in cars). We stopped in Oklahoma City to visit friends and then visited eight of the National Parks, including Bryce, the Grand Canyon, Zion National Park, and the Painted Desert. We drove through the desert entirely at night to avoid the extreme heat of the day. In Los Angeles, we visited with Eve and Ed Clark. Ed was Rubbermaid's Western Division Manager. They had just installed a swimming pool in their yard, which we initiated. We drove north along the coast, stopping in San Francisco, and then headed east to Estes Park, Colorado, where we stayed at the Stanley Hotel for three days while I attended the West Coast Pot and Kettle Club Convention. This was a Housewares Club which I was attending as Rubbermaid's representative. We had a memorable trip out west. Nancy, who was six years old, played Gin Rummy with the other children sitting on the back seat and she often beat them. Dave, who was 15 years old, had studied up on all of the National Parks and other points of historical interest, and so he was our tour guide.

I always thought that vacations were necessary for good productivity. I know that in my own case I could tell when I needed a vacation because I could sense an irritability within me. Of course, I tried not to show it, but whenever it appeared I knew that it was time for me to take a vacation. I never took more than one week of vacation at a time except for the vacation where we drove out west when I took three weeks. I found that one week of the type of vacations I took was adequate to get me recharged and rested up and also got rid of the feelings of irritability. I never took more than three such one-week vacations during a year, but it was very important for me to take those vacations.

Many people say that an executive needs to take three weeks of vacation at one time because it takes ten days for him or her to get unwound and then a week to rest. This was not true of me when I took skiing vacations. When I would get to the top of a mountain on skis and look down the run, it took only three minutes for me to relax because the instinct for self-preservation clutched in and focused my mind on getting to the bottom of the run safely. I always felt that at the top of a mountain my mind became clear of business problems and it reminded me of taking an eraser to a blackboard and erasing the words on it. I could not possibly think about business concerns or problems when I was downhill skiing. The same was true of cross-country skiing, but for an entirely different reason. Cross-country skiing was so exhausting that it did not leave me with any energy to think about business concerns or problems. This same feeling of relaxation occurred on the weekends when we took the family water skiing. When I would get behind the rope on water skis, again the instinct for self-preservation took over and erased all business concerns and problems from my mind. I think executives make a serious mistake if they try to keep going for six months or a year without a vacation because I think a vacation recharges the batteries so that the executive can accomplish more and make better decisions coming back from a total change and total relaxation.

Since I mentioned our four children earlier in this chapter, I want to include some information on their subsequent education, careers, and families. When our son, Dave, was in the 9th grade, his teacher asked each student in the class what job or profession they would like to go into when they became adults. Dave's response was, "I don't know because the job I may want to do may not be in existence today." He was fascinated with the prospect of astronauts going into space, a job which was not in existence at that time.

When Dave and Dick were in their early years of high school, I told them that they could enter any honorable profession or job that they chose. They could work anywhere they wished except for one place – Rubbermaid. Even in those early years before I was Chief Executive Officer, I was a firm believer in a policy of no nepotism (see Chapter 32). I felt that it would not be fair to the boys to allow them to work at Rubbermaid, because if they were really good and competent and rose through the ranks to a position of responsibility, they would be accused of having received advancement because their father was a Company executive. The boys told me later that at the time I told them this, they thought that I was being cruel, but later they thanked me profusely for permitting them to choose what they wanted to do and prove themselves without help from their father. Even for summer jobs I would not permit them to work at Rubbermaid. Dave worked one summer at B & F Transfer taking care of trucks and helping to move household furniture from one home to another. Another summer he worked at Steel Storage File Company in a factory job. He spent a third summer on a dairy farm in Vermont.

As each of our children reached the middle years of high school, we took them to visit many different college campuses. Whenever we would take a summer vacation, we would try to include one or two or three campuses in our tours. In our home, there was never any discussion of whether or not to go to college. There was only a discussion of where to go. After looking at many campuses, Dave chose to go to Wesleyan University in Middletown, Connecticut, a very fine school, but taking him there was a terrible cultural shock for Alice and me. We were used to schools where they had many rules – rules about drinking, smoking, class attendance, curfews, and traveling away from campus. When we got to Wesleyan University, we found that they had none of these rules. In fact, the only rule at Wesleyan was that the students had to get passing grades. We saw liquor bottles on the window sills and we discovered that students could travel wherever they wished without checking with anyone. We were very teary-eyed when we drove away from campus. We felt as though we were leaving our little boy (who was a strapping six feet, five inches tall!) to all of the temptations of a very bad society.

Dick also had a variety of summer jobs. One summer he followed Dave by working at B & F Transfer where he took care of trucks and moved furniture. For a couple of summers he painted houses as part of a crew put together by William Sadler, one of his high school teachers. As I mention in Chapter 33, Dick was a football player on a high school football team that in his senior year had an undefeated season. Dick was selected as an "All Ohio End" and also was a straight "A" student. His academic achievements combined with his football ability made him sought after by four of the Big Ten universities and by many other colleges. He was kept busy many weekends being entertained by some college or university. After one weekend spent visiting one of the Big Ten schools, he came to his mother and me and said, "I have decided I don't want to play Big Ten football." I asked him why and he said, "Because it's a business and I'm not ready to go into business." We thought this was very perceptive.

After several more weekends of visiting various campuses, Dick said he wanted to talk to both his mother and me. He said, "The college that I would like to attend, I will go to only if you will agree to act as though I'm 500 miles away from home." We agreed that we would do this and he said the college he would like to attend was The College of Wooster in our hometown. We lived up to our agreement and our only communication with him up until Thanksgiving was his regular Sunday morning phone call. About Thanksgiving time, Dick found that by coming home, or by permitting us to come to the campus, he could get his laundry done, and when he came home, he also could raid the icebox. So our agreement was modified accordingly.

After Dave found out that Dick was getting along well going to The College of Wooster in his own hometown, in the middle of his third year he transferred from Wesleyan University to attend The College of Wooster, where he graduated a year and a half later. Dave had majored in history because he felt that left many options open as to what field he might enter. During his senior year at Wooster he applied to and was accepted at Duke University Law School in Durham, North Carolina. He said he was applying to law school, not because he was sure he wanted to be a lawyer, but because again it left more options open than anything else. He felt that after going to law school he would be able to practice law, teach in a law school, teach history in a college, or enter government service – at the time he was particularly interested in the diplomatic service. After law school Dave did go into the law, working first for the most prominent law firm in Washington, D.C., where he was assigned for a year and a half to a case in Chicago. He then switched jobs to work for the Critchfield law firm in Wooster, Ohio and later opened his own law firm in Millersburg, Ohio. Eventually he moved his firm to Cleveland, where he has successfully run his own law firm ever since.

Dave is married to Gayle, a psychological consultant. They have four children:

- Donald Noble II, who graduated from Purdue and is in charge of human resources at United Titanium in Wooster. He is married to Theresa, who is a sales administrator at the Prentke Romich Company in Wooster.
- Robinson, who graduated from The College of Wooster and has a Master's degree in geology from the University of Colorado at Boulder. He is working for Sheppard & Company in Ft. Collins, Colorado. He is married to Carrie, a public school teacher who teaches seventh grade.
- Elizabeth, who is studying at Middlesex University in London, England, after completing two years at Skidmore College in Saratoga Springs, New York.
- Matthew, who recently graduated from Orange High School in Orange, Ohio, is attending Duke University.

Dick was a pre-med student at The College of Wooster, planning to go to medical school and then specializing in surgery. Dick finished at The College of Wooster in three years, and in his senior year he was awarded a Rhodes Scholarship which paid the entire cost of two years of post graduate work at Oxford University in England, even including his travel expenses. While he was at Oxford, Dick became interested in philosophy. After finishing his two years at

Oxford, he came back and took further post graduate work at the University of California at Santa Cruz while he was teaching philosophy. He continued his studies at the University of Michigan in Ann Arbor, Michigan, while he was teaching there. He is still in the Philosophy Department at the University of Michigan, but for many years he has been teaching most of his classes at the University of Michigan Medical School where he teaches medical ethics. Dick is married to Marianne, a vice president of Blue Cross of Michigan in Ann Arbor, Michigan. They have a son:

- Andrew, who just graduated from Wooster High School as class valedictorian. He was on the tennis team all four years of high school and earned a letter in tennis each of those years. He is attending Carleton College in Northfield, Minnesota.

Our daughter Jeanne attended The College of Wooster for one year and then transferred to Augustana College in Rock Island, Illinois, where she majored in the French language and in French history. She then went on to do two years of graduate work in French language and French history at the Sorbonne University in Paris, France. Following this, she wanted to stay in France and get a job. We encouraged her to go to Ottawa, Ontario, Canada to look for a job where I contended her knowledge of French and her ability to speak the language fluently would be of more value than even in France. She reluctantly agreed to try it. She got a job with the Canadian Government and 20 years later she still lives there and still works for the Canadian Government. She met and married Stuart Langford, a native of Ottawa, who is a lawyer and currently editor of the Journal for the National Canadian Bar Association. They have three daughters:

- Katherine, a high school sophomore;
- Sarah, a seventh grader; and
- Laura, who is in the fifth grade.

Our daughter Nancy went to Swarthmore College in Swarthmore, Pennsylvania, and graduated with a major in English. She married James Holland, who had graduated from Swarthmore the year before. For many years, both Nancy and her husband taught English in private academies, first in Hawaii and then in Palos Verdes, California. Nancy also studied music in night classes at the University of California in Los Angeles. Nancy and her husband then moved to England to begin further studies. While James was studying at Oxford University, Nancy studied music for two years at the London Conservatory of Music. The two of them returned to continue teaching in Palos Verdes, California, but Nancy switched to teaching music and conducting choral groups. They then moved to Boston so James could work on a Doctorate degree in childhood learning at Harvard University and Nancy could study and receive a Master's degree in choral conducting at the New England Conservatory of Music. They have two children:

- Lilly, who is in the fourth grade, and
- Stephen, who is in the second grade.

As much as our family enjoyed traveling, our various houses have always been our focal point. Alice and I built four houses. We never got to live in the first one built in Berea in 1941 because we moved to Wooster so I could accept Rubbermaid's job offer. The second house was built in 1950 at 211 Oakley Road in Wooster, where we lived for 19 years. The third house was built in 1969 at 1677 Christmas Run Boulevard in Wooster, and we lived there for five years. The fourth house was built in 1974 at 1488 Morgan Street in Wooster, where we still live 22 years later.

In the spring of 1960, we decided to build a swimming pool in our back yard on Oakley Road. Dave, at that point, was in his first year at Wesleyan University in Connecticut, and the swimming pool was a big surprise for him when we brought him home from college for his summer vacation. The swimming pool was a great success because it was something all of us enjoyed. It made a wonderful place for our children to bring their friends and it provided a great opportunity for me to relax with the family on weekends.

My "career" as an outside director at other companies began relatively early and in a rather unusual way. In the fall of 1949, after I had been at Rubbermaid for eight years, Alice and I bought a lot on Oakley Road in Wooster and started planning to build a new house. I knew that we would require the maximum available for a mortgage loan because Alice and I had been able to save up only the bare minimum for a down payment. I went to all of the banks and savings and loan institutions in Wooster to see where I could get the lowest interest rate on a mortgage loan.

While I was very careful to look into the stability of a financial institution where I had a savings or checking account, I did not feel that an institution's stability was a concern as long as I was borrowing their money. Therefore, I felt that my only consideration was getting the lowest possible rate of interest. The interest rates quoted to me ranged from 4-1/4 percent to 4-1/2 percent from all the institutions except one savings and loan that quoted me 4 percent. When I was about to sign up with that institution, David Taggart, President of the Wayne County National Bank, called me at the Company and asked me to come to his office. When I got there he said, "Ceylon Hudson, our Chairman of the Board, and I were not going to tell you this for a while, but because you are applying for a mortgage and because we don't want you to go to any other institution to borrow money, we have to tell you now that we want to invite you to become a member of the Board of Directors of the Wayne County National Bank. If you accept and become a director, we would not want you borrowing money from another financial institution here in Wooster."

David Taggart went on to say that he and Ceylon Hudson were managers of the endowment fund at the Wooster Cemetery and that they would be glad to lend me money from that fund at 4 percent interest. He said that Edmond Secrest, Director of the Ohio State Experimental Station, would be retiring from the board at their next annual meeting to be held in February 1950 and that they would like to have me replace him at that time. After checking with Jim Caldwell and getting his enthusiastic blessing, I accepted their invitation to join the Wayne County National Bank's board and arranged for my mortgage through the Wooster Cemetery endowment fund at 4 percent. I was only 34 years old and I felt very highly complimented to have been asked to go on the Bank's board. This was the first of many boards which I have been asked to join – over the years I have served on the boards of 21 business corporations (see Appendix 1). Adding up all of the years I have served on these 21 corporate boards equals 179 years. That figure, of course, does not take into account all the years I served on the boards of trade associations, charitable organizations, and other non-profit organizations; otherwise it would be much higher.

Each time I have been invited to join a corporate board, I have told several things to the person or committee extending the invitation. They are:

- Thank you. I am highly complimented and flattered to be invited to become a member of your board.
- Do not invite me to join your board, however, if you take pride in having all unanimous votes from your board members, because if I feel strongly about an issue, I will vote my convictions even if I am part of a minority of only a few other members or even a minority of one.
- I will not go on your board if I am to represent some particular group of stockholders. I will join only if I can represent all the company's stockholders.
- I will join your board only if I can learn something that will help me to manage Rubbermaid and I will remain on your board only so long as I continue to learn from the experience. After I retired from being Chief Executive Officer of Rubbermaid, this, of course, was no longer a consideration.

A few months after I joined Wayne County National Bank's board in 1950, I was invited to become a member of the Board of Directors of Rubbermaid. In 1942, I had been made Secretary of the Company. During the eight years to 1950, I attended every single Rubbermaid Board meeting as Secretary and then every single Board meeting for the 35 years I was a Board member. I never missed a single Rubbermaid Board meeting for 43 years.

The list of corporate boards on which I have served, shown in Appendix 2, shows considerable diversity, with everything from banks to high technology manufacturing and communications companies. As a result of these board memberships, I have had the privilege of serving with and associating with many fine men and women who were or are very influential in the business world. One of the richest of these experiences was serving on the Federal Reserve Bank of Cleveland Board which was a tremendous learning experience for me. The Board of Directors of the Federal Reserve Bank of Cleveland is made up of three classes of directors. One class represents the large city banks. Another class represents the small regional banks. The third class is appointed by the Federal Reserve Board of Governors to represent the community at large. Several large city banks usually each sponsor someone for the job and then campaign to have their person elected. The National City Bank of Cleveland, after requesting my permission to do so, proposed my being a member and successfully campaigned for my election to the Board of Directors of the Federal Reserve Bank of Cleveland. Periodically, members of the Federal Reserve Board of Governors in Washington, D.C. would come to Cleveland to speak to our board and occasionally some of the Cleveland board members would be invited to Washington.

Twice I was asked to come to work on a full-time basis as a member of the Board of Governors of the Federal Reserve System in Washington, D.C. The first request came from Arthur Burns, who was then Chairman of the Board of Governors of the Federal Reserve System. He asked me to come to Washington so that he could describe to me what the job involved and so he could try to talk me into taking the job. During my interview with Burns, he asked me to read a paper he was planning to present to Congress suggesting that the government be the employer of last resort. He was suggesting that the wage rate for this type of employment should be the minimum wage established by the Federal Government. I told him that I thought it was a great idea, but that if he set the wage rate at the federal minimum wage, a great many people who were currently working below the minimum wage would want to go to work under the government program. It would constitute a higher wage for them. Burns registered great surprise that there were people in the country working below the federally established minimum wage. I explained to him that the federal minimum wage only applied (at that time) to companies involved in interstate commerce and that there were many companies which were not involved in interstate commerce, such as retail stores and restaurants, and they paid less than the minimum wage. After I left, Burns, of course, had his economists research this point to verify what I had told him. Later, he wrote to me thanking me profusely for the information saying that my calling this to his attention had saved him considerable embarrassment.

The second invitation for me to become a full-time member of the Board of Governors of the Federal Reserve System came from Bill Miller, who, as Chairman of the Board of Governors, asked me to again come to Washington so he could present his case for my becoming a member of the Board of Governors. In both cases, although it was a very great compliment and very flattering to have been asked, I declined because I felt that I had so much of importance yet to do at Rubbermaid that I did not feel I wanted to leave my work at the Company uncompleted.

In addition to being asked to serve on the boards which I did join, I was asked to serve on at least 15 other industrial company boards which, for one reason or another, I declined. Most of these offers were turned down on the basis that I did not have time to serve on any more boards. Some were declined for other reasons such as the company involved being a business in which I was not interested, a company that I did not think had the highest ethical standards, or a company where I did not think the board membership would add to my knowledge in a way that would help me in managing Rubbermaid.

The corporate boards on which I served met anywhere from six times a year to 12 times a year. Several of them met ten times a year, which meant every month except December and July. These variable meeting schedules required me to attend and prepare for many different meetings at many different locations during the course of a year. Inasmuch as I always felt I was learning something from the board meetings that helped me in running Rubbermaid, the meetings were justified. But I also rationalized that because I was putting in an average of 64 hours per week at the Company, another way to look at it was that I was actually serving on these boards on my own time and still putting in more time than would be expected on the job at Rubbermaid.

Based on my long experience as a member of corporate boards – Rubbermaid's and those of other industrial companies – I have formed some strong opinions about the responsibilities that board membership carries with it. For example, I am firmly convinced that the most important responsibility of a corporate board is to choose the Chief Executive Officer of the corporation. To my mind, the selection of the best possible candidate is so important that everything else fades by comparison. After a Chief Executive Officer has been selected, the board is responsible for monitoring and appraising his work and for counseling and advising him so he can perform as effectively as possible.

In addition to these "group" responsibilities of the entire board, I believe that whenever it is appropriate each individual board member should counsel and advise the Chief Executive Officer on a one-on-one basis to give him the advantage of a different point of view, as well as the advantage of whatever special expertise the board member has. When a Chief Executive Officer fails to perform satisfactorily despite the board's assistance, the next most important responsibility of the board is to fire the Chief Executive Officer. If it becomes necessary for the board to fire a Chief Executive Officer, the board is back again to its most important responsibility – identifying and choosing a new Chief Executive Officer.

To provide overall direction to the organization, the board of directors must work with management to formulate a mission statement and a statement of philosophy and fundamental business practices. The board should also play a significant role in developing procedures to assure that the mission statement and the statement of philosophy and principles are distributed throughout the organization and that they are used as guidelines by all employees in their day-to-day work. Successful implementation of these procedures should be an important part of the board's evaluation of the performance of the Chief Executive Officer and his management team.

Similarly, the board must work with management to develop financial growth objectives that will serve as clear operational guidelines for the entire organization. These should include short-term and long-term objectives for the growth of:

- Net sales,
- Net earnings,
- Net earnings per share,
- Book value, and
- Book value per share.

The board must also work with management to develop procedures for timely announcement of the established financial growth objectives to all employees throughout the organization and to the financial community. In addition, the board should develop a dividend pay-out policy consistent with the financial growth objectives it has established with the company's management.

To encourage superior management performance, the board must develop policies for determining the salary of senior officers that are based on salary norms for the industry in which the corporation competes and are consistent with good management practices. The board is also responsible, either as a whole or through its appropriate committees, for developing short-term and long-term incentive pay plans for corporate officers and other key members of the company's management.

Finally, as the representatives of the corporation's stockholders, the board members must work with management to develop policies on mergers and acquisitions. Such policies should require completion of thorough "due diligence" analyses of all proposed mergers and acquisitions and should be formulated to assure that the board's approval or disapproval of any proposal is in the best interests of all the stockholders and employees of the corporation.

In addition to being a director on the boards of industrial corporations, I served on the boards of two trade associations that were very important to Rubbermaid – the National Housewares Manufacturers Association and the American Hardware Manufacturers Association (my years of service and positions are shown in Appendix 2). The National Housewares Manufacturers Association (NHMA) is an association of manufacturers who make and market products which are sold in the housewares departments of department stores, discount houses, hardware stores, and other retail outlets. The NHMA was founded in 1948 for the express purpose of putting on two housewares shows each year. I have discussed these shows and their importance to Rubbermaid in Chapter 22. Prior to the formation of the NHMA, housewares shows were put on by an independent profit-making organization. The NHMA was run very efficiently and saved the manufacturers a great deal of money compared to having an outside organization do the shows. Caldwell was part of the group that first organized the NHMA. For many years the NHMA was headed by Dolph Zapfel, a very good executive who did a fine job as Executive Director.

The American Hardware Manufacturers Association was an association of manufacturers who made products which were sold through hardware stores. These included everything from bolts and nuts, tools and paints to housewares such as Rubbermaid's products. The prime purpose of this association was to put on a hardware show where all of the manufacturers could display their wares and which buyers from wholesale hardware companies as well as major hardware dealers could attend and see the new products and compare the product lines of various manufacturers. The Association also put on a convention in which no products were displayed but instead a program was arranged for the manufacturers and wholesalers with speakers on subjects of general interest to both those groups.

In both the Housewares and Hardware Associations, board members were elected for three years, not subject to reappointment. I served on the Housewares Manufacturers board for six years and on the Hardware Manufacturers board for eight years because I had been selected to climb the ladder of offices and ended up serving in both organizations as President for one year. A person stayed on the board during the period of time he served as an officer plus one year following his service as President.

The person serving as President of the National Housewares Manufacturers Association was asked to speak at most of the regional housewares clubs, called Pot and Kettle Clubs. These regional clubs were made up of housewares buyers for department stores, discount houses, wholesale hardware companies, and also the salesmen and manufacturers' representatives selling to them. During the year that I served as NHMA President, I spoke to most of these clubs which entailed a great deal of traveling and speech-making, but I felt that it was worthwhile for Rubbermaid because I made so many valuable contacts.

Similarly, the person serving as President of the American Hardware Manufacturers Association was asked to speak at most of the regional wholesale hardware association meetings. I did this and felt that it gave Rubbermaid good exposure to our wholesale hardware customers and helped support our merchandising efforts.

In addition to my corporate directorships and trade association directorships, I also served on many local civic organizations which are listed in Appendix 2. I also served on several national civic organizations. One of these that was extremely interesting was being a member of the New York Stock Exchange Listed Company Advisory Committee. This Committee met four times a year at the New York Stock Exchange. The purpose of the group was to consider matters which would enable the New York Stock Exchange to better serve its listed companies.

James Caldwell had a wonderful business philosophy based in no small measure on his own tremendous trust in people. He paid little attention to a person's position and treated everyone alike with dignity and respect whether they were a janitor, a factory worker, or a vice president. In my opinion, because of his tremendous trust and faith in people, two percent of the people he dealt with took advantage of him but the other 98 percent of the people rewarded his trust with outstanding effort, performance, and loyalty.

Another philosophical principle that Caldwell tried to establish throughout Rubbermaid was that no one should be afraid of making a mistake. He told us that anyone who was accomplishing anything would make some mistakes and, therefore, one should try to learn from the mistakes and move forward. I remember so well when I made a mistake that cost the Company $1,500. It seemed like a monumental mistake to me and a monumental cost to the Company at the time. I very sheepishly went to Caldwell and told him that I had made a mistake which had cost the company $1,500. I was thinking that he would at least be cross with me or at worst might fire me. Instead, he merely said to me, "Don, did you learn something from the mistake?" Of course I answered, "Yes" and he said, "Well, then don't worry about it!" He said the only way not to make any mistakes was to do nothing and he believed that if employees were afraid of making mistakes, they would never try anything new. That is how he encouraged innovation – making sure people knew that they would not be fired for trying a new approach, even if it failed.

It was Caldwell's concern for the dignity and well-being of employees which led to the creation of the Company's first retirement plan. In 1943, Dan Guthrie, who had been firing the Company's boiler since before the war, had a heart attack and could no longer work. Once a week, Caldwell would visit Dan at his home. While he was there, Caldwell would dig down into his own pocket and give Dan some money for groceries and rent. Following each of these visits, he would come back and tell me that the Company should establish some kind of retirement plan that would permit employees to retire with dignity or to have some money to live on without having to accept charity if they became disabled like Dan. As a result, in September 1944, Caldwell and I sat with Bob Critchfield, the Company's attorney, and Oscar Carlin, a pension consultant, in Caldwell's kitchen and designed the Profit Sharing Retirement Plan, which went into effect September 30, 1944, and, until recently, remained in effect with very few changes.

- The plan provided that each year 25 percent of pre-tax profit, subject to a maximum of 15 percent of eligible payroll, would be deposited into the plan. It was then credited to each employee's profit-sharing retirement account based on a formula that took into account the earnings of an employee for the year and his or her length of service.
- The plan also provided that there would be no vesting until an employee had five years of service with the Company, at which time the plan would become 25 percent vested. Thereafter, the employee's account would vest five percent more for each additional year of service until, with 20 years service, the plan would become 100 percent vested.
- If an employee terminated after five years of service, he or she would get 25 percent of the amount that had been put into the profit sharing plan account up to that time plus the dividends, interest, appreciation, and forfeitures.
- If an employee worked one additional year, he or she would get 30 percent and so on until, after 20 years, he or she would be entitled to 100 percent of the account.
- The difference between the vested amount an employee received on termination and the total amount in his or her plan account would be forfeited and would be distributed to the remaining employees, in proportion to how much each employee had in the plan. This provision in the plan was a strong inducement for people to stay with the Company.

This has been a wonderful plan for Rubbermaid employees, permitting long-service employees to retire with a substantial retirement benefit. The plan also incorporates a loan feature which entitles employees to borrow up to 25 percent of the amount they have vested in the fund for emergency uses or to purchase a home. I remember John Beck, a factory employee, telling me at one of the Quarter Century Banquets honoring long-term employees, that the profit sharing retirement plan was responsible for his long service with the Company. He said there were times he would get discouraged with some aspect of his job and go home and tell his wife he wanted to quit. She would tell him that if he would only put in another two or three months, he would get an extra five percent from his profit sharing plan because he would reach another anniversary date; or she would tell him that in two or three months another deposit would be made in his profit sharing plan account because new deposits were made at the end of the Company's fiscal year, which in those days ended on September 30. He said that those wifely pep talks would encourage him to stay, and by the time one of the events she described had happened, he would be over his discouragement and he would stay with the Company.

In my opinion, the profit sharing retirement plan has been one of the major reasons for the extremely low rate of employee turnover that Rubbermaid has always enjoyed. In more recent years, however, the Federal Government has issued rules requiring all retirement plans to have a shorter vesting period, which is now a maximum of seven years. This has taken away some of the incentive for employees to stay with the Company which was built into the original plan.

In 1950, Caldwell told me that just as the Company had for many years carried Key Man Insurance* on him, he was thinking

---

* Key Man Insurance is insurance coverage taken out by a company on members of its senior management team whose skills, experience, and responsibilities are considered critical to its continued success. These individuals are difficult and costly to replace, and the insurance is payable to the company when such key executives die to cover at least part of the cost of replacing them.

of also buying Key Man Insurance on Forrest Shaw, who was Vice President of Manufacturing; on Jim Buckwalter, who was Vice President of Sales; and on myself as Vice President, Secretary and Treasurer. He thought that this would be appropriate because of the key positions that each of us held in the Company.

I thought about this overnight and the next morning told Caldwell that while I thought it was extremely important for the Company to have Key Man Insurance on him as President, I thought there was a better way to spend the insurance premium money as far as the three of us were concerned. It happened that each of us was then looking for an assistant. I said that if we would increase the salary we were planning to offer each of these assistants, we could hire more capable individuals. That would give more protection to the shareholders than buying Key Man Insurance. My idea was that by hiring more capable people, the Company would automatically have someone in place to take over our duties if something happened to us. Because our assistants would already be familiar with the Company and its day-to-day operations, the management transition would cause less disruption and less profit loss than bringing in someone from outside. Caldwell agreed with my idea and each of us did raise our sights to hire a more capable person. In my case, I discontinued my search and started all over again from scratch, making it my objective to hire someone who was more capable than I.

As a result of this upgrading of the assistant positions, Shaw hired Lester Gigax, who went on to become Factory Manager, then Vice President of Manufacturing, and finally President and Chief Operating Officer of the Company. Buckwalter hired J. Robert S. Conybeare, who later became Vice President of Sales and Marketing and made a great contribution to the Company. I hired Charles R. Snyder as Controller, and he went on to become Vice President and Sales Manager and eventually President of the Company's Consumer Goods Division. This experience led me to believe in and adopt the policy that it is best to pay executives at a level that is somewhat higher than the pay offered by the competition for similar jobs.

Later, Rubbermaid established a policy of paying a competitive base salary but also paying a bonus that was considerably higher than the average bonus paid by similar companies. The reason that I think this was a good policy was that it enabled the Company not only to attract better caliber executives but also to retain them. I think most companies underestimate the real cost of employee turnover and particularly the tremendous cost of executive turnover. An executive who knows a company and who has learned its corporate culture by being part of it for several years can operate so much more effectively than most executives recruited from outside. It may take a newcomer many months of on-the-job training before he or she knows how to get things done in the new environment and that can have disastrous effects on both profits and employee morale. In the worst-case scenario, the outside executive never learns how to operate in the new corporate culture but instead tries to impose the management techniques and procedures that worked in his or her previous job and were suited to another kind of culture. All too often, this leads to the executive being fired and a costly search for a replacement has to be started, which may take quite some time and adversely affect the business.

There are exceptions, of course, in which executives recruited from outside Rubbermaid have done brilliant jobs. For the most part, however, our policy of hiring the best possible people in the first instance, giving them responsible jobs that build their confidence and skills, and then promoting them to fill vacant senior positions has produced many benefits in terms of effective management practices that are consistent with our stated philosophy and fundamental principles. To help retain outstanding employees, Rubbermaid had a very firm and often-stated policy of promoting from within and most of our promotions did come from inside the Company. We stated in our promotion policy, however, that when there was no one in the organization who was qualified and ready to take on the new responsibilities of an open position, we would go outside to find a person who was qualified. This gave our management confidence that when a position became open, all qualified inside people would be considered first for that position. If a person were qualified and ready for it, he or she would be given an opportunity to fill the position, even though it caused disruption and inconvenience on the part of the department or division he or she would be leaving. Often we would promote someone who was not quite as well-qualified as a person we might have hired from the outside. The payoff came from increased loyalty and from the fact that the inside person was familiar with the Rubbermaid culture and how we did business. On the other hand, because we reserved the right to go to the outside if no one on the inside was close enough to being ready, it assured that we would get a qualified person for the job. Because there were occasionally situations of this kind, it meant that we could hire people from outside who would bring fresh, new thinking and different perspectives into the organization, which prevented us from becoming stale.

After I became Chief Executive Officer, every six months I would write a paper on the subject of top management succession. I wrote this paper out by hand and shared it with no one. In the paper, I discussed the strengths and weaknesses of each member of the Operating Committee and of some executives in the next echelon. I named those who I thought should be considered to succeed me, setting forth the reasons why, and those that I thought should not be considered to succeed me, again listing the reasons why. This paper I put into a sealed envelope and gave to Bob Critchfield, our outside attorney, telling him to give it to the Board if something happened to me so the Board members could see what my thinking was on succession planning. The Board knew that this was being done and that the paper was available if they needed it. I asked Bob to save all the past copies of these succession papers so that the Board could not only see my most recent thinking, but also could see the evolutionary changes in my opinions over time.

I did something similar with succession planning for the top management ranks throughout the Company. Once a year we had what we called "Let's Talk People Day." I would spend a full day with each General Manager talking about his succession and promotional plans for his entire management team. He would come prepared with an organizational chart, showing for each box on the chart the names of two executives who could be considered for promotion into that position if the incumbent was promoted to another job. The General Manager was responsible for indicating which of the two candidates for the position was best qualified and why. He also prepared a list of what each of the candidates should do to become totally qualified for consideration. Finally, the General Manager was required to provide information on what he was doing to help the person get the necessary education or training to qualify for promotion. We would then discuss each executive, analyzing his strengths and weaknesses and what could be done to further enhance his upward mobility. A few executives in each business organization were designated "high potential executives." In the case of this high potential group, we tried to make sure that they did not stay in any given assignment for more than three years.

I spent so much of my own time and that of other executives on promotional matters because I viewed a sound promotion policy as critical for the Company's future success. I also knew it had to be handled carefully because promotion, oddly enough, can be one of the greatest challenges that an individual faces during a business career. I often said that the most difficult career move a person ever makes is from being a "doer" to becoming a supervisor of doers. Examples of such moves include moving from being a production worker to becoming a foreman or from being an accountant to becoming an accounting supervisor.

There are many reasons for the stress involved in such a move, the most important of which is that when a person is a doer, he or she "belongs" to and is accepted by a group of doers. Everyone likes to belong to a group and likes to be accepted by that group. But when a person becomes a supervisor of doers, he or she no longer belongs to his or her previous group and has not yet been accepted into the supervisory group. It can become quite lonely for a newly appointed supervisor unless he or she is an outgoing person who quickly develops a new circle of friends.

Sometimes a person who is promoted into a supervisory position cannot make the necessary adjustment and asks to be returned to the prior level of being a doer. I believe the first-line supervisory level is one that many businesses tend to neglect, when it actually should be given a great deal of attention because of the major adjustment a new supervisor has to make. To help ease the transition period, companies should form first-line supervisory groups that meet periodically after work. This would provide a new supervisor with a chance to belong to a group that understands and shares the pressures he or she is feeling.

The next most difficult career move that a person ever makes in business is from being a supervisor of one discipline to being the supervisor of several disciplines, such as becoming a General Manager of an operating unit or a Chief Executive Officer. The reason that this is such a difficult move is that up until being promoted, the executive has supervised a discipline with which he is totally familiar – an area in which *he* is the expert. Then suddenly, the new General Manager or Chief Executive Officer is responsible for supervising disciplines with which he is not familiar and the people he is supervising are the experts – which is a totally new ball game with a completely different set of rules.

One major adjustment that a promoted executive must make in that new ball game is trusting the managers reporting to him to provide accurate information. Another is to learn as much as possible about how the other disciplines function, which is a very steep learning curve. While the new General Manager or Chief Executive Officer may never become as familiar with other disciplines as he is with his own, he has to at least become skilled enough to detect whether each manager reporting to him is giving him honest information. This is very difficult and he must terminate immediately any manager who tells him less than the whole truth by trying to gloss over problems or hide something. He cannot delay demoting or firing such a manager because he cannot convert a person from a liar into a totally honest person. So severe and demanding is the transition required that I have often said, "You cannot know whether a person can be a General Manager until he is a General Manger." There is no training course that can prepare a person to meet a career challenge of such magnitude – it is literally a form of "on-the-job" training.

In succession planning, I always stressed the responsibility of senior executives for making sure that the persons they were placing on the list of candidates for promotion received the education and training needed to make them ready to assume new and more demanding responsibilities. That reflects the section of our *Statement of Rubbermaid Philosophy and Fundamental Principles* which says, "We will strive to provide each employee with opportunity for career growth and advancement within the Company based upon individual ability and performance." One of my greatest satisfactions in business came from seeing young people develop by taking on greater responsibilities and growing into the job. That was exciting for me because I had learned that I liked to teach when I taught Economics at Heidelberg College for a year. I enjoyed the teaching aspect of being an executive and I have often said that every executive has to be half teacher. It takes a lot of teaching, training, and patience to develop people, but I think that it is fundamental for building a business and making it into a great enterprise. Without it, our policy of promoting from within would simply not have been effective.

I had an interesting experience in advising young people several years ago when I was asked by the Graduate School of Business at Indiana University to be "Executive in Residence" for three days. This involved speaking to three or four graduate classes each day and joining students for discussions at lunch and dinner. During a question and answer session in one graduate class, a student asked me what were the three most important things to be considered when promoting a person into middle management. I answered by saying, "I can tell you right away what number one is – it's the ability to get along with people." Then I went on to tell the class that the ability to relate well with other people, understanding their problems and respecting their abilities and contributions, was one of the most important qualities for being an effective supervisor. On the promotion point, I said that often a person who otherwise was highly qualified in a business discipline and highly productive as a "doer" would be passed over for promotion because, in management's opinion, he or she lacked that quality and, therefore, would not be a good supervisor of other employees. That evening, before dinner, I was talking to two business school professors – one from the class in which I had made the statement and the other from a class that I was scheduled to talk with the next day. The first professor commented that he had been impressed with my answer to the student and repeated it to the other professor. That gentleman laughed and said that if I gave his class that answer, the students would think that he and I were in collusion because he had been telling them exactly the same thing. After thinking about that, I got up at 3:00 a.m. and wrote out some notes on what I meant by the ability to get along with people in a business setting. This is what I said to the class the next day:

"In business you have many bosses, not just your immediate supervisor. The appraisals of you that are made by three groups of people will have an impact on your progress or lack of progress. The three groups are first your peers, second your supervisors and their peers and their supervisors, and third, your subordinates – when you become a supervisor. Therefore, it is important to make a favorable impression on all three groups and that is why it is so important to know how to get along with them

In your relationship with your peers, be helpful. Get your own work done quickly and thoroughly, always reaching a little beyond your precise job description so that you make your co-worker's job a little easier. Never engage in a dispute about, 'That is not my job. It is yours.' When you see a co-worker getting behind in his or her work, offer to help even if it means working extra time without extra pay. Compliment your co-

workers. In addition to complimenting a co-worker directly, when you talk with others in your department, tell them that you have observed something very nice about the person you were complimenting. Do not criticize co-workers, either directly or to other co-workers. If you talk unfavorably about a co-worker to another co-worker, the one to whom you are talking may likely suspect that you are being critical of all your fellow workers. Show an interest in your co-workers, but never gossip.

The same things that I am suggesting for your relationship with your peers also apply to your relationship with your supervisor. He or she is interested in how well you get along with your peers and if you do get along with your peers, it makes his or her job easier. Obviously, from your supervisor's point of view, the most important thing is for you to do your job well, but also show your supervisor that you think beyond the boundaries of your job description. Always try to find out why you are doing what you are doing and how it fits into other departments of the business. Make suggestions as to how the job can be done better to help the other departments with their work. If you do not know why you are doing a certain job, try to insist on finding out why, because without knowing why, you cannot improve the way the job is being done. Sometimes when you find out why the job is being done, you may find that the job does not need to be done at all. Try to know as much as you can about your supervisor's job without being nosy, of course. By knowing what your supervisor's job is, you will find ways that you can help him or her by doing your job somewhat differently or by going beyond your job description to help him or her. Such voluntary assistance is usually greatly appreciated. Show a willingness to work some extra time without extra pay to demonstrate your desire to help. Also, show a willingness to stay after regular working hours when necessary to complete an urgent job. These kinds of activities will come to the attention of your supervisor's supervisor and to the attention of your supervisor's peers, many of whom will have input on your career progress.

When you become a supervisor, be sure to compliment employees when a job is done well. Make your compliment directly to the employees and do so in front of others with their peers and your own supervisor present whenever possible. Conversely, you should criticize very sparingly and never in front of other people. It is amazing to me how many supervisors make the mistake, over and over again, of criticizing an employee in front of others. This causes resentment on the part of the person being criticized. When you must criticize an employee one-on-one, try to precede the criticism with a sincere compliment and try to follow the criticism with another sincere compliment. This is called sandwiching the criticism with compliments. When an honest mistake is made, do not criticize it, but be sure the associate has learned something from the error. To criticize a mistake too severely will make the employee not want to try anything new or not want to try to improve the way things are done. Conduct regular performance reviews with each of the people reporting directly to you. This should be done no less frequently than every six months and, in some cases, every three months. At this time, be sure to compliment the individual on good performance while making your comments on any weak performance constructive criticism focused on how the employee can do things better and improve performance. When your department is recognized for something good that has happened, give full credit to the employees working for you. On the other hand, when the department is criticized for something bad, take full responsibility for it publicly.

As I said, in business everyone has many bosses. Your co-workers, all of your supervisors as well as their supervisor and their peers, and the people reporting to you when you become a supervisor, all have a voice in your career progress. When people are being considered for a promotion, all of the comments that are made by all of these groups have an impact on a promotional decision. That is the reason I say that when we are considering a promotion to middle management, it is important to know whether the candidate knows how to get along with people."

My comments were well received, and I believe what I told the class that day is still sound advice for young people when they are beginning a career in business.

The need for great sensitivity in handling promotions was driven home to me when I had to fill an opening for a Vice President of Marketing and Sales, an important position in any company but one with particular significance given Rubbermaid's strong marketing and sales orientation. The problem was that I had two executives who were almost equally qualified for promotion. I knew that telling the one who did not get the promotion would have to be done in a way that would encourage him to continue doing his job enthusiastically and to go on working well with his colleague who had been promoted to Vice President. We were scheduled to announce the move on a Monday morning. I called in the man who was not going to get the promotion and told him about the change. He said that he felt he was qualified for the job, that he was hoping to get it, that he was bitterly disappointed that he did not get it, and that he wanted to know why. It happened that just the day before, on Sunday, the downhill slalom ski races in Austria had been televised. I told him I had watched the downhill races and that the skier who came in second was only four one-hundredths of a second behind the winner. I told him that he was well-qualified for the position, but, unfortunately, just as in the downhill race, there could only be one winner and that even though he was a very, very close second, he *was* second. He responded with another question, "But Don, where did I fall down?" I replied, "That is just it. You did not fall down. If the racer who came in second yesterday had fallen down, he would not have been second. He would have been in last place. But he did not fall down. You did not fall down, but you ended up in second place – a very close second place." This seemed to satisfy him and he agreed to stay with us and worked very cooperatively with the man who became his boss through the promotion. I was very glad that I had watched that ski race!

Another thing we tried to foster was an unusual freedom of communications throughout Rubbermaid. I say it was unusual because most companies tend to be pretty rigid about communications going through the "chain of command." In many organizations, an employee is reluctant to talk to his supervisor's supervisor and even more reluctant to talk to a supervisor two levels higher. Frequently in such situations, an employee is told that this practice is frowned on, if not actually forbidden. Similarly, executives are actively discouraged from talking with an employee two or three levels down in the organization without clearing it with the person's immediate supervisor.

At Rubbermaid we encouraged quite the opposite of both those policies. We encouraged people to talk to anyone in the organization, up or down the line, on any business subject without clearing it with the supervisors in between. We felt that answers to questions and solutions to problems were often arrived at much more quickly and better solutions were reached by having complete freedom of communications. It takes supervisors with considerable self confidence to feel comfortable with this kind of "open door" policy, but I do believe it worked well for us and it is still the Company's communications policy today.

Another way in which we further encouraged openness at Rubbermaid was to bring employees together in social situations. This was a terrific morale builder and it gave everyone a sense of belonging to a "family" instead of just a commercial enterprise. For example, Marge McClelland frequently reminds me of the ice-skating parties we had during the 1940s, up until 1948 when the Wooster Community Hospital was built. In those days, there was a pond where the Hospital is now located that was kept clear of snow and was wonderful for ice-skating. All of the office and supervisory personnel were invited to bring their spouses or a friend for ice-skating on the pond. After ice-skating, we would all go up to our house where Alice would have ready a large bowl of hot chili, her homemade pecan rolls (known as "sticky buns"), and hot chocolate. We would sit around the living room on chairs or on the floor eating chili, drinking hot chocolate, and having lively conversations. These parties would happen two or three times each winter.

We also usually had a Christmas office party on the 24th of December, the last afternoon before Christmas Day. We would quit work about 3:30 p.m. and would all move to the Company cafeteria where there would be group singing with office people performing in groups or quartets or duets. After the group singing and performances, there would be coffee and cake. For the 1952 Christmas party, the office girls talked me into singing as a solo the song, "I Saw Mommy Kissing Santa Claus," which was popular that year. Alice sent over to my office a costume that made me look like a small boy with shorts and a short-sleeved shirt with a big bow tie. The girls gave me a big panda bear to hold and I sang the song going through all the motions. We have a photograph of me singing the solo and, as I look at that picture, it makes me reflect on how such social events welded us into a closer knit organization.

I also think the philosophy and principles under which Jim Caldwell operated and which were set out in the *Statement of Rubbermaid Philosophy and Fundamental Principles* that I had published and distributed to all employees in 1960 established a pattern of honesty which was not violated by anyone, or at least not violated sufficiently to come to light. One of the best tributes to the personnel policies of Rubbermaid is that during the entire period of 39 years from when I joined Rubbermaid in June 1941 until I retired as Chief Executive Officer in May 1980, there never was a case of a known defalcation, embezzlement, or stealing from the Company. Of course, there were times when we had problems with employees taking products for their own use, but I am talking about what is commonly known as "White Collar Crime," namely embezzlement or stealing money through fraud.

I think that in other companies embezzlement sometimes results from the feeling – right or wrong – that the top officers of the company are benefiting personally from various kinds of irregularities, such as supplier kickbacks or taking undue advantage of fringe benefits and perks. When that is the case, people down the line begin to believe it is equally acceptable for them to also benefit from unethical behavior. In my opinion, because the top officers of

Rubbermaid tried to behave in a completely ethical manner and not take advantage of their positions, it made all the other employees of the Company feel that they also should play it straight. The top officers of Rubbermaid, myself included, paid for every Rubbermaid product we took home for personal use or gifts. We never used the Company airplanes for personal trips. We never tried to get friends or relatives on the payroll. We never had personal work done at our houses by Rubbermaid employees. All of these things I think set a pattern for honest dealing with the Company, which was followed by all employees down to the lowest levels.

One of the unwritten policies of Rubbermaid that began with my becoming Chief Executive Officer, was a policy against nepotism. This meant that we would not hire the children or close family relatives of any executive of the Company. This did not apply to factory or office employees. In the factory we, of course, have many members of a single family and this has worked out very well. And we always have had good experience with the children of factory employees working for us during vacations while they were going to college, because they did not want to embarrass their parents and, therefore, were very diligent workers. But our policy was not to hire the children of an executive.

One reason that I established a no nepotism policy for executives was that I did not think it was fair to a young person to be hired at a company where his father or mother was in an executive position. If a young person is capable and is successful in being promoted, he or she will not be given credit by his co-workers for his good performance. They will say that the kid is being promoted solely because his "old man" is influencing the decision. Another reason to avoid hiring a child of an executive is that if the young person is not capable and does not do a good job, it is very difficult to handle the disciplining or dismissal because of the parent's executive position. It is better and fairer to everyone concerned to have a firm policy that avoids all these sticky problems. We had cases where an executive found it very hard to understand our no nepotism policy and felt that it was discriminating against his children because they wanted to work at Rubbermaid. But often such an executive would come back after his son or daughter had obtained a job elsewhere and acknowledge that the policy had worked out better for everyone concerned.

Another unwritten personnel policy concerned promotions which required executives to relocate their families – a policy quite different from that of most companies. When we offered an executive a promotion requiring a family move, we always told the executive that we wanted him to accept the promotion only if the move were acceptable to his family. We would pay the expenses for the family to visit the new location and look at schools, housing, and the general quality of life. If the family decided after such a visit that it would not be in their best interest to make the move, we did not want the executive to accept the promotion. We told him it would not be held against him in considering him for future promotions. In other words, we would not, as most companies would do, put him on the back burner. This policy paid off for us in many ways. When a company insists on an executive moving, it is sometimes against the desires of the wife. After she gets moved to the new location and is unhappy, the company has an unhappy, less effective, and less productive executive. This can lead to poor performance or even to a resignation so the executive can move his family back to where they really want to live. Or, if the company chooses to bring the executive back, it involves the additional cost of a second household move, which can be substantial. Another way Rubbermaid benefited from this policy was a sincere appreciation on the part of the executive and his wife and family for such considerate treatment. This was true whether or not the executive accepted the promotion and the relocation. In either case, the executive responded with additional enthusiasm and loyalty to the Company. We also tried not to offer a promotion requiring relocation to executives with children in the 11th or 12th grade of high school, because our experience was that children in those grades find it very traumatic to move. This was not an ironclad rule but we applied it with good results several times.

While I was Chief Executive Officer, we had yet another unwritten personnel policy. When an executive told us that he had found a job elsewhere, we would never offer a salary increase to encourage him to stay. I did not want our executives to feel that they had to search for another job with higher pay in order to whipsaw us into giving them a salary increase. I wanted them to know that they were being paid competitively for the job they were performing and that they would get increases when appropriate. If a person was truly being offered a job with more responsibility and, therefore, worth more money, I would recommend taking it and say "God bless you, I wish you success."

We spent a great deal of time evaluating jobs and comparing what we were paying to what was being paid for similar work outside the Company. We also compared similar jobs among the divisions of Rubbermaid. Giving an increase to a person to stay with us would have put the pay for that job out of line with what was being paid both externally and internally. On the other hand, our policy was to re-hire an individual who had left for another job provided, of course, that the person had been doing a good job before leaving. Many companies refuse to re-hire anyone who has left, feeling that it shows disloyalty. We always have had a different point of view. When people who had left in good standing decided Rubbermaid was a better place to work, we welcomed them back. They usually became very loyal, productive employees and they would often tell other employees that the grass was not always greener on the other side of the fence.

Except for our plants in Wooster, Ohio, and Mississauga, Canada, which were already unionized, we tried to develop strong "union avoidance programs" at our other plant locations. The union avoidance programs were really just effective human resources programs involving good communications with all workers and fair industrial relations practices such as frequent reviews of wages and fringe benefits, to assure that we were meeting local competition. We trained supervisors to listen to employees and if something was bothering them, determine what it was and what could be done about it. We wanted to have a strong union avoidance program at each of the non-union locations, not because we wanted to save money, not because we wanted to pay lower wages, not because we wanted to have fewer fringe benefits, but because we felt that employees would be happier and get greater job satisfaction in a non-union set up. The fact that employees could move from one job to another with no union to restrict them meant that they could seek out the type of work that they would enjoy most. The fact that they could talk to their supervisors freely and tell them what was bothering them and reach an agreement quickly meant that they would be happier on the job. All this, we believed, would result in greater productivity without anyone working harder – as a matter of fact, workers would expend less nervous energy than in a union environment where tension usually results from an outside union business representative trying to justify his job by creating an adversarial relationship with management.

CHAPTER THIRTY-THREE • TEAMWORK AS A WAY OF LIFE

Today, Rubbermaid is noted for its successful use of team management, but that was not always the case. Caldwell was a one-man band. He made all the important decisions and he gave all the important directions. He expected each member of his management team to do what he told us to do and he expected it all to fit together. It was not a harsh one-man rule, but it was one-man rule. Perhaps that is why I stressed teamwork so vigorously when I was in a position to do so.

When I became Chief Executive Officer, I strongly supported the concept of teamwork almost to the point of making it become hackneyed. The concept of teamwork sounds corny to some people now and it probably sounded corny back then, but I believed and still do that it was very important in Rubbermaid's past success and that it is the key to the Company's future success. Many times in talking about teamwork, I used the example of several men trying to push a car out of the mud. All of the men can be working extremely hard and straining themselves to move the car, but nothing happens if they are not all putting forth their maximum effort at the same time. It is when a leader calls out "one, two, three, push," and all of them push together with their utmost strength at the same instant, that the car moves out of the mud. Someone has to be the signals caller, and I used to say that while any one of our team could have been the signal caller, the Board had chosen to designate me for that job. I said we would succeed when we had everyone pushing in the same direction and putting their maximum effort forth at the same time.

Another illustration that I often used to emphasize the importance of teamwork was an incident that occurred around the kitchen table at our home. My son Dick played football at Wooster High School and, just as he was entering his senior year, the boy who had been the team's quarterback moved to Florida. The team decided that they would like to have one of their friends, Teddy Huxley – the son of Arlene Huxley, a Rubbermaid factory employee – become their quarterback even though he had never played football. The same group of boys played basketball and Teddy was on the basketball team; although he was only about 5' 7" tall and very light weight, he was a great ball handler and an important asset for the basketball team. The boys invited Teddy to a meeting in our kitchen. Alice and I were sitting in our living room and could not help but overhear them. The boys told Teddy they wanted him to be their quarterback for the coming season. Teddy said, "I have never played football. I do not know anything about football. I do not want to play football. And, finally, I am just too little to play football." The team members said emphatically that although he had never played football, they were certain that he could play the game well because he was a good ball handler in basketball. They assured him that they would protect him against ever being hit by opposing players. They also said that they desperately needed him as quarterback. Teddy kept saying that he was too small to play football while they kept assuring him that they would protect him. Finally, they convinced him to be the quarterback on the team, which went on to have an undefeated season that year. I think they were undefeated not because they had the best football players in Ohio, but because none of them were trying to be stars in their own right. They were truly working together as a team in trying to protect Teddy as they had said they would. In every play, every player did his very best, expending every ounce of energy in first of all protecting Teddy, and secondly, moving the ball forward. I always thought this was a great example of what teamwork really meant and I used it frequently in describing what we needed to do to succeed at Rubbermaid.

In discussing the need for teamwork, I told our top management team that I thought as much as 15 percent of executive time and effectiveness was being lost in many companies through internal politics, bickering about non-essential matters, petty jealousies, and attempts to gain advancement at the expense of others. I said that if we could keep these disruptive activities to a minimum, we might be able to cut our losses in executive time and effectiveness to only 10 percent. That would give us a five percentage point edge on our competition, and I said that I would be glad to take such an advantage anytime. When I shared this idea with Jim Kemp, an industrial psychologist whom we used on a consulting basis, I asked him whether he agreed that as much as 15 percent of executive time and effectiveness was being lost through the kinds of disruption I have described. He replied, "Don, would you believe as much as 50 percent?" Frankly, I was amazed. I am confident that at Rubbermaid we had less of this disruptive infighting than existed at most companies. I told our management team that I had kept a plaque on my desk – the only plaque, in fact, that was there – for 25 years which said, "There is no limit to what a man can do or where he can go if he doesn't mind who gets the credit." I think our management team took that to heart and worked together with a high degree of harmony as the result of each person working as part of a team and not trying to take credit for their individual efforts.

After I had been Chief Executive Officer for several years, I told my Operating Committee members that I had delegated to them almost every aspect of running Rubbermaid. I had, of course, never delegated to them my relationship with the Board of Directors, my relationship with stockholders, my responsibility for strategic planning, or my responsibility for setting management incentive plans. Other than these few things, however, I had delegated to them all the responsibilities involved in the day-to-day management of Rubbermaid. I said that because I had delegated almost everything to them, there was very little left for me to do and, therefore, it was up to them to determine and let me know how my time could best be spent to benefit Rubbermaid. I told the Committee members that since my job was to assist each of them in getting their jobs done, they could ask for my help when they needed me or, perhaps more accurately, needed my title. For example, they could call on me when they needed to use my title to arrange meetings with the Chief Executive Officer of a customer or a supplier, or to add emphasis at the sales or management meetings of the Company's operating divisions. They realized that I genuinely wanted them to think of me as an assistant and as a resource to help them get their job done. And that is how we worked together as an effective team for many years.

Another approach I used to get the best performance from Rubbermaid management people was to tell them how much I always had been impressed with the deeds of people during an emergency. Many people respond to the emergency conditions created by natural disasters like floods or blizzards with efforts that seem to be superhuman. They perform incredible feats of strength, such as a small woman lifting a car off her child, or feats of great endurance, such as a man running for many miles to get help for an injured friend. While those acts may seem to be beyond human capacity, they really are not. An emergency stimulates human beings and causes them to use all of their strength and endurance in one big burst of energy instead of just coasting along as we all do, using only about a quarter of our true capacity. My point was how great it would be if we could achieve something of that same stimulation while at work. I think that during the course of a day's work, we put forth perhaps only 25 percent of our capacity to think and accomplish things compared to what we could do if we were as stimulated as we would be in an emergency. I told managers that if we regularly used only 25 percent of our energy and brain power, we could move up to 35 percent of our true capacity through better concentration and expending a little extra effort. Those added ten percentage points would result in an overall gain of 40 percent more accomplishment each day. Back then, I thought that type of gain was possible and I seemed to get some good results from the managers I told about my theory. Their productivity certainly went up in a measurable way. Today, I am pleased to see that some scientific experiments are verifying just how much more human beings are capable of when they are properly motivated.

After I had been Chief Executive Officer for about six or seven years, I developed a new idea for keeping the Board of Directors informed about management's concerns. Twice a year, I would ask the members of the Corporate Operating Committee to bring to our next meeting subjects that they considered of greatest immediate concern to them as individual managers. In the meeting, we would discuss all of these subjects and pick out the ten which we as a group considered to be the matters of greatest concern. We would have this list typed up and I would take it to the Board of Directors to discuss each of the subjects with them. This gave the Board not only a sense of what our concerns were, but also a sense of which of the problems were the most troublesome and represented the greatest risk for the Company. What was perhaps even more important was for our management team to discuss the list which focused our consideration on concerns that might otherwise have been neglected or at least not given the full attention they deserved. As Chief Executive Officer, I found it particularly useful to know the concerns of the people working for me and the order in which they ranked those concerns.

At Rubbermaid, we often used a technique for decision-making which we called listing the "musts and wants." An example of this kind of decision-making procedure was our identification of the best site for building a new plant. Under our list of "musts" would be those things which we felt were absolutely essential for us to chose a site. They were the kinds of things that, if they were not present, we would not consider a particular site.

The "musts" were such things as a railroad siding. We would absolutely not consider a place where a railroad siding could not be brought in. Another "must" might be that the site had to be within 70 miles of a major airport. If this were a "must," we would not even consider a location further than 70 miles from a major airport. Another example was that the site must have an adequate water supply, while another might be that the local community had to have a good fire-fighting organization.

On the list of "wants," we would put down the things which we would like to have, but could do without. Sometimes, even though we could do without a particular item, certain costly substitutions might be necessary. In that case, it was a matter of evaluating what the cost was to provide a substitute or the cost of doing without a specific thing. Typically, the list of "wants" would take into account some of the ·available alternatives and their cost. For example, we would want a building site that was flat, so we would not need to move a lot of dirt. If everything else was right, however, but it was a hilly site, we had to compare the cost of moving dirt against the costs of other locations. Another "want" might be to have a good sewer system. That would involve an analysis of the cost of building a system of septic tanks and leeching beds versus the costs of building somewhere else. Another "want" might be for a site to be within a few miles of an interstate freeway. The further away from the freeway an otherwise acceptable site might be, the more we had to consider the cost of building or improving roads to provide access to the freeway. This method of decision-making sometimes made it possible to walk away from a potential plant site quickly when the place did not meet our "must" requirements.

An executive search was another example of a decision-making process in which the "must" and "want" technique could be used. We would list the abilities and experiences a candidate absolutely must have, and we would also list the abilities and experiences that would be "wants" and we would try to get as many of those as possible. But if the person who was applying did not have every one of the "must" abilities, we would quickly be able to say no. This listing of "musts" and "wants" worked well for making many types of decisions. I think it resulted in less time being taken to make decisions and often resulted in our reaching better decisions than we would have otherwise.

CHAPTER THIRTY-FOUR • RUBBERMAID GOES PUBLIC

In 1954 and early 1955, Grable, Ebert, and Caldwell began to be concerned about how their estates would pay estate taxes when they died. In those days, federal estate taxes were actually confiscatory and, of course, The Wooster Rubber Company stock each of them held had appreciated to a sizable value. They concluded that the best way to solve their potential tax problem would be to have public trading in the Company's stock. Therefore, they engaged Milton Hulme of the brokerage firm of Hulme, Applegate, and Humphrey in Pittsburgh to make a public offering with each of them selling a small portion of their holdings. Milt Hulme put together a group of securities dealers throughout Pennsylvania and Ohio to handle the public offering which was made in June 1955. Prior to the offering, the number of shareholders had increased from 35 to 79 in 1941, when Caldwell sold some of his stock to management people, manufacturers' representatives, and friends. The public offering was at $10 per share and in one day, the number of The Wooster Rubber Company shareholders increased from 79 to more than 1,400. One hundred shares which were bought 41 years ago for $1,000 would today be 10,031 shares (as the result of stock dividends and stock splits over the years) and would be worth approximately $300,000.

Having the ownership of the Company go public made a dramatic and drastic change in the way we handled financial information at Rubbermaid. Prior to going public, all information on sales, profits, and balance sheets were kept extremely confidential. Suddenly, this information had to be made public in substantial detail. This was a very drastic change which was difficult for me to get used to because such information obviously would be of substantial value to our competitors.

In 1956, the Company made its first long-term borrowing from Equitable Life Assurance Association. We borrowed $1,500,000 to be repaid in annual installments through the year 1967 – a 10-year payback – at an interest rate of five percent. By 1961, the Company had paid this loan down to an outstanding balance of $900,000.

The following year, 1962, we went back to Equitable and increased the long-term loan to $3,000,000, this time at 5-1/4 percent payable in annual installments over the period to 1977 – a 15-year payback. By 1965, this was paid down to $2,400,000.

During 1966, the Company negotiated a new loan with Equitable in the amount of $7,200,000 at 5-3/4 percent interest payable in annual installments through 1981 – another 15-year payback. By 1975, this note had been paid down to under $3,000,000. In 1976, the Company borrowed $15,000,000 at 9-1/4 percent interest to be paid back in annual installments through 1991. Of that amount, $5,000,000 was taken down in 1976 and the balance was taken down in 1977.

Whenever I went to Equitable Life to talk to George Stoddard, who handled all of these loans over the years, I would tell him that Equitable should start lending money to Rubbermaid in a different manner. Because Equitable always provided for annual re-payments, Rubbermaid had to borrow more than we needed each time to provide the ability to pay back. Because we were a growing business, I told George that Equitable really should be lending us additional money each year because as our business grew so did our requirements for buildings and equipment, and that meant our long-term financial needs were increasing as well. I think it was a sound argument, but George could never see it that way.

In 1957, in order to capitalize on the name Rubbermaid, which by that time had become a very well-known brand name and trademark throughout the United States, the decision was made to change the corporate name from The Wooster Rubber Company to Rubbermaid Incorporated. The name change became effective December 12, 1957. Another reason for making the change at that time was our anticipation of eventually qualifying Rubbermaid stock to be listed for trading on the New York Stock Exchange. It was felt that the name Rubbermaid would help people to identify the Company with its diverse product lines and quality reputation in a way which we could never achieve by continuing to call it The Wooster Rubber Company.

In 1959, Grable became unhappy with the way the brokers were handling Rubbermaid stock on the over-the-counter market. He thought the brokers who were "making a market" in Rubbermaid stock were quoting too wide a spread between the bid and ask for the stock, making too big a profit on each transaction. He asked me to investigate what it would take to have Rubbermaid stock listed for trading on the New York Stock Exchange. There were several qualifications, such as the volume of sales, the amount of profit, and a minimum number of shareholders. Rubbermaid just barely qualified on the basis of sales and profits, but with only 1,400 shareholders we fell quite a bit short of the minimum 2,000 shareholders required. So once more, Grable, Ebert, and Caldwell agreed to sell a small portion of their holdings in a new public offering of the stock. Milt Hulme again headed up a syndicate of brokerage firms that handled this new public offering of the stock and achieved the necessary number of new shareholders to have the stock qualify for trading on the New York Stock Exchange.

On June 22, 1959, several of us went to New York to observe the first trading of the stock on the New York Stock Exchange. In the group were James Caldwell, Forrest Shaw, Bob Critchfield, John Johnston, Bob Ingram, and I. The first symbol we requested for our stock was RBM, which we thought was a good abbreviation of the word Rubbermaid. On the second day of trading, however, the New York Stock Exchange said that we would have to change our symbol because it was too close to IBM and they were afraid of confusion. So we changed the symbol to RBD, which is what it is today.

From 1956 through 1963, the Company issued five percent or three percent dividends in the form of stock shares. I became very much opposed to the Company's issuing stock dividends for the following reason. Some of the brokers who were handling the stock, would tell prospective buyers to whom they were trying to sell the stock that Rubbermaid paid a cash dividend equal to approximately four percent of the market price of the stock and, in addition, the Company issued a five percent stock dividend. Then they would either say or imply that this made an investment on which the buyer could expect to get a nine percent return. That troubled me because the five percent stock dividend really gave the shareholders nothing other than an additional piece of paper. It did not increase their percent of ownership of the Company. They merely had more shares representing the same investment they had before. I considered it dishonest on the part of the brokers to represent the potential investment in this manner. In 1965, we discontinued issuing stock dividends and waited until we had enough additional value built into the Company to make a two-for-one stock split.

The first stock split occurred in 1970. A stock split seemed to be much better understood by the shareholders than a stock dividend. It was very clear to everyone that when they received a stock split, they were not getting any additional value – they were merely holding more shares representing the same investment. The stock split approach could not be presented in the dishonest fashion that some brokers had used on the stock dividends. Another reason for the stock split was to keep the stock price within a range of roughly $20 to $60 per share. When the price of the stock got to be $60 per share, 100 shares – a block of shares normally viewed as a "round lot" – would cost $6,000, which would rule it out as a round lot investment for many people.

There were other considerations besides price that were used to determine when to split the stock, such as the amount of dividends per share. I wanted the quarterly dividend per share to be large enough after a split to permit a 10 percent increase in the dividend without going to a fraction of a penny. This meant that the quarterly dividend had to be at least 10 cents per share.

The graph below shows the market value of 100 shares of Rubbermaid stock purchased in June 1955 at the time of the first public offering of the stock. The highest and lowest values of the stock shares are shown for each year from 1955 to 1980.

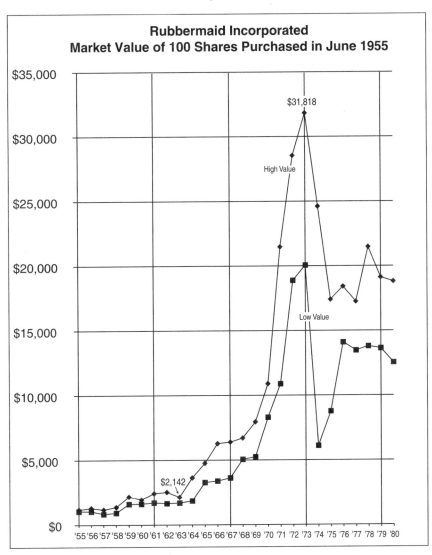

Rubbermaid Incorporated
Market Value of 100 Shares Purchased in June 1955

As the graph indicates, the stock's value increased from a 1963 high of $2,142 to a 1973 high of $32,818, a compounded annual rate of increase of 31 percent.

During this period of time, the stocks of all the consumer goods companies were popular with security analysts and were being pushed up to very high price earnings ratios, but Rubbermaid's stock was being bid up to an even higher price earnings ratio. In September 1973, Rubbermaid stock was bid up to a price earnings ratio of 43 times earnings – which was considerably higher than the ratios for the other consumer goods companies. Just as the market had been overpricing Rubbermaid stock in 1973, it under-priced the stock in 1974 in reaction to an international event which affected the entire U.S. economy and had a sharply negative impact on our financial results.

In 1960, Iran and several other nations formed the Organization of Petroleum Exporting Countries (OPEC) to increase oil prices by restricting oil production. By 1974, the resulting oil shortage had created a serious shortage of plastic raw materials, which are largely made from petroleum, and the dramatic increase in the price of oil drove up the price of the plastic raw materials used by Rubbermaid.

This shortage of plastic raw materials was further aggravated by President Carter's imposing price controls. This put a ceiling on what the producers of plastic raw materials could charge in the United States, so they shipped to Europe and Japan an increased amount of their output which otherwise would have been available to American companies. Because Rubbermaid had built up long-term working relationships with our raw materials suppliers, we were given preferential treatment for the scanty supplies that existed.

We had to pass along what we could of the sharp increases in the price of our raw materials by increasing our finished product prices. Although we did so, the plastics price run-up still hurt our profits because we had committed to our customers to maintain prices for a six-month period so they could plan their activities. Until we could play catch up by making our price increases effective and by printing new catalogs, we suffered profit erosion, paying higher prices for raw materials but not being able to collect more revenue for our products.

Over the 13-month period from September 28, 1973, when Rubbermaid hit its high, to October 29, 1974, our stock lost 80.8 percent of its market value, dropping from $50.75 per share to $9.75 per share. The price earnings ratio dropped from 43 times earnings to eight times earnings. During the five-year period 1976 to 1980, the price of Rubbermaid stock was flat, as the financial community waited for the Company's performance to catch up with the overpriced evaluation of its stock by the market in earlier years.

In recent years, the Securities and Exchange Commission has been encouraging companies to reward executives based on stock price. The graph shows why I do not think that is a sound basis for executive incentive. It illustrates how the market at times highly overvalues a stock but later drastically undervalues that same stock. There is little that the officers of a company can do, or should even try to do, to influence these overvaluations and undervaluations.

Rubbermaid, throughout these wide stock price fluctuations, was a sound company achieving sales and earnings increases, good returns on its assets, and good returns on its net worth. It is true that 1974 earnings were off somewhat because of rapid increases in the cost of plastic, Rubbermaid's principal raw material, but the Company was just as sound that year as it was in the preceding or following years. Nevertheless, as the graph demonstrates, Rubbermaid stock lost 80.8 percent of its value as a result.

During the period 1953 to 1959, approximately 30 companies showed an interest in acquiring Rubbermaid because of the Company's consistently impressive growth. In many of these cases, the company wishing to make the acquisition actually made an offer specifying the price they would pay for Rubbermaid stock, either in cash or in their own common stock. Some of our major shareholders were undecided as to whether their best interests would be to sell or to continue operating as an independent company. The problem was that those shareholders who really did not want to sell would not come out and say so. Instead, they said that they were willing to sell but at a price much higher than the current market value of the Company's stock. As the market value of Rubbermaid stock increased, of course, their acceptable price level increased in direct proportion. So each time there was an offer, those shareholders who were in the majority took the position that the proposed acquisition price was not high enough.

While most of the acquisition overtures were made by serious businessmen, one approach about a possible merger was – in retrospect – rather comic. In 1956, a man by the name of Kaufman, whom Caldwell had never heard of, called Caldwell and said that Eddie Thomas, who was Chairman of the Board and Chief Executive Officer of Goodyear, would like to meet with him. Caldwell's response was, "I know Eddie Thomas very well and I don't understand his coming through an outsider to ask for a meeting, but, of course, I will meet with Eddie any time he wants to." So a date was set up for Caldwell to go to Akron to meet with Thomas. Caldwell took me along with him. When we arrived at Goodyear, we were ushered into a conference room. There sat Kaufman, whom we did not know. Soon, Thomas and a couple of other Goodyear executives entered the room. Thomas opened the discussion by saying to Kaufman, "Now, Mr. Kaufman, you told me that Mr. Caldwell wanted to meet with me and I told you that it was a peculiar way for him to ask for a meeting. I know Mr. Caldwell and he could call me personally if he wanted to have a meeting with me. But I respect Mr. Caldwell and would meet with him any time he asked me to do so. What's this all about?" Kaufman, with a very red face, said, "Well, I wanted the two of you to get together because I think it would be a good idea for Goodyear to acquire The Wooster Rubber Company and if you ever do, I want to be the one who brought you two together." At this point, it was Thomas' turn to get red faced. He angrily exclaimed to Kaufman that, "It's not necessary for you to introduce The Wooster Rubber Company to Goodyear. We have had a very close working relationship for many years and if we wanted to talk about a merger, we certainly did not need you to bring us together nor to help us in any merger." He loudly told Kaufman to leave, which he did in a hurry, with a sheepish expression on his face.

Once a year for several years after this odd meeting, Kaufman wrote a letter to Goodyear and one to The Wooster Rubber Company stating that he had introduced the two companies to each other and that he would expect a finder's fee in the event there was ever a merger between them. This upset the executives of both companies. Each year, I would respond to Kaufman's letter by saying that he did not introduce us and that he would not be entitled to a finder's fee if we ever merged. Goodyear also wrote a similar letter to Kaufman every year. Looking back, it is funny, but then it was a sad chore having to write repeatedly to a man who was devious.

For several years after I became Chief Executive Officer of Rubbermaid in August 1959 and had told the Board I did not want to waste time talking to companies who wanted to acquire us, we still had several takeover approaches. One of the more serious of these approaches was made by the W.R. Grace Company. Their Chief Executive Officer, Peter Grace, called me several times indicating that he wanted to make an offer to our Board of Directors. I told him that we were not interested, but he kept coming back saying that he wanted to meet with a Board committee to discuss his offer. I, of course, conveyed his interest to the Board, but did not encourage them to set up a committee to meet with Grace.

Then Peter Grace called one day to tell me that he was tired of waiting for me to act and that he was going to make a tender offer for the stock of Rubbermaid at $22 per share when our stock was selling for $17 a share. In other words, he was offering a premium of 30 percent over the market value at that time. I told him I thought we could get a committee together to talk to him and that he should hold back on making a tender offer. He set a deadline of seven days hence, saying that if I had not brought a Board committee to his office to meet with him during that period, he would go ahead with the tender offer. I arranged for a committee of the Board to go and meet with him within the time frame he had set. The committee was made up of James R. Caldwell, Horatio Ebert, Charles Burke, Bob Critchfield, and me. We met with Grace, but registered no interest in his offer, and in the meantime the price of Rubbermaid stock had risen, so the meeting was concluded with no decisions made. The price of the stock continued to rise and Grace lost interest.

Another experience with a takeover attempt further strengthened my conviction of the important difference between a long-range point of view and a short-range outlook. After we had considered more than 20 acquisition offers, one of my very best friends in business, Lee Waterman, the Chairman and Chief Executive Officer of Corning Glass Works in Corning, New York, came to me in 1969 and said that Corning would like to acquire Rubbermaid on a friendly basis. Lee said that Corning would offer 140 percent of the then current market price of Rubbermaid stock in the form of shares of Corning stock. I called a special meeting of the Rubbermaid Board of Directors and told them about Lee's offer. My recommendation to the Board members was that if they were going to consider any acquisition offer over the next five years, they should accept Corning's offer. The reason I gave to the Board was that I knew Corning to be a growth company with a management committed to high principles and the highest standards of business ethics and integrity – people with whom I was sure we could work well as true partners. A portion of

Corning's business was in the housewares industry and, therefore, I believed that they would bring to the table a better understanding of our business than any other potential buyer. In talking with the Board, however, I added that our own Rubbermaid management team – the Operating Committee – felt that if we were given a chance, we could increase the market value of the Company's stock to produce a better deal in the future than would result now from acceptance of the current Corning offer. Essentially, I told the Board members that if they would give us the opportunity to manage the Company without taking time to review other acquisition offers, we were confident that we could increase the value of Rubbermaid stock to more than 140 percent of the value of Corning's stock within five years. After a day and a half of meetings and deliberation, the Board decided not to sell to Corning and to give us the chance to prove ourselves.

Because we had announced Corning's offer at the outset, arbitrageurs and brokers were busily acquiring Rubbermaid stock. The day after our Board turned down the Corning offer, I was on the telephone most of the day taking calls from brokers. Each caller asked basically the same question, "How could your Board turn down an offer of 140 percent of the market value of your stock?" My response was, "It's easy. Our Board believes we can make Rubbermaid stock worth more than 140 percent of what the price of Corning stock will be in five years." This typically evoked a loud and incredulous, "Five years?" That time frame was an alien concept to a financial community that, even in those days, seldom looked beyond a company's next quarterly results. But establishing that target made it possible for me to take a long-range point of view in managing Rubbermaid because I knew, in no uncertain terms, that I was working for shareholders whose time frame for success was five years. I am proud of the fact that we succeeded in meeting that deadline. As a matter of fact, we greatly exceeded it. Within five months, Rubbermaid stock was worth more than 140 percent of the value of Corning's stock and it has maintained a higher value in relationship to Corning's shares ever since.

During the period from 1970 to 1976, we continued to be concerned that some larger company would make an unfriendly tender offer for Rubbermaid stock. At that time, it was a practice of companies making acquisitions to make an unfriendly offer for 51 percent of the stock at a very substantial premium over the market price. Once they had acquired a majority interest in the acquired company, they then offered to buy out its minority stockholders at a much lower price, sometimes in the form of preferred stock with a much lower value than the price paid to the first group of stockholders. This caused stockholders, when they heard of an offer for a company in which they held stock, to rush quickly to accept the first offer because they were concerned that if they did not, they would be left behind as minority holders and as such would get a very inferior price for their holdings. This made tender offers very successful during those years.

In 1976, I started working with William Steinbrink of the Jones Day law firm in Cleveland to design measures for combating hostile takeover attempts in an effort to prevent Rubbermaid from suffering what was happening to so many good U.S. companies. Bill was very innovative in suggesting new approaches for such measures. He and I worked well together, and we came up with a measure against hostile takeovers that our Board recommended to our shareholders for adoption. As a result, in 1978, Rubbermaid adopted amendments to its by-laws which created a totally new takeover defense never used before by any company. The amendments provided that if any single holder acquired as much as 50 percent of Rubbermaid stock, the Company guaranteed that it would pay to all remaining stockholders the highest price paid to any of the first group of stockholders selling their shares to the acquiring company. This meant that stockholders did not have to rush to accept the first offer, but could relax knowing that they would get the highest price paid to stockholders who responded quickly. This was a very effective measure and resulted in Rubbermaid not getting a single hostile takeover offer after its adoption. This provision for guarding against takeovers was subsequently copied by many corporations throughout the country and is still considered one of the best measures against hostile takeovers ever invented.

CHAPTER THIRTY-SEVEN • FIRST INTERNATIONAL STEPS

Shortly after World War II, Rubbermaid took its first steps into international business when Caldwell engaged Walter Levy in Toronto, Canada, to be the national distributor for Rubbermaid products in Canada. Levy took orders from department stores and wholesalers for products which were shipped from the United States directly to the customers. Levy also had a warehouse where he stored an inventory of Rubbermaid products which he re-shipped to fill smaller orders. By 1950, his business had increased to the point that we decided to open a warehouse in Canada and begin making rubber-coated wire dish drainers. A man in the wire-forming business was getting ready to construct a new building in Port Credit, Ontario. Learning of his plans, we arranged with him to make the building twice as large as he needed – he would use half of it and rent the other half to us. In our half of the building, we would dip the dish drainers we purchased from him and we would also have adequate space for warehousing our finished products.

We advertised in a Toronto newspaper for a manager. I went to Toronto, interviewed candidates, and we hired Wally Sholdice. We operated in that building for five years, buying the wire dish drainers which were produced in one half of the building and moved to our half of the building for dipping. We shipped large quantities of other rubber products from Wooster to Port Credit, storing them in the warehouse and shipping them throughout Canada. Early in 1955, we decided it was time to expand our operation by buying land and constructing our own building. Caldwell sent Forrest Shaw and me to Canada to pick out a site for the new building.

We scoured an area within a 70-mile radius of Toronto, looking at farms for sale where a railroad siding could be brought in. We looked at more than 30 sites. When we returned to Wooster, we recommended to Caldwell that we buy five acres of land on Stanfield Road, north of the Queen Elizabeth Way and just south of Dundas Road in what is now Mississauga. The five acres was part of an apple orchard on a large farm with nothing for miles around but farm land. The price was $5,000 an acre or a total of $25,000. Caldwell frankly thought that we had lost our minds. The reasons he thought we had gone crazy included the fact that all of Rubbermaid's worldwide operations at that time were sitting on less than three acres of land on Bowman Street, plus the fact that farm land around Wooster was selling for only $300 an acre. He decided that all three of us should go back and look again at each of the sites to see where we had gone wrong. After reviewing all of the most desirable sites, he concluded that we had picked the best one and we bought the land. Later, we bought 11 acres on the other side of Stanfield Road, and recently one acre of that land sold for $1 million. So, it appears that $5,000 an acre was not too bad a price since it turned out to be a rather good investment. We built a factory and office building on the five acres of land and moved the wire-dipping operation from the rented facility into that building. We also bought new rubber molding presses, a Banbury, and a mill to start manufacturing other rubber products in Canada.

In 1963, Frank Russell, who was our manufacturers' representative for the sale of our automotive floor mats in Texas, brought to our attention an opportunity to license a Mexican company to make automotive mats in that country. Frank introduced us to Andres Salomon, who owned Productos Monarca, a company in Mexico City, Mexico. This company was in the business of bottling perfume under license from two or three companies in France. It seemed a far cry from the perfume business to the business of manufacturing automotive floor mats, but Salomon convinced us that he was serious and that he could start up and manage such a business. I took Bob Critchfield, our General Counsel, and Bill Coulter, our Vice President, Automotive, with me on two or three trips to Mexico where we entered into a licensing agreement with Salomon under which Productos Monarca would produce and market automotive accessory mats with our molds and pay us for the use of the molds and a royalty on the licensing agreement. At first, Salomon set up manufacturing in Mexico City but later moved the operation to Guadalajara, Mexico. The business was very successful and we collected a substantial amount of royalties from the business until we ourselves went out of the automotive mat business in 1978.

Early in 1965, Al Strunck, who was head of our International Operations, came to the management team with a recommendation that we acquire Dupol GmbH, a small manufacturing business located in Sprendlingen (now Dreieich), Germany. He proposed that we use Dupol as a base for introducing Rubbermaid manufacturing and distribution, first into Germany and then into all of Europe. I made a trip to Germany with Strunck to look at the facility and to meet the owner of the business and his management team. Dupol primarily manufactured bar accessories, such as plastic swivel sticks for mixing drinks, plastic toothpicks, ice cube trays, and some products that were similar to those in our line at the time, such as a dishpan and a plastic plate and bowl scraper. We told Kurt Krusche, the owner of Dupol, about our interest in acquiring his company, and he indicated a willingness to sell but at a price we felt was twice what the company was worth.

Strunck and I made two more trips to Germany to negotiate the deal, taking Bob Critchfield, Rubbermaid's General Counsel, with us. I remember one afternoon during the course of the negotiations when I thought we were not getting together on price and it appeared very likely that we would never agree. I said that I felt we were not making any progress and that Bob Critchfield, Al Strunck, and I were leaving to take the next plane back to the United States. I picked up my papers and briefcase and started out the door. Krusche followed me out into the hall to say, "Don't give up, I think we can get together." I said I would not go back in unless he could be more flexible and change his asking price to one closer to the maximum we could afford to pay. He agreed to that and we resumed negotiations. It took a while but we finally did arrive at a price and we acquired his company as a subsidiary, Dupol-Rubbermaid GmbH. Part of the deal was that Krusche would continue as General Manager after we acquired the business. We immediately shipped some molds, which were obsolete in the United States, to Germany so Dupol could produce the products necessary to develop a German housewares line. The business remained modestly profitable and about three years later we built a new and very large building on a separate site to accommodate expansion of the business. We experienced extreme difficulty in trying to establish the Rubbermaid philosophy, our business principles, and our corporate culture at Dupol-Rubbermaid. I have since thought that we would have been far better off to have gone to Germany, bought some land, built a building, hired local management, and started a business from scratch. But after a few years of struggle and changing managers three times, we succeeded in increasing our volume and making the business somewhat more profitable.

In April 1966, Fusion Rubbermaid Corporation joined with a company in the Netherlands, Vaessen-Schoemaker Holding NV, to form a joint venture, Vaessen-Schoemaker Rubbermaid NV, in Deventer, Holland, to manufacture and market heavy-duty plastic products for commercial and industrial use in the European Common Market using the powdered plastic and rotational-casting manufacturing method. Fusion Rubbermaid owned 50 percent of the new venture. Bob Ebert, who was managing Fusion Rubbermaid at the time, was responsible for developing this joint venture with Paul Schoemaker, the manager of Vaessen-Schoemaker Holding NV.

Through our business dealings, I became friends with Paul Schoemaker and our relationship resulted in Paul making a rather unusual request. One day in August he called me from the Netherlands and said, "Don, my son is on his way to the United States and he is going to visit you. Would you please try to assist him in getting into Notre Dame University?" I told Paul that I doubted anything could be done because classes would start the next month and I was certain that the University had closed its freshman class in the spring or early summer at the latest. Paul said that he knew it was short notice but would appreciate anything I could do. Sure enough, the young man showed up on our doorstep and I called the Director of Admissions at Notre Dame in South Bend, Indiana. He confirmed what I thought about the freshman class being closed and added, "Another problem we have with these young fellows from Europe is that they have not taken their SAT examination, so we can't really tell whether they're qualified for admission." I said that I recognized the problem of the SAT examination as well as the problem of simply applying too late. Nevertheless, I asked the Director if he would just talk to Paul's son with the idea of perhaps qualifying him for consideration the following year. The Director agreed and we arranged for the boy's visit to South Bend. He left that evening. I was quite surprised when the Director of Admissions called the very next day and said, "Mr. Noble, thank you for sending Mr. Schoemaker to see me. He is taking his SAT exam even as we speak, and we are so favorably impressed by him that we are going to make a place for him in our freshman class." Of course, I was delighted, particularly since the young man had made it on his own merits. All I had done was open the door just a crack for him. Nevertheless, it was one of the more unusual results of our global operations.

CHAPTER THIRTY-EIGHT • RUBBERMAID TAKES TO THE AIR

As Rubbermaid grew and we expanded our facilities around the country, it became a very time-consuming task to travel by train or car to attend the many different meetings at various locations. Starting in 1948 when I was still Treasurer of the Company, I engaged Walter Shuey, who operated the Wooster Airport at that time, to fly me in his single engine, two-seater Piper Cub to Columbus, Pittsburgh, or even as far away as Chicago on business trips. Walter's plane, of course, had no instruments and so it was all visual flight, which meant that we had to guide our course by the landmarks that we could see below us on the ground, mostly highways but sometimes natural features of the terrain such as rivers or the shoreline of one of the Great Lakes.

Les Gigax was a qualified pilot so when he became Factory

Manager, he chartered planes which he piloted himself. Frequently I would go with him on these flights – just the two of us. My flights with Les became even more frequent after I became Chief Executive Officer. Rubbermaid continued to add plant sites after Les became President and Chief Operating Officer, which made it impossible for him to visit each plant as frequently as he should to supervise the various operations. We considered hiring a full-time assistant for Les so the two of them could divide up the plant visits between them. We also thought that another solution might be to purchase an airplane that Les could fly. Compared with the delays of commercial flights, we thought having a plane would enable Les to save enough time to be able to make all the necessary plant visits himself. After calculating the costs both ways, we found that it would cost more to hire a full-time assistant, including fringe benefits, than it would to buy and operate an airplane. Our analysis showed another advantage to buying an airplane – better use of a senior executive's time. If Les had hired an assistant, he would have had to spend a lot of time listening to the assistant's reports on plant visits, but if Les himself visited all of the plants, he would have the same information first-hand. So in 1974, the Company bought its first corporate airplane, a twin-engined Beech Travel Air with room for five people, which included the pilot or pilots. Les and I used this plane frequently, particularly for visiting the Company's subsidiaries in Canada, Winchester, Virginia, and Statesville, North Carolina. It was a lot more convenient going into small airports near the plant sites and we could pretty much make our own time schedule instead of having to run for commercial flights. We were very happy with our decision.

Later, when we were calculating the cost of operating a corporate airplane with a full-time pilot and copilot, I said that it was also important to calculate how much more an executive could accomplish during the time he saved by flying on a corporate airplane versus the time he or she would spend traveling on a commercial flight. The time saved should be calculated as a savings in terms of the executive's total compensation including not only salary but also bonus and fringe benefits. In our calculations of the time savings made possible by a corporate airplane, I said that we should include both the extra working hours and the added time the executive would be able to spend with his or her family. To me, it was an extremely important and valuable benefit for Rubbermaid that our executives, who had to spend so much time away from home traveling, should be able to get home and spend as much time as possible with their families.

Les and I began logging so many miles of air travel in the corporate plane that the Board members became concerned. They let us know that they thought Les and I should not be flying without a copilot. So, in 1974, we engaged George Hunyadi on a part-time basis to be copilot when Les and I went flying together. The first time George Hunyadi came along as a copilot was an early morning flight. He brought with him a bag of donuts and a thermos jug of hot coffee, which I thought was wonderful. It was such a hit that George brought along donuts and coffee on all early morning flights and he probably still does because George is now the Company's chief pilot.

In 1975, we traded in the Beech Travel Air for a Merlin twin-engined, turboprop plane with room for six passengers and two crew members. It was a more comfortable and more sophisticated aircraft in terms of instruments. In 1978, the Board of Directors put their collective feet down and said that they did not want Les and me flying together. So either we would have to charter a second plane or one of us would have to take a commercial flight. That same year, we put into the Company's five-year plan a provision for the purchase of a jet airplane three years later, in 1981. As it turned out, that was exactly the year when the Company traded in the Merlin turboprop plane for a Cessna Citation II jet airplane, a wonderful little airplane that got you to your destination in a hurry.

This look back at Rubbermaid's use of airplanes reminds me of a sales meeting held in 1960 at McAllen, Texas, when Bob Conybeare was Sales Manager and I had only recently become

Chief Executive Officer. I was told to be in the Dallas Airport at 3:00 p.m. where I would be picked up and flown by chartered plane from Dallas to McAllen, Texas. When I arrived at the appointed time and place, I saw that all of our Rubbermaid executives were there. All of the sales staff were there. All of the sales managers and salesmen were there. We all went out onto the tarmac and boarded a chartered plane, a very large turboprop aircraft called a Convair which was the same kind of plane that Eastern Airlines used on its domestic routes.

After all of us had boarded, I sat in my seat feeling stunned. I could not help but think during the entire flight what a disaster it would be for Rubbermaid if something happened to the plane and everyone on board was killed. During all of my prior flying, I had never been what you would call a "white knuckled flyer," but I was on that trip! When we landed without incident at the little airport in McAllen, Texas, we sat in the plane on the tarmac close to the administration building for several minutes without anybody getting off. I was so relieved to have arrived safely that I did not think much about it for a few minutes, but then I began to get impatient. I inquired as to what the problem was and found out that the airport did not have a gantry, one of those aluminum staircases with wheels, that was big enough to reach up to the height of the plane's exit door. An airplane that large had apparently never landed at the McAllen airport and no one had given any thought to how we would get off the airplane when we arrived.

At that point, the humor of the thing got to us and there was quite a bit of joking about holding the meeting on the plane. After about 20 minutes, the airport ground crew brought out an extension ladder and put it against the side of the plane. Then we all crawled out of the plane door and scrambled awkwardly down the ladder. It seemed a very long way down to the ground and I thought how funny we must look, a bunch of usually dignified businessmen in a very undignified situation. Fortunately, there were almost no people around except the airport ground crew and they were too embarrassed by their lack of proper equipment to laugh at us.

The first thing I did after we were on the ground was to declare firmly that no more than half of the executives, no more than half of the sales managers, and no more than half of the salesmen could use that plane or any other single plane for the return trip. We all got back safely, but half of us made the return flight by commercial aircraft. When I reached my Wooster office, I issued a written policy stating that certain key executives could not fly together and that not more than half of the executives in any department could fly together. That policy is still in effect today at Rubbermaid, and I believe something along the same lines is a common practice in most American corporations.

Another funny story involving a chartered airplane comes to mind. In November 1964, we scheduled a Board Meeting to be held in Statesville, North Carolina, at the offices of Fusion Rubbermaid so that the Board members could see that operation. We chartered a twin-engined plane with a single pilot to take the officers and local directors from Wooster to Statesville. Dick Raeder, Tom Clark, Bob Critchfield, Jim Dawson and I went out to the Wooster Airport and a snow flurry started just before we boarded. Being naturally cautious as a lawyer, Bob Critchfield expressed some reservations about whether we should be flying in a snow storm and the pilot said, "This is no problem at all; get in and we'll go." As we took off, the snow flurry intensified and Bob asked the pilot how long he had been flying chartered planes and he answered, "Oh, this is my first flight." Bob asked him what he had been doing before that and he said, "I was a crop dusting pilot." Bob turned to me and said "I don't think we should continue this flight any further than necessary." We made an immediate executive decision to land in Pittsburgh rather than continuing on to Statesville with the crop duster. We all got out and waited for a commercial flight to go from Pittsburgh to Charlotte, North Carolina. Bob and the rest of us were much more relaxed on that flight and we got to our destination, which was not the case for all of the other attendees. On that same trip, several directors were coming in from Florida where they were living – Bob Becker, Milt

Hulme, Horatio Ebert, and Carl Towne. The same snow storm we experienced up in Ohio was also raging over the southern states. Their commercial plane had to land in Montgomery, Alabama, and they were unable to charter a flight so they never made it to Statesville for the meeting.

CHAPTER THIRTY-NINE • THE RUBBERMAID BOARD

The members of Rubbermaid's Board of Directors have been extremely important to the Company's success since it was founded. We were always fortunate in having well-qualified directors who took their responsibilities seriously. One of the reasons they made such significant contributions is that many Board members of The Wooster Rubber Company and later Rubbermaid Incorporated were truly representative of the stockholders since they themselves had significant holdings in the Company's stock.

From 1920 to 1926, they were the original founders and investors in the Company. In 1926, Horatio B. Ebert and Errett M. Grable bought all of The Wooster Rubber Company's stock and then sold some of it to their colleagues at the Wear-Ever Division of the Aluminum Cooking Utensil Company, who included: Carl G. Towne, Robert L. Becker, Arthur P. Miller, and Levi Smith. Along with Ebert and Grable, all of these individuals except Levi Smith served as Directors of the Company long after Rubbermaid went public in 1955, when their business positions were described as follows:

- Horatio B. Ebert, Sales Manager, Retail Stores Division, Aluminum Cooking Utensil Company (retired);
- Errett M. Grable, President, Wear-Ever International, Inc. (He assumed this position after his retirement as President of Aluminum Cooking Utensil Company);
- Robert L. Becker, Vice President in charge of Sales, Aluminum Cooking Utensil Company (He later became President of Aluminum Cooking Utensil Company);
- Arthur P. Miller, Vice President and General Manager, Wear-

Ever International, Inc. (He assumed this position after his retirement as Vice President in charge of Direct Sales for Aluminum Cooking Utensil Company); and

- Carl G. Towne, President, Aluminum Cooking Utensil Company (He took over Errett Grable's position when Grable retired from being President of the company. Prior to becoming President, Towne had served as Vice President of Finance at the Aluminum Cooking Utensil Company for many years).

All of these directors from Wear-Ever were active, contributing members of the Board of Rubbermaid Incorporated. The other five Board members in 1955 were all members of Rubbermaid's senior management team, namely: James R. Caldwell, President and General Manager; James K. Buckwalter, General Sales Manager; Lewis E. Glezen, President and General Manager; Midwest Metallic Products Company; Donald E. Noble, Secretary and Treasurer; and Forrest B. Shaw, Vice President in charge of Production.

Until the Company went public, there was an Executive Committee of the Board made up of Errett M. Grable, Horatio B. Ebert, Carl G. Towne, and James R. Caldwell. The Executive Committee was very active, making decisions between Board meetings and holding meetings – often over the telephone – prior to regular meetings to make their recommendations to the Board.

Each director brought different strengths to the Board based on his own business experience and position. Over the years that he served, Errett M. Grable made tremendous contributions to the Board which were based on his strong financial background and expertise. He was responsible for the initial public offering of stock that was traded on the over-the-counter market and he was responsible for the initial listing of the Company's stock on the New York Stock Exchange. When Errett Grable died in December 1959, he was replaced on the Board by his son-in-law, Charles Burke, the husband of Patricia Grable Burke. Charlie served for 33 years and made tremendous contributions to the Company's success. He brought sound business understanding as well as a legal approach to Board discussions which helped us make sound decisions, and he provided very helpful counsel to me between Board meetings. He retired in 1993 at age 70 in accordance with corporate policy. Charlie was replaced by Jan Nicholson, who is the daughter of Marion Grable Nicholson and William Nicholson and the granddaughter of Errett Grable.

I have mentioned elsewhere the tremendous contributions to Rubbermaid's success made by Horatio B. Ebert. I vividly remember another contribution he made back in 1955. Ebert said he thought we should have a dividend policy that would increase the amount of dividends paid per share, saying, "I think we should nudge the dividend each year." Whenever the question of dividend policy was discussed, he repeated that same phrase and, as a result, Rubbermaid's dividend per share has increased every year for 40 years. When Ebert retired from the Board in 1976, he was replaced by his son, Robert O. Ebert, who is still serving on the Board as of 1996. Bob brought to Board discussions not only a very sound understanding of business in general, but also a very broad understanding of the Company itself, because he had worked here as an executive for many years.

These replacements continue representation on the Rubbermaid Board of the substantial stock ownership of the Grable and Ebert families who have contributed so much over the years to the Company's success. Other individuals with substantial stock ownership serving as members of the Board included: James R. Caldwell from 1935 to 1963; Lewis E. Glezen from 1953 to 1967; Robert P. Ingram from 1970 to 1988; and Quinten Alexander from 1985 to 1990. These stock-owning directors gave the Board true stockholder interest and representation.

Robert Critchfield, the Company's outside legal counsel who came on the Board in 1959, brought sound business skills and a legal perspective to Board discussions. Bob also carefully read the minutes of the preceding meeting and, therefore, was always the Board member who made the motion to approve the minutes of the preceding meeting. A humorous incident occurred following one

Board meeting when only Bob, Tom Clark, and I were still in the Board room standing around the Board table. Bob was patting his suit coat pocket on his right side and then patting the suit coat pocket on the left side and looking through his papers and books which were in front of him on the table. Tom Clark said to him, "Are you looking for something, Bob?" Bob said, "Yes. When I came in I had three pipes. I have one in this pocket." He patted the right pocket. "I have one in this pocket." He patted the left pocket. "But I'm sure I had a third one when I came in." Tom Clark asked, "Bob, are you counting the pipe in your mouth?" He reached up to his mouth and said, "Oh, my gosh! I did not realize I had one in my mouth." Since he smoked so frequently, Bob was not aware of the third pipe in his mouth.

Elsewhere I have mentioned how helpful James M. Dawson was to the Board of Directors and to Rubbermaid management through the economic forecasts he gave at each Board meeting. Because Jim was a professional economist at the National City Bank, these forecasts had great credibility, and they were particularly advantageous when we were going through a recession and Jim would predict when we were going to come out of it. This gave management the confidence to recommend to the Board, and for the Board to approve, major expansions in building additions and in acquiring new manufacturing equipment so that we would be ready for growth and expansion immediately upon the improvement of the business climate. This permitted us to build buildings at a lower cost during the recession and to get special deals on the purchase of new equipment. But even more important was our being ready to use the buildings and equipment immediately upon coming out of the recession. Most businesses waited until they came out of the recession to construct buildings and buy equipment; as a result, they lost the first several months, or even years, of good business before they were ready to meet increased demand.

Norris A. Aldeen of Amerock Corporation, Arthur J. Frens of Gerber Products Company, E. J. O'Leary of GAF Corporation, and

L. Stanton Williams of PPG Industries, Inc., each brought a unique knowledge of business to the Board because each of them was the Chief Executive Officer of the companies for which they worked. As Chief Executive Officers in their own right, they brought a very special understanding to the problems faced by the Rubbermaid Board and the Company's management.

After I became Chief Executive Officer, we never had more than two employee directors. The rest were always "outside directors," which I thought made for a much stronger Board that was truly representative of all stockholders. My own election as Chairman of the Board of Directors was described this way in the following excerpt from the letter to stockholders in the 1973 Annual Report:

> *"Since 1959, our business has more than quadrupled with virtually all of the growth being achieved internally. This rapid increase in size, as well as the anticipation of similar growth in the years ahead, makes it essential that our top management team be restructured. On January 8, 1974, the Board of Directors elected Donald E. Noble Chairman of the Board and Chief Executive Officer. For over 14 years, he has served as President and Chief Executive Officer."*

That same letter announced the Board's election of Lester E. Gigax as President and Chief Operating Officer. Les joined the Company in 1951 and served in a variety of manufacturing posts before being elected Vice President of Manufacturing in 1959. In 1965, he was elected Vice President and General Manager of the Consumer Products Division and in 1971 was elected Executive Vice President in Charge of Operations. Les served as a member of the Board of Directors from 1974 to 1981 and made many contributions to the Company's success in that role.

Since Rubbermaid stock was first sold to the public in June 1955, the Board has met regularly six times a year with occasional special meetings called in between regularly scheduled meetings. Regular meetings were always held on the fourth Tuesday of February, April, June, August, and October. The "December"meeting was held during the first week in January to cover year-end business that could not be handled in December. I think this was a good schedule with our regularly scheduled meetings usually being frequent enough to take care of all matters requiring Board attention.

The February meeting, with spouses invited, was usually held in Florida and lasted at least two days. This gave management time to review operations in depth and it also allowed directors to become better acquainted with one another. I thought the February meetings were worth the time and cost because it gave the directors time to discuss Rubbermaid business matters one-on-one, thus getting a better idea of what each member was thinking and how he or she approached and analyzed Rubbermaid's business and problems. Because we scheduled time for golf and tennis and private dinners together, the February meeting also gave directors a chance to discuss things in a relaxed social setting. I firmly believe these meetings were worthwhile because they saved time during the year and resulted in the Board arriving at better and sounder decisions because the directors had learned how each other thought and respected each other's opinions. These meetings also gave the directors an opportunity to become acquainted with members of top management and to discuss Rubbermaid business with them on a one-on-one basis. It also permitted the directors to evaluate the strengths and weaknesses of members of management for use in considering proposed promotions and succession considerations.

CHAPTER FORTY • CLOSING ONE SET OF BOOKS

In 1974, when I was 59 years old, I told the Compensation Committee of the Board of Directors that I thought Les Gigax was qualified to replace me as Rubbermaid's Chief Executive Officer and that I knew Les had a strong desire for the job. Having worked with him for many years and having observed his progress closely, I felt he had the ability to lead the Company. I also said that if Les were ever to become Chief Executive Officer, it would be important for him to replace me quickly because at 55-1/2 he was only three-and-a-half years younger than I was.

My reasoning was based on my conviction that a Chief Executive Officer should have at least ten years to serve when he assumed the position. During the early years of his term in office, it is important that a Chief Executive Officer be able to make sound long-term decisions that might have a negative effect on profits for two or three years but provide substantial long-term benefits downstream. When an individual has only three or four years to serve, he is not likely to make decisions which will hurt financial results on his watch. I often cited General Motors as an example of this theory. For years, the GM Board elected individuals as Chief Executive Officer who had only four or five years to serve and, therefore, were not willing to make the tough decisions with the inevitable result that the automotive giant suffered real problems. I also cited the tough decisions I had to make when I first became Chief Executive Officer, primarily when I stopped the proposed expansion of the plant at the corner of Palmer and Bowman streets, purchased the 100-acre Steiner farm on State Route 585, and started construction of a whole new complex. That decision had a negative impact on Rubbermaid's earnings for three years and resulted in considerable criticism from some Board members (see Chapter 17). Because I was young enough to have a substantial amount of service ahead of me, I was able to persevere with the project and it did contribute to the long-term growth and profitability of the Company. Based on that thinking, I told the Committee that if they waited until I became 65 when Les would be 61-1/2 years old, I could not recommend that he replace me because he would not have a long enough period to serve. The Board's reaction was to tell me that they wanted me to continue serving as Chief Executive Officer. That, of course, did not resolve the issue and left me with the responsibility for identifying a suitable successor when the time came.

My Operating Committee at that time consisted mostly of the same men who had been members when I became Chief Executive Officer, except for two or three additions made within the first couple of years after I was elected. Even though I was only 44 years old when I took office, every member of the Operating Committee was between 3-1/2 and five years younger than I was. While that made for a very cohesive and compatible group, it also meant that none of them would have ten years to serve if I continued to be Chief Executive Officer until I turned 65. Therefore, I suggested to the Operating Committee that we identify within the Company some men who were at least ten years younger than I was to be groomed as potential successors. I also suggested that potential candidates be rotated among different areas of the business to give them broader experience and seasoning. That sent a clear message to the Committee members that they were out of the running.

Every time I suggested a likely candidate for such training, some Committee members would launch a campaign of criticism, finding fault with the candidate and magnifying any weaknesses in his performance. I suppose their reaction was understandable, but it was frustrating for me. After this had happened several times, it seemed to me that I had only two choices. My first choice was to reach age 65 without having identified an internal candidate who was young enough and properly groomed to succeed me. My second choice was to break up an Operating Committee team which had worked together effectively for many years. This was a matter of great concern to me and I spent a lot of time wrestling with the problem. Because I was reluctant to break up a winning team, I ended up without a qualified internal candidate. The Board asked me to stay on beyond age 65 with the idea that we would search for a successor from outside Rubbermaid.

In mid-1978, the security analysts began to tell me about their concern that there was no apparent successor within the Company. Their concern began to be reflected in their evaluations of Rubbermaid as an investment and this began to have a negative impact on the stock price. Fortunately, the Board and I were able to identify an excellent outside successor – Stan Gault.

I first met Stanley C. Gault when he joined the Board of Trustees of The College of Wooster in 1972. He was then a Sector Executive Vice President at General Electric Company. At one of the College Board meetings, I told him that I knew his father and knew of his father's connection with The Wooster Rubber Company, and I wondered if he would be interested in touring the Rubbermaid plant to see what had happened to the Company in which his father had played such a vital part. His face literally beamed as he said that he would really like to see the plant. So we set up a date for him to visit the plant on his next trip to Wooster for a Board of Trustees meeting at the College. I personally con-ducted a tour of the facility for Stan. I was so impressed with his keen interest in everything that was happening and his very insightful questions that I suggested to the Nominating Committee of the Rubbermaid Board of Directors that we invite Stan to become a member of our Board. They enthusiastically agreed and I made a special trip to New York City to have dinner with Stan and extend to him the Board's invitation to join us.

His immediate response was, "Don, I would very much like to join the Rubbermaid Board, but the General Electric Board has rules prohibiting officers of General Electric from serving on the boards of other corporations." He said it was rather paradoxical that General Electric expected other company executives to serve on their board, but restricted G.E. officers from joining other boards. But he said, "I want so much to join the Rubbermaid

Board that I am going to ask the G.E. board to make an exception to permit me to come on the Rubbermaid Board." He did and the G.E. board made an exception to its policy that allowed Stan to join the Rubbermaid Board in 1978.

As Stan served on our board, I was so impressed with his keen interest and insight as well as his helpfulness and thorough understanding of Rubbermaid's business that I suggested to the Board that he be offered the position of Chairman of the Board and Chief Executive Officer of Rubbermaid after my retirement. I had previously announced to the Board my desire to retire in May 1980 following my 65th birthday. Once again, in December 1978, I made a special trip to New York City to have dinner with Stan and told him of the Board's desire and offer that he replace me as Chairman and Chief Executive Officer of Rubbermaid.

His immediate response was, "Don, I think I have a chance of becoming Chairman and Chief Executive Officer of General Electric and that is my first choice. In case I do not get the top job at G.E., my second choice would be to be Chairman of the Board and Chief Executive Officer of Rubbermaid. However, I will not know for one year whether or not I will get the G.E. position." I said, "Stan, I will wait."

Eight months later, on a Sunday in August 1979, Stan called me at home to say, "I am getting indications that I may not get the job as Chairman and Chief Executive Officer of General Electric. I am ready to talk." A meeting was arranged for Stan to talk to the Nominating Committee of the Board of Directors and he accepted the offer to become Vice Chairman of the Board effective January 1, 1980 with the understanding that at the end of May 1980 he would become Chairman of the Board and Chief Executive Officer. After Stan took office, the price of Rubbermaid's stock continued to be depressed until he had been in place for a few months and the security analysts became comfortable and could see that he was taking hold and would be successful. Stan was very successful, and the fabulous job he did in continuing the growth of Rubbermaid sales and earnings per share is history.

Over the course of the entire 20 years prior to Stan Gault joining Rubbermaid in 1980, the Company's sales and earnings per share all grew continuously and consistently at a rate which exceeded doubling the business every six years. For some reason, however, the editors of many newspapers and magazines insisted on characterizing Rubbermaid, prior to Stan's takeover as Chief Executive Officer, as being a "sleepy little company down in the country." One book author even called Rubbermaid prior to 1980 a "faltering company." The following statistics on sales and earnings increases in the five years immediately prior to 1980 show just how false and misleading these characterizations of Rubbermaid were:

Year	Net Sales	% Increase over Preceding Year	Earnings Per Share	% Increase
1974	$130,598,000	—	$1.14	—
1975	$153,997,000	18%	$1.32	15%
1976	$186,222,000	21%	$1.80	36%
1977	$226,448,000	22%	$2.18	21%
1978	$258,349,000	14%	$2.45	12%
1979	$305,010,000	18%	$2.96	20%

During the five-year period before Stan Gault became Chief Executive Officer, sales had more than doubled from $130 million in 1974 to $305 million in 1979. Earnings per share of $2.96 in 1979 were 2-1/2 times the $1.14 earned in 1974. The balance sheet for December 31, 1979 showed current assets equal to 2.26 times current liabilities and long-term debt equal to only 13 percent of total shareholders' equity – a very sound, solid balance sheet, and certainly not one of a "sleepy" or "faltering" company.

When I was being interviewed recently for a magazine article, I was asked by the reporter, "What do you want to be remembered for at Rubbermaid? What are the accomplishments made during your tenure as Chief Executive Officer which you think are most outstanding?" After giving that question some thought, I have come up with the following accomplishments during my tenure as

Chief Executive Officer with which I am most pleased and that I believe have contributed most to the success of Rubbermaid:

- The issuance of a *Statement of Rubbermaid Philosophy and Fundamental Principles* which was widely used throughout the organization as a basis for daily conduct and recruitment of executives (see Chapter 21 and Appendix 1).
- Setting a growth objective of doubling the business every six years and publicizing it widely, and developing a formula to finance growth from plowed-back earnings while providing for dividends that would increase every year (see Chapter 18).
- Establishing long-term strategic planning on a five-year basis to be done each year and to be participated in by all levels of management (see Chapter 20).
- Purchasing the land on State Route 585 in 1960 and laying out a plan for a facility complex with one million square feet of floor space built at the same floor level to provide space for expanding the business (see Chapter 17).
- Setting the criteria for the type of community where we wanted to build new plants and purchasing eight times as much land as we needed each time we chose a new plant site giving us the room to grow (see Chapter 26 and Appendix 3).
- Having an Operating Committee and entire management team who were happy (relatively happy at least) in their jobs. Having good morale and excellent teamwork and cooperation among the members of our Operating Committee and throughout our entire management team with a minimum amount of politics, resulting in marvelous – almost miraculous – accomplishments (see Chapter 16).
- Setting a goal of having 33-1/3% of sales five years hence be made up of products not currently in existence and setting the climate for the motivation and innovation that would enable this to happen (see Chapter 24).

Looking back at my life and business career, I am very grateful to have been born in the United States under the free enterprise system – a system that really works. Because I feared starvation, or at least feared being hungry, I determined to work more hours than were expected of me at National City Bank which triggered a whole series of events:

- Because I was willing to post a ledger for Earl Biggs past the quitting time of five o'clock, he chose me to be his clerk.
- Because I worked diligently and worked extra hours for Biggs (without any extra pay), Robert Blythe chose me to be a trader in the Bank's Securities Analysis Department, which greatly expanded my knowledge of the free enterprise system.
- Because of those two factors, Biggs made special arrangements for me to work part-time so I could attend college classes during the mornings and evenings.
- Because I worked diligently and did extra work in my college classes, Western Reserve University recommended me when Paul Willour, Assistant Treasurer of The Wooster Rubber Company, asked for a recommendation of a recent graduate.
- For the same reason, the University recommended me again when Dr. Clarence Josephson asked for the name of a recent graduate who could teach economics at Heidelberg College.
- And because I worked diligently and did extra work on weekends at The Wooster Rubber Company while teaching at Heidelberg College, Caldwell asked me to return to become Secretary and Treasurer of the Company.

As the saying goes, "the harder I worked, the luckier I got." Some people might say, "But think of all the sports, social life, and movies you missed." I never felt that way. I was enjoying the pleasure and excitement of jobs completed and I believed that rewards would be forthcoming and they were. My many rewards included:

- Career advancement.
- The challenge of greater responsibilities.
- Enjoying the company of the wonderful people with whom I was privileged to associate throughout my career.
- Being able to help bright and capable young people develop, progress, and succeed in rewarding careers.
- Increases in pay.

That is what is so great about the free enterprise system – dedication, diligence, and hard work *are* rewarded. They also are the best guarantee of job security that I know. Only twice in my life did I have to look for a job. First, when I applied for a job at the soda fountain of a local drug store during my junior year in high school and second, when I looked for a messenger job at National City Bank after high school graduation. During my entire career, I never once asked for a pay increase. All the salary increases I received came without my ever mentioning salary to my superiors.

I believe that in order for our free enterprise system to work, there must be both fear and hope as motivators. On one hand, the fear of poverty and being hungry. On the other, the hope of reward for a job well done. It takes both to motivate people to do their best and for the free enterprise system to work efficiently and create wealth for our society. Unfortunately, many politicians today do not understand the need for both motivators under our free enterprise social and economic system. In their search for votes, they want to take away the fear of poverty with "transfer payments" which has led to generation after generation living on welfare and imposed a heavy tax burden on both business and individual citizens. Politicians also fail to see the need for rewards if people are to deliver their best performance on the job and so they try to tax away the rewards. If they take away the twin motivations of fear and hope that certainly stimulated my work ethic, the whole system will fail.

When I retired from Rubbermaid, I closed the books on a very satisfying and rewarding period in my life although I remain keenly interested in the ongoing success of the Company. In bringing these memoirs to a close, I look back with great pleasure on a long life that has been both exciting and rewarding in so many ways. It has never been dull and – if I had a chance to do so – I can truthfully say, I would do it all over again.

PHILOSOPHY

AND

FUNDAMENTAL PRINCIPLES

RUBBERMAID
CORPORATE PHILOSOPHY

WE BELIEVE in a single standard of conduct which will at all times consider the best interests of the corporation, its stockholders, its employees, its customers, its suppliers and the communities in which it lives.

In the conviction that Rubbermaid must consistently maintain this standard of conduct in order to grow and prosper, we must be able to answer "yes" to the following questions about each activity we undertake:

1. Does it represent a high degree of integrity; is it morally sound and honest?

2. Is it profitable to the Company and does it represent a fair return to all involved—employees, suppliers, customers and others?

3. Does it represent leadership beyond the commonplace?

4. Will it contribute to the long-range growth of the Company?

Donald E. Noble

President and General Manager

RUBBERMAID
FUNDAMENTAL PRINCIPLES

WE BELIEVE that our customers, investors, employees, suppliers and communities are entitled to share in the economic good created by our concerted effort in developing, producing and marketing products of recognized value and utility.

To this end,

FOR OUR CUSTOMERS (wholesalers, retailers, consumers, and users)

we will strive

- to manufacture products of high quality and true value, incorporating in those products leadership in design, style and utility.

- to work consistently and diligently to increase our knowledge of our customers and their requirements.

- to give the best possible service to our customers in prompt response to their needs.

- to price our goods to provide a reasonable profit to wholesalers, retailers and others selling our products.

- to deal with our customers consistently, with honesty and integrity, and without discrimination.

FOR OUR INVESTORS

we will strive

- to earn a reasonable profit.

- to maintain a program of sound growth supported by the profitable reinvestment of retained earnings.

- to communicate effectively and, on a timely basis, keep investors informed of the activities and progress of the Company's operations.

- to build competence and depth in our management organization to support future company growth.

FOR OUR EMPLOYEES

we will strive

- to recognize the intrinsic value of each employee as an individual.

- to provide working conditions and an environment which will maintain the dignity of the individual.

- to treat our employees and applicants for employment without discrimination as to race, creed, color, sex, age or national origin.

- to provide training opportunities which permit employees to enlarge their capacities to perform their jobs in a better and more meaningful manner; to provide each employee with opportunity for career growth and advancement within the Company based upon individual ability and performance.

- to recognize the value and potentials of self-motivation of people who thoroughly understand their jobs . . . not only what they are supposed to do, but the reason why . . . so that individual initiative and thought will be encouraged in the accomplishment of their tasks.

- to provide compensation equal to or better than prevailing rates for comparable services in the business community.

- to provide maximum continuity of employment.

FOR OUR SUPPLIERS
we will strive

- to establish and maintain mutually beneficial, long-term relationships which will result in maximum ultimate value to Rubbermaid for each dollar expended.

- to give prompt and courteous reception to salesmen calling on us.

- to honor and maintain any confidence disclosed.

- to deal equitably and with integrity.

- to deal objectively and with independence of thought avoiding all favors, gifts or personal gratuities which would hamper independence of action.

FOR OUR COMMUNITIES
we will strive

- to support the economic climate of the community through purchasing materials and services locally whenever such purchases are possible and economically feasible.

- to promote the general community welfare by direct financial support and by encouraging officers and employees to participate in community affairs.

- to encourage our employees to assume their civic responsibilities in active support of the kind of government which will maintain and actively promote free enterprise.

- to be a good neighbor by being mindful of the Company's ecological responsibilities.

APPENDIX TWO • BOARD MEMBERSHIPS

Past Corporate Directorships

The Wayne County National Bank - Wooster, OH	1950-1971
Rubbermaid Incorporated - Wooster, OH	1950-1980
Oak Rubber Company - Ravenna, OH	1956-1965
Insilco Corporation - Meriden, CT	1966-1985
The Tappan Company - Mansfield, OH	1967-1978
The Federal Reserve Bank of Cleveland - Cleveland, OH	1972-1977
Thermo Electron Corporation - Waltham, MA	1975-1977
The Stanley Works - New Britain, CT	1976-1985
National City Bank - Cleveland, OH	1978-1983
Libbey-Owens-Ford Company - Toledo, OH	1978-1985
The Ferro Corporation - Cleveland, OH	1980-1985
Times Fiber Communications, Inc. - Wallingford, CT	1984-1986
Seaman Corporation - Wooster, OH	1984-1989
Asian Oceanic Group - New York, NY	1984-1990
Thermo Instruments - Waltham, MA	1985-1992
Communications Group, Inc. - King of Prussia, PA	1986-1990

Current Corporate Directorships

Thermo Electron Corporation - Waltham, MA	1983 - present
Thermo Process Systems Inc. - Waltham, MA	1986 - present
Thermo Power Inc. - Waltham, MA	1990 - present
Thermo Fibertek - Waltham, MA	1992 - present
Thermo Sentron - Waltham, MA	1996 - present

Trade Associations

AMERICAN HARDWARE MANUFACTURERS ASSOCIATION

Member of the Board of Directors	1961-1974
Member of the Executive Committee	1962-1964
Chairman of the Executive Committee	1964-1965
Third Vice President	1965-1966
Second Vice President	1966-1967
First Vice President	1967-1968
President	1968-1969

NATIONAL HOUSEWARES MANUFACTURERS ASSOCIATION

Member of the Board of Directors	1962-1969
Treasurer	1965-1966
Vice President	1966-1967
President	1967-1968

Past Civic Affiliations

Member of the Board of Trustees	
Westminster Presbyterian Church - Wooster, OH	1944-1948
(served as Chairman for two years)	and 1950-1954
Member of the Board of Trustees of Wooster United Way	1946-1949
	and 1957-1960
Member of the Board of Directors of the Wooster Country Club	1948-1955
Member of the Board of Directors	
of the Wooster Chamber of Commerce	1950-1954
President of the Wooster Manufacturers Association	1951-1954
Member of the Board of Trustees	
of the Wooster YMCA (Chairman in 1959)	1954-1960
Member of the Cleveland Treasurers Club	1955-1959
Local Chairman of the State House Conference	
on Education - Columbus, OH	1958 and 1960
Member of the Board of Trustees	
of Boy Scout Camp - Wooster, OH	1959-1960
Member of the Rubber Sub-Council	
of the National Industrial Pollution	
Control Council - Washington, D.C.	1971-1973
Member of the Executive Committee of Wooster United Way	1971-1976
Member of the New York Stock Exchange	
Listed Company Advisory Committee - New York, NY	1978-1982
Member of the Committee of Twenty for Ohio	
Schools Financing Study - Columbus, OH	1978-1983

Current Civic Affiliations

Member of the Wooster Rotary Club, serving two terms	
on the Board of Directors	1942-present
Member of the Board of Trustees of The College of Wooster	1961-present
Member of the Board of Trustees	
of The Greater Wayne County Foundation	1995- present

APPENDIX THREE • CRITERIA FOR A NEW PLANT SITE
(FIRST PREPARED IN 1968)

- A small city of approximately 15,000 to 50,000 population in an
  agricultural surrounding
- A good school system
  - Above-average S.A.T. scores
  - Above-average percentage of high school graduates go on to college
  - Well-maintained school facilities
  - A vocational school
  - A school for the handicapped
  - Adult education and evening classes offered
  - Successfully passed operating levies
- A good college
- Good health facilities
  - A good hospital with modern equipment and well staffed
  - Clinic-type medical facilities also available
  - Above-average number of doctors per 1,000 population
  - Above-average number of dentists per 1,000 population
  - Emergency medical service (EMS) available
  - Rehabilitation programs
- Good recreational facilities
  - Good public swimming pools and parks
  - Swim teams
  - Tennis courts
  - Golf courses
  - Fishing and boating available in nearby lakes or streams
  - Baseball, football, and soccer fields
  - YMCA
- Adequate utilities
  - Adequate water supply with a high degree of purity
    and plenty of pressure
  - Good sewer system for both storm and sanitary sewers
  - Well-maintained streets (no chuckholes)
  - Good fire department with equipment and hydrants with a
    good fire insurance rating
  - Good police department with an adequate number of
    well-trained police officers
  - Adequate number of police cruisers (above-average per 1,000 population)

- Adequate utilities *(continued)*
  - Low incidence of breaking and entering and other crimes
  - Good cooperation among local police, state police,
    and sheriff's department
- A major airport within 70 miles
- A local airport with a runway of at least 4,300 feet
- Located on or near major interstate highways
- Adequate freight-out service for the marketing area
- Adequate housing with a good balance of apartments, duplexes,
  and single houses
  - Reasonably priced housing with a wide range of sizes and price levels
  - Houses that are neat and well-maintained even in
    the poorer sections of town
- Good city government
  - Stable council and administrative heads
  - Good cooperation among the mayor, city council, police,
    and fire department
  - Minimum of bickering on city council
  - Minimum of bickering between mayor and city council
  - Favorably disposed toward business
  - Not a strong union town
- A high degree of civic pride
  - Active service clubs such as Rotary, Kiwanis, Lions, and the Jaycees
  - Active Chamber of Commerce
  - Well-maintained churches, temples, and synagogues
  - Actively seeks to be an "All American" city
  - Celebrates national holidays such as the Fourth of July
    and Memorial Day

INDEX

cess, 88; sells some of his Company stock, 215; sells additional stock, 217; his long service on Rubbermaid Board, 236; member of Board's Executive Committee, 237; his influence on dividend policy, 238

Ebert, Lyda, 63

Ebert, Robert O. (Director), 155-156, 230, 238

E. I. duPont de Nemours and Company, 124

Electric car, 9

Employee turnover cost, 195

Equitable Life Assurance Company, 125, 216

Estes Park, Colorado, 176

Ethical behavior pattern set by senior Rubbermaid executives, 205-206

Executive as teacher, 199-202

Executive Committee of the Rubbermaid Board, 237

Executive order prohibiting civilian use of rubber during World War II, 70

Executives with high potential, 197

Fair Trade Laws, 127-130

Federal Reserve Bank of Cleveland, 41, 185

First-line supervisory level, 198

Fisk Rubber Company, 57

Five-year planning cycle, 117-119, 141, 147, 148, 161, 233

Floor mats, 135, 154

Florida Board Meetings, 241

Fort Wayne, Indiana, 35

Franks, Delroy, 94

Fredericks, Ed, 89

Free enterprise system, 247-249

Freedom of communications encouraged throughout Rubbermaid, 203-204

Fremont, Michigan, 171

Frens, Arthur J. (Director), 239

Ft. Collins, Colorado, 180

Fuller Brush man, 58

Fuller, Smith and Ross, 50, 52

Fusion Rubbermaid B.V., 101

Fusion Rubbermaid Corporation, 156, 230, 235

Gans, John, 154

Garfield Heights, Ohio, 82

Gas lamps and gas streetlights, 5

Gasoline ration stamps in World War II, 75

Gault, Clyde C. (Director), 56

Gault, Stanley C. (Director), mentioned in footnote, 56; part-time work at Rubbermaid as college student, 76; joins Rubbermaid Board, 245; succeeds Noble as Chairman and Chief Executive Officer of Rubbermaid Incorporated, 245

General Electric 225 computers, 69-70, 149-150

General Electric Company, 244-245

General Motors, 158, 242

Georgetown University, 57

Gerber Products Company, 171

German language, 2

Germany, 2, 70, 109, 229-230

Getting along with people, 199-202

Gigax, Lester "Les" (Director), member of Noble's Operating Committee, 89; recommends daily cost-cutting, 122; with Noble at NHMA Show, 134; as Vice President of Manufacturing hires industrial engineers, 151-152; hired by Forrest Shaw, 194; pilots airplanes on Company business, 231-232; election as President and Chief Operating Officer, 240; possible successor to Noble, 242

Glezen, Lewis E. (Director), 237, 238

Glossary of Terms, 90

Goodyear Tire and Rubber Company, 61, 71, 73, 74-75, 77, 79-80, 124, 222-223

Grable, Errett M. (Director), purchases Company with Horatio Ebert, 54; works for Wear-Ever, 55; part-time management of Company, 56; with Ebert, pays Caldwell's salary out of personal funds, 61; develops products, 62-63; contributions to Company based on his financial expertise, 64; death of, 86; calls Donald Noble into Board meeting to announce his election as President and General Manager of the Company, 89; interest in national advertising, 135; sells some of his stock, 215; initiates listing of Rubbermaid stock on New York Stock Exchange, 217; sells additional stock, 217; long service on Rubbermaid Board, 236; member of Board's Executive Committee, 237; contributions as Board member, 237

Grabner, George J., 171

Grace, Peter, 223-224

Great Depression, 18, 36, 37, 38; lasting effects on Noble, 40, 45; a suicide caused by, 46; causes of, 46-48; ended by World War II defense spending, 49, effects on the sales of The Wooster Rubber Company, 57; effects on James Caldwell's career, 57

Growth formula for doubling the business every six years, 96; 103-107, 109, 112, 147, 160

Growth philosophy, 107-109

Guadalajara, Mexico, 229

Gulf Oil, 144

Gushman, John, 170, 171

Guthrie, Dan, 191

Noble, Marianne (daughter-in-law), 181
Noble (Meiche), Mary Martha (mother), birth,
    1; work for Dr. George Crile, 1; German as
    first language, 2; appearance, 2; canning
    done by, 9-10; raising children as a widow,
    31; death of, 32-33
Noble, Matthew (grandson), 180
Noble, Milton (brother), 19, 22, 24, 27, 31
Noble, Nancy (daughter), see Nancy Noble
Holland
Noble, Paul (brother), 31
Noble, Philip Edgar (father), birth, 1; atten-
    dance at Ohio State University, 1; appear-
    ance 3; love of draft horses, 3; lives on
    family farm, 4; moves to East Lansing as
    manager of dairy farm, 4; agent for New
    York Life Insurance Company, 22; bread
    salesman, 24; driving Ford Model T truck,
    24; gives son a time management lesson,
    29; emergency appendectomy 29; death
    of, 30
Noble, Reuben (paternal grandfather),
    1; works at Star Bakery Company and runs
    real estate business, 5; builds new house,
    23
Noble, Richard "Dick" (son), 173, 177; attends
    Oxford University on Rhodes Scholarship,
    179-180; member of Wooster High School
    football team, 210
Noble, Robinson (grandson), 180
Noble, Roger (brother), 31
Noble, Theresa, 180
Noble, Will (great-uncle), 23
North Royalton Methodist Church, 1
North Royalton, Ohio, 1
Northfield, Minnesota, 181
Norton, Massachussetts, 57
Notre Dame University, 230-231

O'Leary, E. J. (Director), 239
Ohio State University and Ohio State
University School of Agriculture, 1
Oil crisis of the 1970s, 220
Old Testament, 35
One-third of earnings paid out in dividends
    and two-thirds plowed back into the
    business, 104, 110
One-year plan, 147, 161
Operating Committee, 89, 90, 91, 105, 106,
    142, 143, 154, 157, 158, 161, 169, 170,
    172, 196, 211, 213, 225, 243, 247
Orange High School, 180
Ottawa, Ontario, Canada, 181
Outlet Company department store, 58
Oviatt, Lincoln, 125

Oxford University, 180, 182
Palos Verdes, California, 182
Paris, France, 181
Park, Leonard, 86
Part-time war work, 76
Pearl Harbor, 70, 72
Peat, Marwick, Mitchell and Company, 86,
    124, 154
Peckham, Perry G., 75
Phillips Petroleum, 144
Pittsburgh, Pennsylvania, 18, 55, 86-87, 215,
    231, 235
Plastic boat project, 142-143
Plastic dish drainer, 83
Plastic dish pan, 83
Plastic garbage can, 144-145
Plastic housewares products, 83
Plastic raw materials price increases, 220
Plowed-back earnings to finance growth, 103,
    104, 105, 107, 109, 247
Policy on executives flying together, 234
Port Credit, Ontario, 227
Preferred stock issuance and redemption, 64
Preliminary planning package, 120
Prentke Romich, 180
President and General Manager of
Rubbermaid, 52, 62, 77, 87, 88, 89, 236
Press luncheons at Housewares Show,
    132-133
Pretty Products Rubber Company, 75, 77, 79
Price earnings ratio, 220
Product Review Committee, 139-140
Product suggestion list, 140
Productos Monarca, 228
Profit Sharing Retirement Plan, 192
Promotion as a challenge, 197
Promotion from within policy, 195
Promotions requiring family relocation, 207
Prospect, Ohio, 1
Providence, Rhode Island, 58

Quality standards, 149
Quarterly dividend per share, 218
Queen Elizabeth Way, 227

Radio, 18, 27, 34, 134
Raeder, Richard "Dick," 89, 98, 235
Re-hiring employees, 208
Rehoboth Beach, Delaware, 176
Republican Party, 46
Research and Development Department,
    105, 117, 119
Restricted Stock Incentive Plan, 115
Return On Assets Employed (ROAE), Noble
    acquires book on use of ROAE analysis,

Strunck, Al, 229
Suerth, John, 171
Sunshine brand rubber balloons, 54, 56
Supervision by asking questions, 164-166
Supplier relationships, 123-125
Swarthmore College, 181
Swarthmore, Pennsylvania, 181

Table protector pad, 63
Taggart, David, 183
Team management, avoiding politics and
    disruptive infighting, 211
Teamwork examples, 209-213
Television advertising, 135, 145
Thanksgiving Day, 8, 10, 21, 68, 72, 78,
    175, 179
The College of Wooster, 76, 92, 179, 180,
    181, 244
The Lincoln Log, 25
The Sorbonne, Paris, France, 181
Thomas, Eddie, 222-223
Tiffin, Ohio, 71, 72, 73
Toledo, Ohio, 171
Toronto, Canada, 227
Towne, Carl G. (Director), 236, 237
Troy, Ohio, 82
TRW, 19
Tullis, Richard, 170

U.S. Army Air Force, 74
U.S. Royal Rubber Company, 58
Union avoidance programs, 208-209
Union Carbide, 124, 144
Union Steel Products, 82
United Rubber Workers Union (URW), 76
University of California at Santa Cruz, 181
University of California in Los Angeles, 182
University of Colorado, Boulder, Colorado,
    180
University of Michigan, Ann Arbor, Michigan,
    181
University School, 19

Vaessen-Schoemaker Holding NV, 230
Vaessen-Schoemaker Rubbermaid NV joint
    venture, 230
Van Sweringen brothers, 47
Vegetable and victory gardens, 53
V-J Day, 79, 80

War work contract cancellations, 79
War work profits, 74
Washington D.C., 180, 185
Waterman, Lee, 224
Wayne County National Bank, 125, 183-184
Wear-Ever Division of the Aluminum Cooking

Utensil Company, 54-55, 61, 236, 237
Welfare, 49, 249
Wesleyan University, 178, 179, 182
West Coast Pot and Kettle Club, 176
West Tech High School, 26, 28, 50
Western Reserve University, 19, 42, 43, 44,
    50, 51, 71, 248
Williams, L. Stanton (Director), 240
Willour, Paul, 51, 248
Winchester, Virginia, 101, 155, 232
Wingerter, Robert "Bob," 171
Winget, Howard, 73-74, 81
Wire dish drainers, 62, 82, 83, 84, 95, 227
Wooster High School, 69, 181, 210
Wayne County Schools Superintendent of, 92
Wooster Rubber Company, The, general top-
    ics, looks for accountant, 51; Donald E.
    Noble joins, 53; purchased by Horatio
    Ebert and Errett Grable, 54; losses during
    Depression, 56; Caldwell joins as President
    and General Manager, 62; first profit of, 64;
    recapitalization of, 64; subcontractor on war
    work, 71; Noble appointed Secretary and
    Treasurer of, 73; Stanley Gault works part
    time at, 76; financial condition after World
    War II, 79; sales in the first post-war year,
    81; first national advertising, 135; first retire-
    ment plan, 192; first public stock offering,
    215; name changed to Rubbermaid
    Incorporated, 217; mentioned, 223, 236,
    244, 248
Wooster Rubber Company, The, in 1941,
    office space, 66; Rubbermaid office staff
    and factory workforce, 66; Rubber Milling
    and Press Department description, 67;
    hourly factory wage in 1941, 67; vacation
    policy of, 67-68; use of IBM equipment, 68;
    holidays at, 68
Wooster Schools Superintendent of, 92
Wooster Office Equipment, 125
Wooster, Ohio, mentioned, 33, 52, 53, 56, 61,
    62, 66, 71, 72, 73, 74, 76, 78, 84, 86, 97,
    106, 129, 131; as a model city for new
    plant sites, 154, 257-258; mentioned, 156,
    175, 182, 183, 227, 228, 235, 244
Work ethic, 7, 31, 40, 45, 249
World War II, 31, 33, 53, 76, 78, 80, 81, 82,
    125, 126, 227
W.R. Grace Company, 223-224
Wright, Edwin, 10, 18, 19
Wright, Francis, 10, 19
Wright, Morris (Morrie), 10, 12, 19, 29
Wylersville, Ohio, option on a farm site in, 96

Yale, 18, 19

Zapfel, Dolph, 133, 189